T0013458

The Kimchi Experiment

Naked Parent Teacher Meetings
and Other Exploits
of a Canadian in South Korea

Beth Ann Knowles

Pottersfield Press, Lawrencetown Beach, Nova Scotia, Canada

Copyright © 2022 Beth Ann Knowles

All rights reserved. No part of this work may be reproduced or used in any form or by any means, electronic or mechanical, including photocopying, recording, or any retrieval system, without the prior written permission of the publisher or a licence from the Canadian Copyright Licensing Agency (Access Copyright). to contact Access Copyright visit www.AccessCopyright.ca or call 1-800-893-5777.

Library and Archives Canada Cataloguing in Publication

Title: The kimchi experiment : naked parent teacher meetings and other exploits of a Canadian in South Korea / Beth Ann Knowles.
Names: Knowles, Beth Ann, author.
Identifiers: Canadiana (print) 20210352906 | Canadiana (ebook) 20210353007 | ISBN 9781989725795 (softcover) | ISBN 9781989725801 (EPUB)
Subjects: LCSH: Knowles, Beth Ann. | LCSH: Teachers—Korea (South)—Biography. | LCSH: Teachers—Nova Scotia—Biography. | LCSH: Canadians—Korea (South)—Biography. | LCSH: Korea (South)—Social life and customs—21st century—Humor. | LCGFT: Autobiographies.
Classification: LCC LA2325.K53 A3 2022 | DDC 371.10092—dc23

Cover image: www.123rf.com/bbtreesubmission

Cover design: Gail LeBlanc

Pottersfield Press gratefully acknowledges the financial support of the Government of Canada for our publishing activities through the Canada Book Fund. We also acknowledge the support of the Canada Council for the Arts and the Province of Nova Scotia which has assisted us to develop and promote our creative industries for the benefit of all Nova Scotians.

Pottersfield Press
248 Leslie Road
East Lawrencetown, Nova Scotia, Canada, B2Z 1T4
Website: www.pottersfieldpress.com
To order, phone 1-800-NIMBUS9 (1-800-646-2879) www.nimbus.ca

Printed in Canada

For Mom, Dad, and Carla-Jo

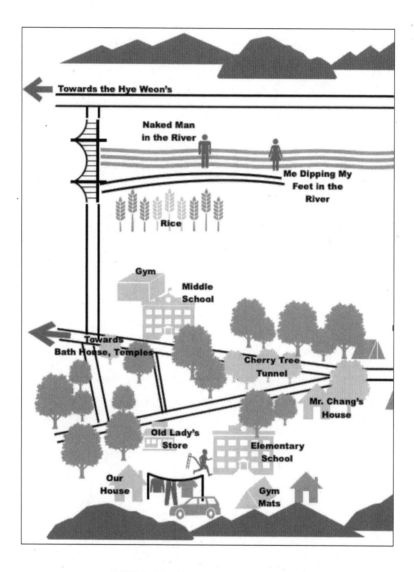

Towards the Hye Weon's

Naked Man
in the River

Me Dipping My
Feet in the
River

Rice

Gym

Middle
School

Towards
Bath House, Temples

Cherry Tree
Tunnel

Mr. Chang's
House

Old Lady's
Store

Elementary
School

Our
House

Gym
Mats

SCHOOL AREA OF HWAGAE

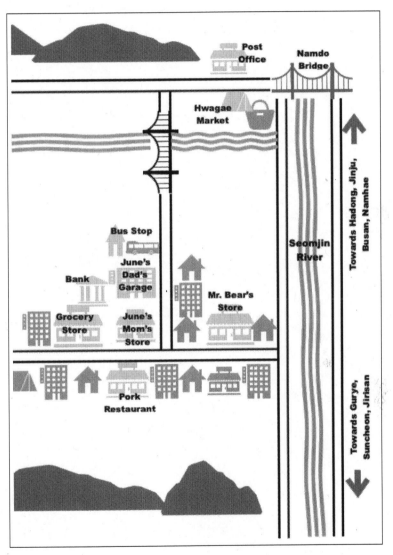

DOWNTOWN AREA OF HWAGAE

ONE

Monday, February 27, 2006, 3:30 a.m.

It is the day before our one-year wedding anniversary, and I have been lying awake on the hardest bed on which I have ever slept, and not slept, in my life.

Dale and I have been in South Korea since Thursday night and I have not been able to sleep past four a.m. yet. I became so desperate this morning, I even tried counting sheep. Does that even work? Are there any documented cases of a person successfully falling asleep as a result of counting sheep? I have not heard of any such evidence, but I gave it a try anyway. By the fourth sheep I had begun counting in my head like the Count from *Sesame Street*, "Four. Four fluffy white sheep. Ah Ah Ah!"

And then I started thinking about *Sesame Street* and then Mr. Snuffleupagus, and then elephants, and elephant tusks, and the earrings made from mink penis bones I had seen at a fair at the Amherst arena years ago, and then my cottage in Amherst, and eating Spam (or my mom's more economical Kam), with potato salad on a summer day, and I realize I am not sleeping and no longer am I counting sheep either. I get frustrated. Frustrated by the person who first suggested counting sheep; maybe had I not tried such an insane ritual my mind wouldn't have taken a turn on a *Sesame Street* tangent and perhaps I would have fallen asleep instead. Frustrated also by the snoring, humphing, grunting, whistling, sleeping sounds coming from my beautiful resting husband beside me. I get out of bed, eat some toast and jam, and begin to write.

*   *   *

It was a crisp morning when we boarded the plane in Halifax, Nova Scotia, on Wednesday, February 22. We would leave behind the frigid Maritime weather, our friends, our family, and our dog to travel around the world and become English teachers for one year. Two hours in flight landed us in Newark, New Jersey, where we transferred by taxi to JFK airport. We viewed the Statue of Liberty from a distance, narrowly avoided seventeen car accidents, and enjoyed our taxi driver's grumbly disposition.

The second leg of our journey had us flying fourteen and a half hours to Seoul. This feat is inhuman, or inhumane, perhaps both. While they provide you with multiple movies, TV shows, music, and video games, everyone starts going a little stir-crazy at the ten-hour twenty-five-minute mark. It may have been the stifling parched air of the cabin and the fact that the plane had no overhead air blower devices; it may have been too many games of Memory and Yahtzee against the plane computer; or it may have been that my eyes were so dry I squinted to see the TV on the seatback in front of me.

I'll never know exactly what caused it, but I started to feel like I was going to have an ugly episode of air rage. Instead of comforting me, Dale rubbing my forearm enraged me even more. I was so hot I couldn't stand any human contact but rubbed my bare feet and arms against any cool metal I could find – my seat buckle, the bottom of the seat in front of me, the arm rests. I was on the verge of freaking out, of giving up all hope of surviving the flight, of snapping another passenger with a steamed towelette and starting the first airborne towel fight. But lunch was served, and the cheesecake on my tray soothed me through the remaining three and a half hours.

We landed in Seoul and gathered our modest 150 pounds of luggage. Without any South Korean currency, we opted to carry our bags instead of renting a cart. Looking back, it was a very stupid decision by both of us. I donned a huge travel backpack, two smaller backpacks, and dragged an overstuffed rolling suitcase. Dale toted another heavy travel backpack and a hockey bag filled to capacity.

Two escalator rides and a 400-metre hike later, the tension in our marriage was at a tipping point. Greater than the time I accidentally shipwrecked our kayak over sharp coral in the Dominican. Greater than the time I inadvertently guided Dale's van into a snowbank during a fierce snowstorm and left him to shovel the van free. Yes, tension was at a max. I feared for the fate of my thong sandals and my long black coat, for two of my three pairs of jeans and four of my five bottles of moisturizer. Perhaps it was the presence of my luxuries that kept me from pointing out to Dale that his long-board skateboard was also contributing to the dead weight of our luggage.

The Seoul airport was the busiest I had ever been in. We saw very few non-Asian people among the thousands, and everyone who was not Asian attracted attention. We sensed many long looks and side stares from strangers: maybe because of my blonde hair and Dale's six-foot-two stature, maybe because they had never seen so much luggage between two people before.

We check our bags for our final flight to Busan. This flight is only about an hour and we doze in and out, sometimes gaping at the beautiful mountains that compose the landscape. We land in Busan around 9:30 p.m. local time, gather our bags (using a cart this time), and step into the arrivals area. The plan our recruiter had communicated to us outlined that someone would be waiting for our arrival, holding a sign with our names. There is no one. We wait about five minutes and still no person, no sign. At this point the airport is almost empty and we are both fatigued beyond belief.

I phone our future vice principal, Mr. Lee. He is very surprised to hear from us, since he expected our arrival the next night (another screw-up by our recruiter ... already we were arriving four days past our contract start date of February 20). Mr. Lee sounds panicked (not exactly reassuring at this point) and tells me to call him back in thirty minutes. I contemplate how limited his English seemed and wonder if I'm going to be teaching the teachers as well. Dale receives the news of a further wait with all the patience of a person who has just been travelling for more than twenty-four hours. We know Mr. Lee is located about two and a half hours from Busan airport so we're anticipating a very long night.

After we sit for about ten minutes, a small group of "police officers," who look about fourteen years old, come along; one tells us the airport is closing and we'll have to leave. We explain we're waiting for a drive and ask if we could wait inside the airport or inside somewhere else. He speaks a little English and asks for the phone number of our drive. Now a serious-looking man carrying a heavy length of chain has come along and speaks hurriedly to the police officer. A third man joins the conversation and he gives the police officer his cell phone and the police officer phones Mr. Lee. The third man, who we now understand to be a taxi driver, talks to Mr. Lee as well, and it goes on. The phone is passed around, everyone speaks rapidly in Korean, and Dale and I look on like spectators at a tennis match. Eventually the conversation with Mr. Lee is ended and the police officer again tells us we have to wait outside.

We must have looked so dejected that he phones Mr. Lee again, and again the police officer and the taxi driver speak on the phone, and then it is passed to me. Mr. Lee tells me the taxi driver will bring us to Jinju where he and Mr. Chang, my future principal, will be waiting. The phone connection is abruptly cut.

This sudden end to the conversation is a pattern I've

noticed from phone conversations with the few Korean people involved in organizing our trip. There is no "Maritime goodbye" like we're used to. No *Okay, well, I guess, well, I guess I'll talk to you tomorrow. Okay then. Take care. Have a great night. Okay. Thanks. See ya. Bye. Bye.* All I got from Mr. Lee and our recruiter, and the woman at the Korean Consulate in Montreal, was "BYE!" Very unceremonious, very final. It left me wanting more, wanting them to say something reassuring, needing a *Take care of yourself,* or *Great to talk to you.*

But Mr. Lee is gone, so I turn to the crowd of men milling around us. The taxi driver says he will take us to Jinju and we load all of our belongings and our exhausted selves into his van. We speak very little with him during the drive, as his English is quite limited and our Korean is nil. He endears himself to us though, when he shows us the audio tapes he plays in his car to learn English. The night is dark so our drive doesn't expose much of Korea. I am aware of steep mountainous shadows looming on each side of the road, and a lonely multilane highway stretching out beyond the headlights.

Our driver takes us to the Dong Bang Tourist Hotel, a name my spent brain finds way too amusing. Standing on the front steps of the hotel are Mr. Chang and Mr. Lee, principal and vice principal respectively of the middle school where I'll be working. We exchange handshakes, they look worriedly at all of our luggage, and they assure us repeatedly that the hotel is the nicest in Jinju. They check us in, and Mr. Lee advises that he will pick us up at nine o'clock the next morning. Everything is paid for and we're told our stay includes an "American breakfast"; I get the feeling they don't think we're ready for Korean food yet and perhaps their assumption is accurate.

We awake barely rested and eat bacon and eggs in the top-floor restaurant. From our high vantage point, Jinju appears to be a pleasant city with a wide, inviting river boldly meandering through its centre. I conclude it is the look of the buildings that tells me I'm on another continent: their arrangement and the unique and distinct Asian architecture.

At nine a.m., Mr. Lee arrives in his car, as does a separate van that will transport our luggage. We drive out of Jinju and into the countryside. I am astounded. Korea is beautiful! Korea is dotted with farmland and hills and mountains and rivers. Korea is beautiful! I had misjudged this country. I had assumed that because South Korea had close to fifty million inhabitants in a square footage not even twice the size of our small Canadian province of Nova Scotia (population not even one million), Korea would be wall-to-wall people and concrete. To my surprise, nature was everywhere and our drive had us winding along river valleys and hugging the mountainsides. We drove through countryside and small villages to Hwagae myeon (town), our home for the next year. Hwagae is located in the southwest of Gyeongsangnam-do (province), in Hadong-gun (county).

Our first impressions were that Hwagae is a very small town with a neighbourly feel, just what we were hoping for. There is a town centre with a few shops and restaurants, and then the businesses and homes spread out along a river valley and into the mountains. Bridges span the valley about every kilometre, to connect life on both sides. Already we are feeling at home and enjoying the protective mountains all around us.

Mr. Lee takes us to our house, which is located about forty metres behind Hwagae Elementary School, where I'll be teaching on Tuesdays. Across the road from the elementary is Hwagae Middle School. I'll teach there the other four days a week. Dale will be teaching twenty kilometres away in a town called Hadong. He'll teach two days a week at a girls' high school and three days a week at a boys' high school.

Our house is a small brick building and I can't wait to see the inside. Excitedly and without any cultural thought, I burst through the door, up the step, and into the living room ... with my shoes on ... a major faux pas in Korea. Mr. Lee politely tells me that shoes are not worn in homes in Korea. We would come to find out that you also do not wear shoes into schools, eating areas of restaurants, and many other places. Everywhere you go you take your shoes off and put on a pair of slippers that conveniently and miraculously appear. In my excitement to see the house I had actually leapt over the two pairs of slippers that were intended for us. Upon Mr. Lee's polite scolding, my first thought was *I'll wear whatever I please in my house ... when nobody else is there of course.* But we would come to appreciate this Mr. Rogers-like ritual of changing out of one's outdoor footwear into a pair of red and blue teddy-bear slippers.

There are two bedrooms in our new little house and we have taken the one on the front overlooking the elementary school. Our bed sits below large windows through which we can gaze up at the mountains. There is a kitchen and living room combination with a big TV. Strangely, the large window in this area looks out onto a small drab yard outlined with a couple of maintenance buildings and another small house. I say "strangely" because had the house been rotated 180 degrees, our living room would have had a wonderful bird's eye view of farmland, the river valley, and beautiful mountainsides. Instead, the bathroom, with its tiny window, too high for me to see out, was built with a view.

The bathroom has another interesting attribute to note: the shower, sink, and toilet are all on the same tile floor. There is no tub or lip to distinguish the shower area or restrain shower water. So the shower water and the water from our yet-to-arrive washing machine both will escape through a drain in the middle of the bathroom floor.

The house is freezing so Mr. Lee turns on the heat, tells us he'll be back in a few hours, and leaves. We start to settle in, unpack, and take inventory. I quickly realize that along with no washing machine, there is no fridge or adapter to plug in our computer and, most importantly, my hair dryer. I start to compile a wish list.

We spend a few hours of intermittent investigation: examining every wall, every corner, and standing in the middle of a room and listening, before we realize the heat is in the floor. This means the house is a bit slow to heat up, and since I know

I'll drive both of us crazy if I go all out unpacking, organizing, arranging, and decorating, we decide to head out and explore.

We walk around to the front of the elementary school and are quickly hailed by a frantically waving lady. Smiling warmly, she leads us into the school and a room holding what appears to be an important meeting. The meeting attendees look at us uncomfortably and then disperse at the command of our hostess. Dale and I are seated and very quickly there are tiny ceramic cups of steaming green tea in front of each of us. I am thankful it isn't strong and there isn't very much. Not being a tea drinker or particularly good at saying no when offered things, I begin having visions of the year ahead of me: faking my enjoyment of smelly green tea as I am forced to choke down cup after cup. But this tea is mild and I can manage one cup, maybe two.

Six teachers stand around us as we drink our tea, smiling and talking about us in Korean; sometimes giggling shyly, sometimes laughing heartily, and sometimes telling us how beautiful I am and how handsome Dale is. Not being used to so many compliments, I don't know if I'm supposed to compliment them as well: give them a friendly Canadian punch to the shoulder and say, *Yeah, you're not bad yourself, eh*, or simply say, *Thank you.*

After about fifteen minutes of watching the newcomers awkwardly drink tea, one of the teachers abruptly shows us out of the school. Apparently, they are done with us and quite frankly, we are scared of them, so we quickly retreat and hide in our house to wait for Mr. Lee. When he arrives, he takes us to the town centre to buy household and food items. Without refrigeration, we stock up on bread, jam, shrimp-flavoured chips, a Korean version of Mr. Noodles, and some fruit. Mr. Lee drives us back home and we continue to settle in.

Saturday is another beautiful Hwagae day, though I'm feeling pretty full of cold and my body is aching. Unpacking and decorating, something I usually love, feels more like a chore today. But I take many breaks and we rearrange and put away and eventually get our house feeling like ours.

In the afternoon we take a walk across the bridge, to the other side of the river, then down the hill towards town where we discover an outdoor market. The Hwagae Jangteo is one of the oldest markets in Korea dating back to around 700 C.E. There are a number of stalls, some with thatched roofs, people selling and cooking various goods, and music playing over a sound system. We get more strange looks and side stares but we just keep smiling and saying, "*Annyeong haseyo!*" Korea's common greeting.

An old lady at a stall hands me a dirty pop bottle cap full of a dark unknown liquid. I stare at it. She stares at me. I wonder if our Korean guidebook includes a phrase I can use to explain that I am allergic to all strange liquids. She stares at me. I am going to have to drink the liquid. What would my mother tell me to do? I think it might be poison; I think if it isn't poison, the filth on the bottle cap might do me in anyway; and I think I don't want to be kicked out of Hwagae on our second day so I knock it back. It is sweet and tasty. I smile, pass her the grimy-looking cap, nod in thanks, and walk away assessing how my body is feeling. My throat isn't closing over, my heart rate seems fine, and I can feel all of my extremities. I will be okay.

We walk across another bridge back to our side of the river and to Hwagae town centre. Our empty stomachs and adventurous spirit take over and we decide to go out for supper, by ourselves, armed with nothing but our Korean travel book. We assume this book to be all-knowing and will help us in any and all situations. However, at this point, we have only read the common phrases chapter and unfortunately haven't yet discovered the food section.

We choose the nearest restaurant and I lead the way inside. The waitress motions for us to go up a step and sit on the floor at one of the low tables. I now have Korean indoor footwear etiquette down to a science, I lived through the dark liquid, and I choked down green tea … I think I've got Korean culture all figured out. With confidence I walk to the step, take off my shoes, and put on the slippers waiting for me there. I step up to the eating area and start across the floor. The waitress begins giggling and then frantically, nervously, almost screaming, she grabs me and guides me back down the step. Indoor footwear faux pas, Number Two. I was not supposed to wear any footwear, even the safe "indoor" slippers, into the eating area. Not only had I worn footwear into the "no-fly" zone, it was the waitress's slippers I had put on. Dale finds this very amusing while I do not.

We get situated on the floor, legs crossed under the low table, and a man brings us a plate carrying about seventeen peanuts in the shell and a bottle of green, Crystal Light-looking liquid. At this point I'm really hoping it is Crystal Light or Kool-Aid or something to quench my thirst but it is cold green tea and I just can't stomach it right now.

The woman gives us menus which are written entirely in Korean aside from the prices. There aren't even pictures to guide us. I get out our travel book and search for some words that will help us explain what we'd like. We have no idea what their restaurant sells or what Korean food even looks like. We truly don't know anything, and from the moment I put on the waitress's teddy-bear slippers, I should have known it would all be downhill.

I find two useful phrases, *another bowl of rice please* and *we are vegetarians*. I imagine even though we don't have a first bowl of rice they might figure out we want rice and just bring us some. I also think, from the tanks of large fish sitting just outside the door, this restaurant might pride itself in serving live fish, so I throw in the vegetarian line for good measure. All of the page flipping and communication attempts take about fifteen minutes, and then suddenly a lady emerges from the kitchen with a tray of food. We are each given a bowl of rice, a bowl of soup containing what looks like baby clams and smells like decaying fish, and some plates with vegetables in sauces.

Aside from the rice and peanuts, we aren't fond of any of the food. We make a valiant effort to eat as much as we can, which is almost nothing, before we pay and leave. It is a worrisome walk home for both of us, discussing the disturbing reality that we might be eating stinky baby clam soup for a year.

During the evening we fill up on noodles and shrimp-flavoured chips and watch a movie. All but three of the twenty channels on our TV are in Korean. Unfortunately, the three English channels seem to only air cheesy Eric Roberts or Gary Busey movies, but because that's our only option, we watch.

TWO

The next morning, Sunday, we know Mr. Chang will be meeting with us. We have no idea when or for how long so we expect him no earlier than nine. I'm just out of the shower at 8:07 when we hear a knock at the door and it is Mr. Chang. He's driven eight hours, all night, to get back from Seoul where he attended his daughter's university graduation. Dale and I are still very jet lagged and I feel miserable, and one would think Mr. Chang would also be tired after driving eight hours through the night with no sleep. However, we would soon discover that sixty-two-year-old Mr. Chang is extremely fatigue-resistant.

We dress quickly, me in cargo pants and a sweater, Dale in casual clothing as well. While we move about the house getting ready, Mr. Chang snoops in and out of our messy rooms. His inspection worries me. Might he send us home because of the mess? Perhaps a messy house in Korea is incredibly disrespectful and punishment is fifteen lashes to the lady of the house. Regardless, he doesn't mention our housekeeping deficiencies and proceeds to take us down the hill, across the street to Hwagae Middle School, where he is the principal. He gives us a short tour before sitting us down in his office.

I study him as he looks around for glasses. His tall and lean frame is capped with jet black hair, parted to one side. I wouldn't have put him at sixty-two and guess that he keeps himself active; his fluid movements don't betray his age. His face is friendly enough and he seems eager to please and impress us. Retrieving a bottle from a shelf, he pours us each a small cup of Korean fruit wine. It is not yet nine a.m. but he seems eager to get alcohol in us ... or maybe in him. I am comforted to discover the wine tastes like the same liquid I drank out of the dirty bottle cap at the market the day before.

Next, he ceremoniously prepares and serves green tea using a beautiful Korean tea set. It is the first time we'd witness the traditional Korean preparation of tea. The tea set is first preheated by pouring hot water into the ceramic teapot as well as the serving bowl and small teacups. After a few minutes the water is drained and any extra water is wiped out of the cups and serving bowl using a towel. Loose green tea leaves are placed in the teapot. Water is boiled and poured into the teapot and the lid is placed on the top. After only about ten seconds all of the water is drained from the teapot. Again, the teapot is filled with boiling water, covered, and this time it is left to steep for a few minutes. When ready, the tea is poured into a serving bowl through a filter that catches any tea leaves. Finally, tea is poured into the individual teacups from the serving bowl.

After tea Mr. Chang serves coffee and slices of an orange fruit known as persimmon. It is the first time Dale and I have seen or heard of persimmons and we really enjoy the sweet juicy slices.

Finally, with a full belly, Mr. Chang gets down to business. He explains to us why we've been invited to Korea. His students are taught English by their Korean teacher, but they are only taught the grammar and technical aspects of English. They don't learn how to converse or use English in everyday situations. Mr. Chang hopes that if I teach the students math by only using English, it will help them speak, use, and understand English better. He gives me the math books which

21

start at the very basics – math skills the students already know. The students' familiarity with the math will help them pick up the language. Mr. Chang believes English sentences are like math equations and he wants the students to learn to write and say the equations and problems in English. The goal is to progress them to conversational English. The students will have no textbooks and the handouts I give them will become the textbook … if my work is good enough.

On Tuesdays, when I'm at Hwagae Elementary School, I won't be teaching math but don't yet know what curriculum will be covered. Dale will be teaching high school students who already have a good English base. Their teachers want him to initiate conversations and discussions.

We are here as part of a two-year research grant from the governor of this province or county, I'm not sure which. Dale and I didn't know any of this before we arrived in Korea but knowing it now, we're very excited to be part of the study. The schools will want us to stay for two years but our contract, and our intentions, state one year, so they will have to replace us next February. Mr. Chang seems very proud that his school and the foreign teachers he recruited are part of this study. He tells us we will even be meeting the governor soon.

We leave Hwagae Middle School and Mr. Chang takes us to his house, another small building on elementary school property. He actually lives in Jinju with his wife but stays in Hwagae during the week, and tells us many of the teachers do the same.

Mr. Chang puts a plate in front of us piled with cakes, cookies, and Timbit-looking things that taste nothing like Timbits, much to my dismay. He serves up more coffee, not giving me a chance to decline, and some very strong wine. He brings me a spoon for my coffee and I notice as he approaches that the spoon is not clean. He rubs the concave side of the spoon with his thumb then seems to consider its cleanliness for a moment. We both stare at him. I half expect him to lick the spoon clean, but he comes to some conclusion and drops the spoon into my coffee.

As we sip our coffees, he fusses around his house which, by the way, is messier than ours and I start to relax about the state of our house. Then he announces we are going to church and suggests I might want to change; apparently cargo pants are not appropriate church attire. Never are we asked if we'd like to go to church; do we have any plans already today; do we want to spend our entire day with him? No, those questions are not necessary. Mr. Chang is our host; we're his "family," as he calls us, and he feels obliged to take good care of us and first on his list of good hosting duties is taking us to church.

I change my clothes, and we set out on our first incredibly painful drive with Mr. Chang. His church is all the way back in Jinju, an hour and a half away, and he putts along well below the speed limit the entire drive. Along the journey I attempt to learn a bit about Korea. I ask Mr. Chang if there is much crime in the area. He responds by telling me, "Yes, many Korean people like to climb the mountain." I notice that talking causes him to drive even slower, so I curb the questions for the time being.

We arrive twenty minutes late for church. It isn't a free-standing structure like the churches back home in Canada, but is a Presbyterian church located on the top floor of a building. There are no pews; instead, everyone sits in chairs at tables that are facing the front of the room, like a university classroom. Similar to churches I've been to, there is a choir and a piano player as well as hymn books. In fact, they have English and Korean hymn books so we can sing along.

Growing up, my family went to the United Church: a very uneventful, predictable, and bland service of listening, singing, and reading prayers written in the weekly church bulletin. As an adult, I realized church wasn't for me and I found other ways to pass my Sunday mornings. Never before had I experienced this kind of worshiping though: the entire congregation chanting to themselves, eyes closed, everyone saying something different, some shouting loudly, and others shuddering and moving about. At one point Dale and I are asked to stand up while the congregation serenades us with a really *really* long welcome song. Some boys are then asked to stand up and the congregation sings them a really REALLY long goodbye song as they soon will be going away to school. Then, during the final prayer, the minister starts sobbing, overcome by sadness that the boys are going away. While I don't find it in the least bit spiritual, it is an exceptionally interesting church service.

After the final prayers, the congregation is invited to greet us and we are swarmed by giggling girls and boys and women and men, shaking our hands, waving, saying hello. I thought we might even be asked for our autographs. We're invited into another room where we're served tea with the minister and he asks us a few questions using the English he knows. He gives us a calendar, as well as two hand towels embossed with the church's name. We eat lunch with the congregation. It is similar-looking food to what we were served during our first Korean restaurant disaster but this time it tastes much better.

Mr. Chang introduces us to his wife, who is a very beautiful sophisticated-looking woman, and the rest of our church visit is spent socializing with the minister's wife. She leads two cute girls in a singsong of English Christian children's songs for us and by the fourth number Dale is belting out the songs right along with them.

At around one p.m. we depart the church, assuming we would be on our way back to Hwagae to rest in the quiet sanctuary of our house. Instead, Mr. Chang drives us to the Jinju fortress where he attempts to educate us on some of the history of the area. The fortress is located in the centre of the city, along the Nam River, and is truly a beautiful site. We wander around trying to absorb some of the history surrounding Japanese invasions at that location. Mr. Chang tells us the story of Nongae, a beautiful Korean courtesan whose husband was killed by Japanese forces during an invasion in

1593. It is said that to avenge her husband's death as well as her country, Nongae lured a Japanese general to the edge of a cliff along the Nam River. She embraced him and then caused them to fall from the cliff into the river, thereby killing them both.

Finally, Mr. Chang decides it is time to head back home. First, he stops by his Jinju house to pick up some supplies for his week in Hwagae. When he returns to the car, he gives us both a bag of ginseng juice. "Good for the health," he tells us as he gulps his down. Eagerly anticipating a delicious beverage, I try to open my juice bag. I cannot so Dale offers me his, which is already open. What a gentleman my husband is. He takes my unopened juice bag and, as he's in the front seat and I cannot see what he's doing, I imagine him opening the bag and slurping back the juice. I take a big gulp. Oh no! I am close to vomiting. Dale asks me how my juice is as he hides the smirk on his face. I manage, "Mmm, great."

For a half hour I valiantly try to down my ginseng juice, not wanting to offend Mr. Chang and thinking Dale must be choking his back in the front seat. My history with car sickness resurfaces at some point along the long winding road back to Hwagae. I know that one more sip will make me vomit. Just the smell of the ginseng juice coupled with Mr. Chang's air freshener might push me past the breaking point. I discreetly place my bag of juice in the pocket of the car door, wondering how Dale can possibly stomach his.

We arrive in Hwagae, drive past our house, and on to a Buddhist temple that Mr. Chang insists we see. Getting out of the car I discover that Dale still has an unopened bag of ginseng juice in his possession. I curse him under my breath.

All of the "hospitality" Mr. Chang is showing us is extremely kind but my head feels like it will soon explode. We are exhausted, we're still experiencing jet lag, I'm full of cold, and, quite frankly, we are both getting a bit Mr. Chang-ed out.

A walk around the temple grounds and a few comments from Dale and me about the beautiful scenery and architecture is sufficient for Mr. Chang to usher us back to his car. However, he again drives past our house and on to a restaurant in Hwagae. Apparently, it is time for us to eat. As exhausted as we are, we really enjoy our meal and are optimistic about the culinary delights that our year in Korea will bring. Pieces of pork are cooked over charcoal on our table. We put the meat on lettuce leaves, add some vegetables and sauce, fold it up, and eat it. We eat and eat, but the food is never-ending. Whenever we finish a dish, more of that dish appears. When finally we are beyond stuffed and Mr. Chang is paying, there is no mention or offer of a doggy bag for the remaining food on our table. As I was raised to clean my plate, in a house that always had a fridge full of leftovers, it took a lot of willpower for me to walk away from a table filled with delicious unspoiled food.

Following supper, the intrepid Mr. Chang seems to feel he has put in a successful day of hosting his "family" and decides to take us home. I am in bed within minutes, but not many more later there is a knock at our door. Dale opens it to find Mr. Chang, panting and straining to hold a metal machine about twice the size of a car battery. Mr. Chang has struggled up a steep embankment and across a hundred metres of uneven ground, in the dark, to bring this machine to us. He explains that it is an adaptor for the North American plugs on our computer and my hair dryer. This is definitely not the same kind of adaptor I could have bought at the luggage store back in Canada but it will work.

He brings up my comment from earlier in the day when I told him we were having problems with our hot water, and he thinks now is a good time for him to fix that too. The problem with the hot water is that we only get about a minute's worth in the shower. Unexpectedly, there is lots of hot water in the back of the toilet.

Dale invites Mr. Chang in. He hasn't brought his glasses, though, so he can't read the dials controlling the water heater. The settings are written in Korean so we also cannot read them. Dale tells Mr. Chang we do not need the water fixed tonight, tomorrow will be fine. Mr. Chang leaves and Dale joins me in bed.

Sometime later that night we are sure we hear footsteps outside. There is a separate small utility room on the outside of the house where you turn the hot water on and off and we think Mr. Chang was in there trying to fix it. The next morning, however, there is still no hot water.

*   *   *

Along one of the outside walls of our bedroom is an air conditioner. The machine isn't plugged in but during that night we hear noises coming from the unit. It sounds like there is something alive and moving around inside of it. Dale gets out of bed and removes the cover from the machine but can see nothing inside. For a while we lay awake imagining what type of animal could be making the noises. They weren't chirps or squeaks so it couldn't be a bird or mouse. Dale thinks the noises might be from chemical reactions happening inside the air conditioner. I am skeptical of his theory and point out the air conditioner isn't even plugged in and shouldn't be making any noises and what chemicals are even in an air conditioner? We sleep very little that night.

My alarm goes off at seven the next morning. I am considering giving our alarm clock away as Mr. Chang's habitual morning visits and calls are rendering it redundant. At 7:05 a.m. Mr. Chang phones to invite us to come for breakfast at his house. He serves up eggs, rice, soup with what he describes as "good ham" (it was Spam, I saw the can on the counter), and kimchi.

We had heard about kimchi before we left Canada. Friends who had been to Korea described kimchi as *Korea's national food*: fermented cabbage often mixed with spices from red peppers. Being labelled a national food I had high hopes for kimchi, but wasn't overly impressed with it, especially at breakfast. It was spicy, salty, limp, and cold. Mr. Chang tells us Koreans eat it at every meal and it is very healthy. Seeing as it is healthy, I decide to try my best to eat it with at least *some* meals in the future.

Mr. Chang caps off our meal with what he calls "Korean coffee." He takes the pot he'd cooked the rice in, adds water to the rice that is stuck to the bottom of the pot, boils it, and serves it to us as "coffee."

After breakfast, we head to Hwagae Middle School where Mr. Chang serves us green tea in his office and shows us his bamboo flute/recorder instrument. Much to our surprise and slight horror, he proceeds to play us a number of songs while we sit there awkwardly smiling and listening. We hear "Auld Lang Syne," "Amazing Grace," as well as some Scottish and Korean folk songs. We wonder when it will end; we wonder if he subjects all of his teachers to his serenades or are we the only lucky ones; and, most importantly, we wonder if and when we'll ever teach.

We had arrived in South Korea during the break between school years. The first day of classes will be in three days, and I don't know if I can take three more days of being "hosted" by Mr. Chang. Eventually the concert ends and Dale and I escape home to prepare our house for the fridge and washing machine which will be delivered that day.

Mr. Chang phones just before lunch to invite us to eat with all of the middle school teachers. Dale had already eaten and didn't feel like spending any more time with Mr. Chang, but as it was my school and my colleagues, I felt I should go. Mr. Chang is disappointed to see me alone. He tells me, "Husband should protect wife." I don't like his comment. He smirks at me. I insist it will be fine if I join the teachers myself.

Still, he won't take no for an answer. Mr. Chang phones our house and we wait for Dale. We are going to a restaurant for lunch but Dale thinks, as I had as well, that we are eating at the school. He takes his time.

Mr. Chang, a somber-looking male teacher, and myself await Dale and finally we spot him flying down the hill towards us on his skateboard. I am horrified. I have no idea how Dale's actions will be received. I have already been told that ice cream, my favourite, is only eaten by children in Korea. How will they react to a twenty-seven-year-old man on a skateboard? Mr. Chang and the other man are surprised, but seemingly amused.

We have another delicious meal and Mr. Chang, Mr. Lee, Dale, and I walk back to the school. I tell Mr. Lee about my family. He is interested in the ages of my parents. He asks my religion and when Dale and I will have kids. My mother would be shocked by his bold questions. I tell him about Keno, the dog Dale and I left behind in Canada, and I say how much I miss him. Mr. Lee tells me, "In Korea we eat dogs." I tell him I am not happy about that custom. We proceed to have a debate on the eating of various animals and our beliefs. I think, if Keno could have just ten minutes with Mr. Lee he'd change his tune about eating all dogs forever. I ask him if he has any pets. He tells me a Persian cat. I want to say, "Mmm, sounds tasty," but I refrain.

I am missing Keno terribly. I missed him the most the day before we left for Korea. Since we weren't exactly sure of our departure date due to some ticket mishaps, we decided to say goodbye to him early. Two days before our departure we'd dropped him off with a friend who would take care of him until my parents got home from Florida. All the next day I looked for him around the house, in his bed where he often is, and by my feet when I went up and down the stairs. His food and water dishes were gone as were all his toys, and I cried for hours. Dale offered to pick him up and bring him home for the day but I thought that would be harder for all of us, mostly me.

We had contemplated bringing Keno with us to Korea, but I was scared the fourteen-hour flight would be too hard on him and we didn't know how difficult it would be for us to have a dog here. It bothers me greatly, though, to think he might not remember us when we get back. Maybe he'll like it better at the sitter's and not want to live with us again. Maybe they'll let him up on their furniture and feed him lots of people food and he'll resent Dale and me forever because we were so strict with him. How will I ever deal with parenting real children if I worry so much about my dog?

We walk by the spot where we usually see Pedro and Simba. They are two absolutely adorable puppies who have chased us down the sidewalk a few times, the yellow one behind me and the dark one behind Dale. He named the dark one Pedro, the name of his father's childhood dog, and I named the yellow one Simba as he is identical to the lion cub from *The Lion King*.

The first time we saw them I thought they belonged to no one and maybe we could rescue them from their street life. Dale said they were too fat to belong to no one. The next time we saw them we discovered their parents, each attached by a very short chain to a doghouse. Dale figures the dogs are being raised for eating. This makes me want to rescue them even more. I start concocting a scheme involving a nighttime heist, black clothing, and my quietest teddy-bear slippers. Dale will have nothing of the plan.

As we near the school Dale asks Mr. Lee if he'd like to try his skateboard. Mr. Lee has already told me he doesn't play any sports. He doesn't appear to be very athletic or coordinated and he's fifty-six years old. I don't think it's a good idea, but Mr. Lee gives it a try anyway. After about ten seconds of teetering along he thankfully decides to call it quits and escapes with all his skin, bones, and teeth intact.

Later in the afternoon we drive with Mr. Chang to Hadong to meet with the principals of Dale's two schools. Hadong is about twenty minutes away by car and is on the route to Jinju. The town is bigger than Hwagae and is where students from our area go to high school.

Still wondering if our area is a safe place to live, I rephrase my question from the day before and ask if there are many criminals in the area. Mr. Chang launches into a detailed description of the many types of cameras he knows of.

The meetings go well. We sit on display as the principals and vice principals (all male) rapidly talk about us, sometimes laughing, sometimes serious, and again tell us how good-looking we are. We tour both the boys' high school and the girls' high school, and are served beverages at both sites as well.

On the drive home, Dale finally gets Mr. Chang to understand my question concerning crime in the area. He reassures us that Korea is very safe. He asks us to join him for dinner, but we decline and enjoy an evening at home.

This morning, Tuesday, I am up at 3:20 a.m., wide awake.

Mr. Chang calls at 7:05 a.m. for us to come to breakfast at his house again. I say I am going jogging, but thank you anyway. He asks, "When, then, can you come?" Again I thank him and say we're just going to grab some jam and toast at our house.

I meet all the teachers at Hwagae Middle School today, and I am assigned a desk in the teachers' office. There are four other new teachers at the school this year. The five of us watch while the others move desks. I don't know why those who already had desks can't just keep them, and we new teachers can take over the empty ones. For most of the morning the office is in chaos while teachers empty the hoards of items from their old desk area and transport their belongings across the room to their new desk.

We are taken out for lunch as a staff with Mr. Chang footing the bill again. He is always quick to point out how much he is spending on us – our hotel room in the Dong Bang and each of the meals he insists on treating us to.

Surprisingly, we have no obligations all afternoon so Dale and I relax at home for the rest of the day. Tomorrow is a national holiday, not that we haven't been on holiday since we arrived, and then it will be the first day of school. Finally!

THREE

I can hear the trumpet sounding, *Dun, Dun, Na Na!* Success! Success at what? you might ask. Success in the bathroom department. While it certainly isn't dinner conversation appropriate, pooping is something I've been working on since we arrived in Korea, one week ago today. Getting backed up is often a problem for travellers and I have experienced it before. Usually I can find something fibrous – some All-Bran, some prunes, something to get me going, but I haven't found anything. I imagine not pooping for a week isn't good for you, and I'd like to know the science behind it. How can I go a full week without pooping and still have an intact midsection? At times, though, the noises and movement in my stomach did worry me that I might be about to explode.

Although coffee is a diuretic, drinking it didn't help. Normally, I never drink coffee, I don't like it. I hadn't even drunk a full cup in all my twenty-six years prior to landing in Korea. But I've been given coffees by a number of hospitable Koreans since we arrived, and I have to say it isn't bad. Dale says it's not really coffee. What we've been served comes in single-serve sachets. The sachet contains one serving of coffee and the perfect amount of powdered milk and sugar. You empty the sleeve into your cup, add some water, and voila, even I can't screw it up. But, despite my coffee consumption, it wasn't until today that I had a BM (bowel movement as my mom would prefer me to call it) and I feel like dancing.

Yesterday, the "holiday," our phone rang at 7:20 a.m. I answered but nobody was there. We both breathed a sigh of relief – no Chang! We were supposed to go hiking in the mountains with his church congregation, but the night before he told us it was supposed to snow and rain so the hike would be cancelled. We were looking forward to the hike, some exercise, and new scenery. However, not hiking meant we could spend our holiday without Mr. Chang, and a Chang-free day of rest before the first day of school sounded good to both of us. Mr. Chang had other plans.

He knocked on our door at ten a.m. He didn't reveal his exact intentions, but we understood that he wanted us to go to the school to have coffee, again. Mr. Bear, another teacher at Hwagae Middle School, would also be part of the plan and there was something happening related to pictures or albums. As Mr. Bear is our favourite Korean person, we didn't mind going to the school with him and Mr. Chang on the holiday.

I'd like to tell you why Mr. Bear is our favourite Korean, but I can't pinpoint a specific reason. During our first month in Korea, he endeared himself to us so much but said barely anything at all. It might have been his name. I believe his family name is actually Bae but we heard "Bear" when we were first introduced and nobody corrected us, so he lovingly became Mr. Bear. He stands about five feet, is in his fifties, and has a shaggy bowl-cut hair-do which he coifs to perfection. Each day he arrives at school in a suit that is too big for him, and he always accentuates his outfit with a pastel striped tie. Mr. Bear knows very little English but comes out with a word every now and again, and says it with vim and vigour, and after hooking up the internet in our house Mr. Bear gave Dale high tens. Many times, we've spied him strolling along singing merrily to himself. Taking long, straight-legged strides, he swings his arms and claps his hands to the beat of his gait, and his song. At meals,

Mr. Bear makes sure Dale and I know all of the customs, and at work he's spent countless hours fixing my computer. And not only does Mr. Bear teach computer technology, he is also the cooking teacher. Mr. Bear wearing an apron over his baggy suit is an image that always makes me smile.

We like Mr. Bear for so many reasons, and each day there is something he *doesn't* say that makes us like him even more. One day it was when I looked up from my work and saw him peacefully sleeping at his desk, his toothbrush sticking out of his shirt pocket. Two days ago, it was when Dale was walking in downtown Hwagae and Mr. Bear drove up to him, beeping a few times on his approach. When he had Dale beside him, he rolled down his window, smiled big, beeped five or six more times, and drove away. He never spoke a word, just smiled and beeped.

With Mr. Chang waiting in our living room, we agreed to his request and headed to the school.

The mountains were incredible yesterday morning. It had snowed through the night, but the snow only made it partway down the mountain. It looked like spring had captured the valley but the mountains were still clinging to winter.

We met Mr. Bear, who was wearing a very puffy white jacket, at the school. Mr. Chang explained to us that Mr. Bear knows a good place at the base of some mountains where he'll take pictures of us for the school website.

We boarded Mr. Bear's Korean Land Rover-looking vehicle and started driving. Eventually we stopped and Mr. Bear posed Dale and me in the centre of a winding mountain road. He took two pictures. Then Mr. Chang joined us and two more pictures were taken. Then Mr. Chang took the camera and Mr. Bear joined Dale and me and two more pictures were taken. Then Mr. Bear gave Dale the camera, saying, "Single," and Dale took two pictures of me. Mr. Bear then said, "Switchy," and I took two pictures of Dale. The camera was handed around a bit more and a few more combinations of pictures were taken. The entire time the photoshoot was happening, we were dodging in and out of the middle of the road to avoid the cars speeding up and down the mountain.

"Whew! Glad that's over," I whispered to Dale after we got back in Mr. Bear's vehicle. But it had only just begun. We climbed the mountain further and stopped and took more shots, each time taking sets of two pictures then doing "switchy" to capture every possible combination of us. We posed in front of many different backdrops on the way up the mountains and the higher we reached the more snow there was.

Some time later we arrived at a Buddhist temple to explore and, of course, to take more pictures. A stranger with a very expensive-looking camera and tripod grabbed Dale and me and asked us to be models in his pictures. He posed us. He had me point at a temple building in a very Sears catalogue-like shot. Dale was placed beside me and we were both instructed to smile. He took about thirty pictures, but no "switchy," thank goodness. I wondered if our pictures would end up on a billboard, in a Korean tourism brochure, or on the cover of *Buddhist Temple Weekly*.

After enjoying the grounds around the temple, we headed home. But "First we eat!" Mr. Chang said, "What fun it is to eat together!"

He took us out for lunch again, but this time Mr. Bear was there so I wasn't disappointed. As we've grown accustomed to, the meal included twenty-plus plates of vegetables prepared in various ways. The main dish this time was a delicious stew and a boiled chicken which the hostess brought to the table whole and broke into pieces, cracking bones and tearing meat apart, in front of us. The food was great and finally Mr. Chang let us go home for the night.

The next morning there is no phone call – we unplugged the phone. It is the first day of the school year and we dress in our best "teacher clothes." Dale asks me to look up Half Windsor Knot tying on the internet. The last wedding we went to, Dale attended the ceremony while his tie sat in the car. When he got a moment at the reception he had one of his buddies assemble his tie. Now he'd like me to read the tutorial on a Half Windsor and attempt it with his tie. The last time I wore a tie was in elementary school when skinny leather ties on girls were in style. I had a gray one but I don't think I ever knew how to tie it. I run through "8½ Steps to a Half Windsor," but my effort looks messy. Finally, Dale takes the time to learn for himself and is successful.

We walk to the middle school, past hoards of smiling, giggling, and blushing kids. Many of them yell, "Hello!" and wave, then turn away covering their mouths with their hands. Those who are immersed in conversation with their schoolmates stop dead in their tracks when they look up and see us approaching. One girl dropped all the books she was carrying. If we say, "Hello!" back to them, they scream or start fanning their faces like they're having hot flashes.

All the teachers are buzzing about the teachers' office. It seems they are very disorganized, and we will be glad to be teaching instead of sitting around doing nothing while people rearrange things and hold meetings in Korean.

Dale, myself, and the other four new teachers are introduced to the students during an assembly in the gym. They seem very excited to see us and go wild when I say, "Hello!" into the microphone.

Mr. Chang is to take us to set up our Korean bank accounts this morning. Before leaving, he asks us if we have ID. Dale and I both have our driver's licenses on us, but our passports are home. We ask if we need our passports and Mr. Chang tells us, "No."

As we near the bank I sense his stress rising. He always hates parking. Instead of looking for a parking spot he stops right in front of the bank door, blocking three parked cars, turns his car off, and ushers us into the bank. We are guided to sit down, and are served energy drinks resembling Red Bull in look and taste. Bank staff speak in Korean to Mr. Chang and he turns to us and asks us if we have our passports. My hands clench under the table. *No, Mr. Chang, you told us we wouldn't need our passports and we haven't left your side since we first told you our passports were home, so how could we possibly have our freakin' passports?* I manage to keep these thoughts to myself. We leave the bank, much to the pleasure of the drivers who were blocked in by Mr. Chang's car. We drive home, collect our passports, return to the bank, block three other vehicles in their parking spots, and begin the banking process again.

Setting up our accounts takes more time than Mr. Chang anticipated, and we are supposed to be in Hadong for 11:30. At 11:10 we rush out of the bank and Mr. Chang says we must "make haste." He drives forty-five kilometres an hour the whole way to Hadong. It is painful. Perhaps he drives so slowly because his singalong during the trip distracted him from applying the gas pedal. Sometime between "The Farmer in the Dell" and "Here We Go Loopty Loo," Dale suggests we should drive faster and Mr. Chang responds by asking if we know "You Are My Sunshine." The last ten minutes of the drive are filled with "Auld Lang Syne," "Doe, a Deer," and "Home on the Range."

"What fun it is to sing!" Mr. Chang says to us. I am dangerously close to peeing my pants, so I pinch my leg to stop myself from laughing hysterically.

We are in Hadong to attend a ceremony christening the new shuttle buses that transport students to and from school. Dale will actually take one of the buses from Hwagae to Hadong each day when he goes to work. We are met by a crowd of teenagers who react as the students in Hwagae did – like we are The Beatles or some Korean pop band. We are introduced to the governor of Gyeongsangnam-do, a small man in a sharp navy suit with a pink tie. The girls swoon over the governor as they do us. He keeps grabbing my hand, saying, "Beautiful!" and making sure I'm beside him in the pictures. Thankfully, the ceremony is short, as it is cold and windy outside. I feel bad for the female students whose school uniform is a knee-length skirt.

Once back in Hwagae we go out for lunch with the

middle school teachers again. Mr. Bear is very attentive to us and guides us through the technicalities of the meal. This time there is no meat but everyone instead gets a big steaming pot of rice. We are given a variety of vegetables to mix with the rice and eat. Once the pot is empty, we add water to the rice stuck to the bottom of the pot and we eat this as a "treat," or as Mr. Chang taught us, "Korean coffee."

Our first official school day has come and gone without us teaching. *Perhaps tomorrow,* we think.

The second day of school, a Friday, sees Dale heading to Hadong on his own to teach at one of the high schools, and me heading down the hill to teach at the middle school. Still, though, we do not teach, but instead hang out in the teachers' office and get introduced in yet another assembly.

We've met all of our teaching colleagues by this time. Out of the fifteen teachers at my school, four have the last name Kim, and four have the surname Lee. One Mr. Kim is one of the two Korean English teachers. His own English is so limited that I don't understand how he could ever be put in charge of teaching someone else English. He is a very sweet man, however, and I try to help him as much as possible.

Following my school's introductory ceremony on Friday, Mr. Kim drives me to Hadong to pick up Dale. He is to take us to Sacheon to apply for our alien registration cards, a necessary step to having health insurance in Korea. Sacheon is about an hour and a half drive from Hwagae, and Mr. Kim has never been there before but is armed with instructions. He invites Dale and me to both sit in the backseat of his car. He points to the cross hanging from his rearview mirror and asks if we are Christians. He tells us he would like to take us to his church sometime. We say, "Maybe at Christmas or Easter."

About halfway to Sacheon, Mr. Kim begins fussing. It seems that despite having directions, he isn't sure we are going the right way. When Mr. Kim fusses, he puts his teeth together and takes a deep inhale, making a distinctive seething sound. Mr. Kim is making this sound every few minutes as he looks again and again at his directions. Finally, he pulls over to ask for help and nods understandingly at the person who gives him instructions.

We arrive in Sacheon, but now Mr. Kim must find the Immigration Office. He pulls over and asks directions three times in a one-block radius. After hearing each set of directions, he nods, smiles, says, "Aah!" and drives off. He rounds the block, searches the buildings, does his fussing sound, pulls over, and asks another person for directions. Eventually, after driving past it four times, we arrive at our destination.

Following the paperwork, Mr. Kim takes us out for Korean pizza. Dale and I are very excited! We haven't eaten cheese since we left Canada and pizza is one of our favourite meals. I order Hawaiian. The pizza arrives and not only is there the traditional pineapple on my Hawaiian pizza, there is also corn, peas, plus all the other fruit a can of fruit cocktail includes – peaches, pears, and cherries. The pizza was a bit of comfort food that reminded us of home, but it left us feeling sluggish and bloated and made us realize how much we had already grown accustomed to Korean food.

We return to Hwagae in time for our first teacher wellness activity: volleyball. I really enjoy volleyball so I'm looking forward to it. It's one of my favourite sports and I'm pretty good at it. After the game with the teachers, however, I never wanted to play volleyball again. We played with nine people per side on a larger court. This allowed for everyone to play at the same time but fewer opportunities to actually touch the ball. There was no rotating; everyone stayed in the position where they started the game. This meant the women and less-skilled male players were hidden at the back of the court and the good hitters and players were at the front of the court. I was never passed the ball and the ball was actually stolen from me many times by various men on my team.

I have lost many hard-fought volleyball matches in my life. I have played with and coached men and women who were much older than I, and who were much more skilled than the teachers from Hwagae Middle School. My family even has an outdoor volleyball court at our cottage. The court – my dad's creation – includes a net attached to a pole on one side and a metal shed on the other. The lines are not parallel and one side is definitely larger than the other. When we played, my dad changed the rules just about every point, depending on if his team was losing or winning. Over the years of highly competitive cottage games, where sometimes the ball could be played off the shed, I have learned to be patient and to have fun whether losing or winning, or whether my dad was playing by the rules or not. But I did not have the patience for volleyball in Hwagae.

As I stood, a motionless pylon on the court, seething from every orifice of my body, I thought, *My God, Beth Ann, get a grip on yourself. This is just a game. It's volleyball. Why are you getting so worked up? You're being childish.*

Then another male teacher jumped in front of me and took my pass. I knew if I told him he was out of position and, in fact, that was my ball he'd just hit, he would have no clue what I was saying. And I also knew that even if he could understand English, he wouldn't care what I was saying. I stood, and I seethed.

FOUR

"The Creature," as we've started to call it, in our air conditioner, has not left us yet. Maybe it never goes home. Maybe the air conditioner is its home. We haven't figured out just what type of creature it is, but we know he or she is in our air conditioner doing jumping jacks every night. Many times, we've looked into the machine but can see nothing. We determined it must be nocturnal as it only makes noise at night. We checked all around the outside of our house but could not find a passage for The Creature to enter or leave the air conditioner – nothing we could block off.

During the third night of fitful sleep due to The Creature's nocturnal fumblings, I dreamt Dale took the cover off the air conditioner again. This time three sets of crustaceous claws poked out of the top. Then three-clawed Transformers made of Maxwell House coffee cans emerged. I grabbed a weapon. I can't remember what my weapon was, but it must have been very sharp because I sliced through the Transformers, cutting them in half at the waist. I woke up. It was 3:30 a.m., and it was still making noise.

Two nights ago, The Creature was driving us crazy again. I jumped out of bed and started viciously banging on the air conditioner. I kept the torment up for at least two minutes but still The Creature would not rest. We slept in the spare bedroom that night and I lay awake feeling sorry for him or her and the fright I might have caused it.

Yesterday afternoon we had had enough and we went hunting. Dale slowly removed the entire air conditioner unit from the wall and found a small sickly-looking bat hiding behind the machine. With army-like precision – me armed with a garbage pail and Dale with our Lonely Planet calendar – we managed to catch the bat in the pail and trap it using the calendar. We then released the bat in the yard behind our house where it tumbled into the grass and lay there motionless.

The next time we checked on The Creature, a few hours later, it was gone. Dale thinks it either flew away to a better life or was eaten by a cat. I suggested he might have found his way back through our wall into the air conditioner. We both joined in a spontaneous rendition of "The Bat Came Back, the Very Next Day." For a few nights after that I lay awake listening for it, but our Creature did not return.

* * *

We continue to experience water problems at our house. The shower, or, more appropriately named, dribble, is hot for maybe a minute. You must wash your hair in the kitchen sink, as there isn't enough pressure or hot water to wash it in the shower. If you shower with the nozzle in the nozzle holder on the wall, you have to press your body into the cold tiles of the wall in order to get wet. So soap goes in one hand, nozzle in the other, "switchy" halfway through, and out in less than fifty seconds, before the water turns cold.

As our showers have to be quick, it has become necessary to spot check each other for lingering soap residue.

"Wait, Dale, you've still got soap behind your ears."

"Beth Ann, check your eyebrows before you leave the house."

The funny thing that neither of us finds funny is there continues to be an abundance of hot water in the back of the toilet. This frustrates us to no end. When either of us is planning a shower, we try not to flush the toilet for several hours beforehand, to salvage the full sixty seconds of hot water. We've seen no evidence that the hot water in the toilet tank even affects the water temperature in the shower, but we're missing a nice hot shower so much we'll try anything.

Why there is hot water in the toilet is beyond our imaginations. But now, every time I visit a bathroom in Korea, I feel the back of the toilet to see if their water is hot too. So far only ours is this deluxe.

Our washing machine was delivered on Monday along with our fridge. The fridge is slightly bigger than a bar fridge and was taken from one of the rooms at Hwagae Middle School, possibly from Mr. Bear's cooking room. The washing machine is a top-loading Samsung and is a similar size to our machine at home. But, instead of flipping up, the top is in two pieces and folds onto itself. All of the buttons are in Korean but some of them have pictures so I can figure out load size and water temperature at least. However, I have no idea what type of washing cycle or how many rinses I have chosen.

Each load seems to take a while but I'm not going to mess with the settings. When a load finishes the machine chimes a little tune to let me know my wash is ready. A similar chiming sound comes from somewhere near our front door if we've left it open for more than thirty seconds. And all of the school bells play pleasant chiming songs as well. Their tune sounds like the Christmas carol "What Child is This," but Dale claims it is "Greensleeves." I'm thinking they might be the same song. Nonetheless, I much prefer the chiming school bells in Korea to the harsh, honking bells in our Canadian schools.

Our little bathroom houses the washing machine, shower, sink, and toilet. If one wanted, one could be using the toilet while putting a load of whites in the washing machine, lathering up one's body with soap, and spitting mouthwash into the sink, all in one go. But, while our bathroom has been engineered with efficiency in mind, the drain in the centre of the floor is for both the washing machine and the shower, which makes going to the washroom during a spin cycle, when the water is draining, particularly tricky. When wet, the tiles are very slippery and I've hydroplaned a number of times in my teddy-bear slippers while trying to get to the sink.

We have no dryer for our laundry. We didn't have one at home either, so it doesn't bother me. I picked up a package of clothespins, labelled "laundry pinchers," at the little grocery store in Hwagae and I hang our clothes to dry outside. Our clothesline is tied between two trees and supported in the middle by a bamboo post. Bamboo is extremely plentiful in Korea and can grow into plants twelve metres high – nothing like the little bamboo plant I have in a vase back home, the one that hasn't grown but also hasn't died in two years.

My favourite part of doing laundry here, after I dance to the washing machine song, is hanging the clothes out to dry. I love that there is a bamboo post holding up my clothesline and I love that when I look up from my basket of clothes, I am gazing into incredible mountains all around me. We are so lucky.

FIVE

I wonder what ever possessed me to give up my government job, leave our beautiful house and dog, and come here to teach these horrible children. Had I written yesterday, after my first day of teaching at Hwagae Middle School, I would have described the satisfaction of being a teacher, of influencing young minds, and broadening the horizons of today's youth. Yes, I loved every minute of it. I only taught two classes, however, both grade threes (grade nine in Canada). The kids were about fourteen years old and were interested in me. I brought pictures of my family and of Canada to share with them and they politely passed them around the room as I told my story. They listened to me, they asked questions, they were quiet when I asked them to be quiet, we joked, we laughed, we connected, and we looked forward to seeing each other again.

Mr. Kim accompanied me to class but left soon after he introduced me. I was happy and comfortable having the kids to myself. "More freedom," Mr. Kim had said when he suggested it. I agreed, knowing he would rather be fussing about his desk in the teachers' office anyway. I didn't tell him, though, that I thought his own English might benefit from sitting in on my classes.

Then today arrived, my one day a week to teach eight- to twelve-year-olds at Hwagae Elementary School. I didn't have to teach until eleven a.m. so the morning was mine to relax and enjoy.

When I do arrive at school, I am given teaching materials – textbooks and CDs, as well as a schedule, something the middle school has trouble providing for me. I was impressed. So impressed I ignored the fact that none of the teachers at the elementary school could speak very much English or communicate with me. *Who needs the teachers?* I thought. *I've got books and my own merits, and these kids will be a breeze.*

I had arrived early so I sat down to go through the textbooks and prepare my introductory lessons. Some of the teachers buzzed around me, obviously talking about me in Korean. They told me I was beautiful, and one male teacher was able to inquire if I was married.

I open the students' textbook and brightly coloured cartoons jumped out at me. The few words in the textbook were in Korean. Not a problem, I also have a *Teacher's Guidebook* for each grade. I open my Guidebook and I see pages and pages of Korean. I flip ahead to Lesson 1, "How are you?" Half of the text is in Korean and half is in English. It is apparent these books are for Korean teachers who are teaching English. If I can learn Korean in the next half-hour I will be set. Then I will be able to explain all the instructions in Korean, and the children will understand me and they will learn so much from me, and I will be their favourite teacher and the world will be perfect.

The half-hour passes and still all I can say in Korean is *annyeong haseyo* (hello), *gamsahabnida* (thank you), and *eolmaibnikka* (how much is this?). I am worried.

My first class, grade five, goes well. The teacher, a small pleasant-looking man with a quiet nature, stays to help out and possibly to better his own English. The students were respectful, quiet, and we even managed to do some partner work.

Then came grade six. I thought, "Great! A bit older, wiser, more mature." Their teacher couldn't get out the door fast enough and I would soon understand why. These kids were a handful.

Instead of repeating after me just once, they chanted mockingly. "Nice to meet you. Nice to meet you too. Nice to meet you. Nice to meet you too. Nice to meet you. Nice to meet you too." They also repeated everything I didn't want them to say. Every "very good" and "okay" was echoed enthusiastically by twenty-five smiling faces. I passed around my pictures from home, as I had done with the other classes. They laughed and pointed at them, joking in Korean about somebody or something in the photograph. The pictures were thrown forward and back, ripped out of hands, dropped on the floor, bent, and smudged. The kids understood, "Quiet down!" But when I said the words, they just repeated them to me, and then said it to each other pretending to be me.

The classroom was getting louder by the minute. One boy kept rocking his desk back and forth, banging it harder and harder on the floor, and then started dropping his books repeatedly. This needed to stop. I got right in Desk Rocker's face, grabbed both sides of his desk to stop the banging, put my hand up, and very firmly told him, "Stop!" He stopped ... for about thirty seconds.

Finally, the lunch bell chimed and my first class with the grade sixes was over. I would need the lunch hour to regroup and get my head back on straight.

Lunch is served to everyone in the school so students and teachers need not bring a packed lunch. In the cafeteria I pick up a metal tray and join the line of students. The tray has five divots. The two bigger divots are for rice and soup and the three smaller ones are for kimchi, some type of vegetable side dish, and the meat or fish of the day. I sit down with my tray and dig in with my chopsticks, as much as one with limited chopsticks experience can dig in with chopsticks. The principal and vice principal wave their own chopsticks at me and give me a few head nods and thumbs-up. They are impressed with my chopstick skills. Midway through my fish, as I try to avoid its head and eyes, and hope I am not offending anyone by not eating the head and eyes, I look up and find thirty pairs of eyes staring at me. Many of the children have strategically placed themselves on the far side of tables so they can face me. The ones who have the misfortune of sitting with their backs to me turn after every bite, so they too might stare.

I finish my lunch, walk through the schoolyard filled with children yelling, "Hello! What's your name?" at me, and escape to the safety of my house and bathroom. Since both schools I teach at are so close to our house, I go home every day at lunch for five minutes to use the bathroom. There are many washrooms in the schools but they are only squatters, and I'm not great at squatting yet.

To me a squatter is like a miniature urinal that, instead of being against a wall, is lying on the floor. The idea is to straddle the squatter, squat, and drop your business into the little trough below. I tried using a squatter for a quick pee before the volleyball game last week and it didn't go well. I don't know how other women pee, but I don't always pee straight down and once I start the flow it isn't easy to stop it or redirect it. I've wondered if something about me is slightly crooked. I've been to the gynecologist many times but he never looked at me down there and said, "Huh?" Or maybe he did see something listing a little to the side but didn't think it mattered, didn't anticipate that one day I'd be trying not to pee on my shoes in a squatter in Korea.

Rotating my hips around and back and forth like a Hula-Hoop champ, I had straddled, squatted, and managed to get most of my pee into the trough. Then I reached for some toilet paper and there was none. There was also nobody there to pass me any toilet paper. Moreover, if there had been another person in the bathroom, they likely wouldn't have understood that I required toilet paper. So I gave a little shake and flushed.

Being nosey, I then checked the other stalls for toilet paper and there wasn't a square to be found. There wasn't even paper towel. Since that day I have checked each of the washroom stalls in the two schools and the gymnasium and have found zero toilet paper. Maybe there's a *bring your own roll* policy that nobody thought to tell me about.

Instead of bringing my own roll, I have been choosing to "hold it" and use the bathroom when I get home at lunch or after school. Today during my lunch hour those lovely little inquisitive elementary school children decided to follow me home.

As I sat, peacefully enjoying a moment on the toilet, I hear tiny voices approaching. I hear lots of giggling. I hear BANG, BANG, BANG. I keep hearing BANG, BANG, BANG for about five minutes. I am under attack. I don't know if I should open our front door or continue hiding. Eventually, when I can take the noise no longer, I open the door.

Four little girls stand there smiling shyly. I look for the blood that must be dripping from their little knuckles after all the rapping on my door.

"Teacher. House," they say, pointing past me into our home.

I say, "Yes. This is my house."

They continue standing there, waiting for an invitation to come in.

I say, "Okay. Goodbye."

They say, "Goodbye," and I close the door to their giggles.

* * *

My afternoon at the elementary school begins with my youngest students, the grade threes. Their teacher stays for the class and I am grateful, as it is a large class and they are an active and energetic group.

The student with the best English is also the kid with the worst behaviour – he repeats everything I say, very loudly and many times over. I had hoped the teacher would be able to translate my instructions to the kids, but I'm not sure he knew what I was saying either, so now I have twenty-six people who have no idea what I'm saying. He did keep the kids in line somewhat and I decided to keep it simple and stick with teaching, "Hello. My name is …" over and over and over again.

The teacher of my grade four class stays with me for the session as well. His English is the best I've heard at the school. However, he had been trying to pick me up in the teachers' lounge earlier, so I would rather not use him as an ally. His class brings me right back to my own elementary school experiences – kids making fun of kids. The first sweet little girl tells me I have big eyes. If an adult had said this to me, I would have taken it as a compliment. But this little girl says, "Your eyes are so big!" She almost phrases it in the form of a question, like I need to explain the enormousness of my eyes to her; like she doesn't approve of me having my own eyes. Then she makes circles with her thumb and index fingers and places the circles over her own eyes to show me how big my eyes are compared to hers.

When I was in grade four I had really big eyes – the same size eyes I have now obviously but my face was smaller so they looked enormous. My mom always told me they were beautiful, but I was skeptical. The kids at school told me I looked like ET and I had never heard anyone call ET beautiful, and grade four kids always know everything so I figured ET eyes were not a good thing.

I stand in front of my students and think about ET, about beauty, and about the beholder. I am feeling like an extraterrestrial on this planet called Korea. Then a second girl grabs on to her little nose and pretends to pull it about a foot off her face and says to me, "Teacher, you have big nose!"

Also when I was in grade four, a kid named Matt told me my nose looked like that of some hockey player I had never heard of. I had never cared what my nose looked like until that point, never considered whether it was big, small, misshapen, or pointy. I blew it now and again, but that was the only time I even noticed it. But now, Matt was telling me my nose was like someone else's and I was interested to see how accurate he was. I asked my dad if he had heard of the hockey player and he had, and I asked him what his nose looked like and my dad smiled and said it was crooked because he'd gotten hit by a puck or been in too many fights.

Staring at these ten-year-old faces, I think of grade four and the mean kids, and the first time you realize somebody is making fun of you. I feel sad for ten-year-old Beth Ann, and then for the kids surrounding me. The kids who will be taunted after school because their sneakers aren't Nike and their mom cuts their hair and they're a bit overweight. I feel grateful that I am done with those years, and I suddenly feel stronger. I want these kids to understand it's not nice to make fun of some-body's appearance. I want to teach them about feelings, and rudeness, and how words can hurt. I want to make a difference.

And then I return to earth, remembering that these kids will have no clue what I'm saying if I give them a lecture about feelings.

I say to the girls, "Yes, I do have big eyes, and a big nose." I say to the class, "Repeat after me. How old are you? I am ten years old." And we move on.

I leave school feeling frustrated because I can't control my classes and, worse, that I can't connect with my students. I had no idea the language barrier would be such an obstacle. I long to be surrounded by English-speaking people. I long for the gym I used to work at and my spinning classes and fitness test-ing and for people who understand my words, my meaning, me.

Dale comes home from his second day of teaching and I vent. He listens. He reminds me that I had hated my old job; that I had felt unsatisfied and bored and useless. He reminds me that we had hated our conflicting work schedules, of how I had felt returning to an empty house with his empty slippers, still warm on the floor. He reminds me how he had felt, each day waking up to a still warm but empty spot beside him. And he reminds me there will be summer vacation and weekends and trips and adventures and, "It *is* only our second day of teaching."

I am comforted, recharged, and ready to make a game plan for next week.

Dale's first two days of school were quite different from mine. He has to commute by bus to Hadong and the bus picks him up near our house at 7:15.

Mr. Chang was at the bus stop waiting to see Dale off on his first day. He asked Dale where I was, and was shocked to hear I was out for a jog and not standing at the bus stop as a "good Korean wife" would be. Then, to show Dale his fitness level, Mr. Chang began to jog on the spot. It wasn't as much jogging as hopping back and forth from foot to foot. He put his hands on his hips, pointed his elbows backwards, and slowly hopped on his left foot a few times, then his right foot, left foot, right foot, and so on and so forth. The bus arrived and Dale left Mr. Chang to his "fitness."

It takes about thirty minutes for Dale's bus to drive to Hadong. Mondays and Tuesdays are his days at the girls' high school, while the rest of the week he's at the boys'.

Monday he was met by class after class of screaming girls. They went nuts for him. His ears hurt. They reached out and touched his arm and swooned, fanning their faces, wiping sweat from their brow, playing like they were going to pass out. They groaned when he told them about me. They screamed again when he told them about his twenty-one-year-old brother Ryan. When he broke a piece of chalk and caught it on the way down, they screamed again. His smiley green-blue eyes and dark tousled hair earned him the nickname Tom Cruise. His day was that of a rock star.

Today the girls were slightly more subdued. He was able to have some discussions with them about pop culture, who their favourite bands were. They mentioned Avril Lavigne and

Dale sang the hook from one of her songs, and the girls went wild again. One student asked him if she was his type. Another girl asked him if he thought she was pretty.

I find it difficult to offer sympathy when Dale complains about girls falling all over him. He gets adoring fans and I get kids screaming "Hello!" repeatedly, and mimicking my shockingly enormous nose and eyes.

*   *   *

In just two days we have become teachers. Each morning I become "Mrs. Knowles"; I wear dress-up clothes, I apply makeup, and, like any good teacher, I make sure to get some lipstick on my teeth. Dale transforms into "Mr. Knowles"; he wears dress clothes – wrinkled dress clothes, but dress clothes nonetheless – and is out of the house shortly after seven a.m. These would be rare occurrences for us in our former Canadian life: with me working at a gym and Dale being a youth care worker, we never wore grown-up clothes; I never had more than lip gloss on my face, and Dale never saw 10:30 a.m. let alone seven a.m.

Each afternoon Mrs. Knowles meets Mr. Knowles at the bus stop in downtown Hwagae and together they walk home. Their hair is a bit messier than it was in the morning, they look wearied, and they have chalk patches spotting their clothes. Slowly, as the evening progresses, you can see them morph back into Dale and Beth Ann, Dale flexing in his Homer Simpson pyjamas and Beth Ann stomping around the house in her outdoor footwear, just because she can.

I've only managed a little bit of stomping in my outdoor shoes, though, as I've somehow managed to injure myself. I always seem to have odd injuries, never a straightforward arm break or traditional sprained ankle.

Once, while working for the Canadian military in Bosnia, I fell off a stationary bike. I had just come in from outside where it was raining. My sneakers were wet and when I stood on the pedals of the bike my feet slipped off and my bum came down hard on the crossbar. Embarrassed by the noise I had made, I tried to act like nothing had happened – like my rear end felt like a million bucks. In actuality, I was in an immense amount of pain. My tailbone was broken but I didn't know it. Sitting on the bike seat to collect my thoughts was my natural reaction. This put pressure on my broken tailbone and suddenly my world clouded over and I woke up on the floor five minutes later. I had passed out while sitting on the bike, fell off, whacked my head on the plywood wall on the way down, and ended up unconscious on the floor with the bike on top of me.

When I regained consciousness, I wondered why it was so bright; why all the people surrounding me were in my bedroom. After a few moments, my brain caught up to the situation and I remembered what had happened. Immediately I started laughing. I think everyone thought I was crazy, and I'm not convinced they believed me when I explained I had hit my bum on the seat and passed out. My hat had splinters in it from the plywood wall and on my forehead was a big blue bump with some scrapes. I'm not sure if the worst part was having to work standing at my desk for weeks, my keyboard propped up on an upside-down garbage can. Or was the worst part explaining the accident to the many people who asked what happened to my head and why I was walking slowly?

"You fell off a bike? Were you going down a big hill? Did the front tire come off? Oh. I see. A stationary bike? You mean one that sits in the gym and doesn't move?"

Just last month, when we were still back in Canada, I was out for a jog and fell – not over anything, not because of anything, I just fell. The tumble badly bruised both of my knees and the timing couldn't have been worse. A week later I was on a shorts-and-bathing-suit-clad trip to Aruba, explaining my knee bruises and wobbly ankles to all.

In junior high I got hit in my right eye with a soccer ball during a game. It didn't hurt, so I continued to play, but soon I noticed I couldn't see out of that eye. After a trip to the hospital, I was diagnosed with hyphema, which is essentially bleeding and blood pooling in the eye. I was put on bedrest for a few days to prevent the blood in my eye from clotting. When I was able to return to school, a few days into grade nine, I had to wear a big metal patch with holes in it (very similar to a slotted spoon) taped over my eye.

At least my Korean injury didn't have any embarrassing visible signs, other than a slight limp. I'm not even sure when I hurt myself but last weekend my left foot started to hurt. The pain reached the point that I couldn't run on it. My self-diagnosis is that I pulled a muscle in the bottom of my foot while walking up a hill.

See! Who hurts themselves walking up a hill? In my defence, if you saw the hills in our neighbourhood you would see the potential for strains. Hwagae is located in a valley surrounded by the mountains of the Jirisan National Park. Our house is perched partway up the side of a mountain, so from our house to school, or town, or pretty much anywhere, one must go downhill. Therefore, to get home one must come back up the hill.

I would estimate the last hill before home, the one that leads to the elementary schoolyard, is at a sixty-degree angle. In order to keep my forward momentum while climbing, I lean in so far that my nose is almost scraping the ground in front of me. By the time I reach the top, I'm gasping and heaving. I stop, bend over, put my hands on my knees, and pant. Often there are elementary students to welcome me home: "Hello! What's your name?" "Teacher! Eyes big!" "Teacher! Face red!"

Behind our house are more hills and farmland. Each morning I can hear roosters crowing, goats squawking, and one cow mooing. I don't think the cow is diseased, but she sure sounds like a "mad cow." I've never heard a cow moo like that before. She's still mooing when I come home from school.

Surprisingly, I've never seen any of the animals that we hear. It has crossed my mind that perhaps they aren't even there. Perhaps it is an elaborate scheme by the Hwagaeonians to create this wholesome farming community vibe to keep us in Hwagae.

It makes me think of a great French movie I once watched, *La grande séduction*. It was about a doctor who travelled to a remote Canadian island to practise medicine. The island inhabitants had lost previous doctors and were scared the new one would also leave, as there was so little to do or see on the island. They came up with scheme after scheme to seduce the doctor into staying. They knew he loved cricket so, as his boat was landing on the island, they set up what appeared to be a huge cricket match. None of the people actually knew how to play cricket, but they wore all of the gear and stood in proper positions on the field. They also tapped his phone calls to find out what foods he liked. Then, each time he dined at the local restaurant, they served his favourite dishes. And each day someone deposited a few dollars in the same spot along the path where they knew he would walk. Each day he would find the money and marvel at the luck he had on this island.

Maybe my imagination is getting the better of me, but sometimes I think the people of Hwagae wouldn't be above such schemes to keep Dale and me from leaving their town. I've found about fifty cents on the ground outside our house, and the little grocery store downtown sells the same body oil I use at home. Did they check up on us before we left Canada? Maybe they know Dale grew up working on farms and lived in a farming community. Maybe they've heard about the cows who woke me up every morning, mooing in the pasture behind my cottage. And maybe, just maybe, these farm animals we hear are merely animal sounds played over loudspeakers so we don't get homesick.

There is a lot of loudspeaker use in Hwagae. For one, there is the Mobile Market. This is a vendor who drives around a few times a day with a truck full of merchandise: fruit, vegetables, household items, etc. We usually hear him at about nine a.m. and four p.m. He announces himself and advertises his wares over a loudspeaker in his truck as he snakes through the valley. His voice echoes for miles. It's all in Korean but when Dale and I imagine out loud what he is saying it goes something like, "Dish detergent! Come and get your dish detergent! Special price for you today. Come and get it!"

Then there are the area loudspeakers that broadcast various announcements or advertisements, or maybe even warnings throughout the day. For all we know they could be reporting our whereabouts around town. "The Canadians are returning home! Cue the mooing sounds!"

At school each day, when 12:30 comes around, a teacher always comes to my desk and announces it is lunchtime. It was a thoughtful gesture the first couple of days of school but eventually it started to annoy me. Lunch is at the same time every day. Then I thought, maybe they announce mealtimes to everyone. Maybe mealtime is what is being announced over the loudspeakers throughout the valley: "Breakfast! Don't forget to eat breakfast. Get out your kimchi. It's breakfast time!"

Sometimes I wonder, if there was a crisis in the world, if Korea were under attack, or if a tsunami was headed our way, would Dale and I even know? If a world crisis was announced over the loudspeaker, would we just assume strawberries were on sale?

* * *

As we live in a farming community that potentially uses pesticides, and we're not sure where our water is sourced, we have chosen not to drink our tap water. Instead, we buy one-and-a-half-litre bottles at about sixty cents Canadian. If we wanted to go all out, we could buy eight litres of maple water for forty dollars Canadian. From what I understand, this is essentially the liquid tapped from a maple tree before it is boiled down to make syrup. The claim to fame of this water is the vitamins and minerals it contains. Mr. Chang told us this, but he also told us parsnips are full of protein.

One of the teachers at my school bought a big jug of maple water to share with the rest of us. It tastes like licking a tree branch. One glass was okay, but they kept forcing it on me.

"Good for health!" they tell me, slapping their chests.

Good for getting splinters in your tongue, I think.

I drink it as they stand watching me, full of pride.

"Mmm. Pretty good!" I manage. They fill my glass again.

On my first day of school, I was force-fed the tree water all day long. Then, as my luck would have it, one of the teachers at the elementary school also brought maple water to share so I was spoiled with tree water my second day of school as well. I'm going to be some healthy by the end of this year.

Aside from the maple water, we are never offered water to drink, so I started bringing my own water bottle to school.

Both times we visited Buddhist temples we were invited to drink out of the freshwater springs. There are two reasons why I did not want to drink from the freshwater springs. First, there are three ladles to scoop the water to your mouth with. Everyone drinks from the same three ladles and there is no dish detergent present to wash the ladles in between uses. And second, there are kids playing with the ladles and throwing them on the ground and, referring back to number one, there is no dish detergent for disinfecting of the ladles. Where is the Mobile Market when you need it?

As we didn't want to offend anybody, we both drank a few hearty gulps from the ladles and we both lived to tell the tale. At some point, though, we're going to say no to some event or task, or decline some offering, but it will be hard. Dale and I are stereotypical Canadians, polite and obliging, never wanting to offend, and always looking to please.

SIX

I think I might have offended everyone. Everyone at my school at least. This week I refused to play volleyball. Refused is a bit of a harsh word. I politely declined engaging in their sexist, pompous, idiotic volleyball match.

By this time, I've played in three matches. If you remember, the first was with the teachers of Hwagae Middle School. Dale played as well and we both left the gym perturbed. My second match was a week ago and was also a "fun" game with my school's teachers. Dale was working in Hadong at the time, so I was on my own to get hip-checked out of the play by my male colleagues. I thoroughly hated the game, and enjoyed the post-game meal just as little. Takeout was ordered, and there were strawberries and beer and juice, and all the other teachers sat around and chatted and laughed, and chatted some more. It would have been great had I understood a word they were saying or had they tried to speak to me even a little. Unfortunately for Dale, I went home fuming.

The next day Hwagae Middle School played volleyball against Hwagae Elementary School. Dale and I were both invited to play. I was the token female and he was to be the blocker. The match went much the same as the previous two. Three people on our team touched the ball, Dale and I and others were knocked out of the way. We were never set the ball once. When, by chance, we did touch the ball, we were great. Dale made some fantastic blocks and I made no mistakes.

I was happiest, though, when we lost. I wanted those three self-important men on my team to be as angry as I was. I have never been so upset over sports in my life!

We returned home after that third match and had a very animated discussion. Dale usually gets over things much quicker than I do, but neither of us could let go of our disgust. We decided we would not play volleyball again. It is easier for Dale to make this decision as he doesn't work at Hwagae Middle School and, typically, he isn't available to play. I, on the other hand, am expected to take part in "teacher wellness activities."

This week, I told Mr. Chang, "I would not like to play volleyball today."

He asked me why and I said, "Because some people play like it is the Olympics. They do not play nicely and it doesn't make me happy. I am much happier when I go running."

He replied, "Please. One more matchy. Today we will play another middle school."

The gym teacher, one of the best players, was not in school and Mr. Chang was short on participants. Mr. Chang is a sore loser and was desperate for me to play. I was tempted. Maybe I would get to touch the ball. Maybe I would be the setter. Maybe they would recognize my skills and incorporate me into the play. Then I thought back to the first match. I thought about when Mr. Chang had said to me, "When it's game point, I give you one."

I remembered how I had gritted my teeth and said, "Don't bother."

He'd replied, "But you can do it."

I had replied, "I know I can do it. I could have done it all game. Don't bother."

I made my decision and told Mr. Chang, "No, I would not like to play."

He said, "Okay. You go running."

At lunch that day he told the other teachers. I didn't understand what he said but I heard *pagu* (volleyball), and he motioned at me with his chopsticks. There was some silence after that. Perhaps they were offended. Perhaps they didn't care. I ran after school on Wednesday and was happy.

* * *

Teaching has gotten much better. We have had a chance to prepare some materials, and we've learned what teaching styles work and don't work with our various classes. Dale's girls have become somewhat more subdued and his male students really like him. The English teachers at his school attend his classes and help out with translating. One particular teacher, Mr. Lee, answers Dale's questions just like the rest of the students. He sits at the back of the classroom, repeats after Dale, waves his arm when he knows an answer, and is very excited when his response is correct.

My middle school students are great. They can misbehave, but I understand why. They start school at 8:30 in the morning, leave at four, and many go straight to Hagwons until eight p.m. or later. A Hagwon is a private school specializing in a certain subject. Parents who want their children to excel at math, English, science, and other subjects pay for their kids to attend a Hagwon after their regular school day. Most foreign teachers in Korea work at English Hagwons and very few teach in public schools as Dale and I do.

I ran into one of my students in Hwagae one afternoon as I waited for Dale's bus. She was on her way to the English Hagwon. I asked her what time her classes finished at the Hagwon and she replied, "Twelve o'clock."

I thought maybe she hadn't understood my question. I asked her a few more times and each time she answered, "Midnight."

When do these kids play? When do they socialize and do sports and have fun and laugh? When do they just get to be kids?

We have heard that for every class the children attend in a day, they should be given an hour of homework to do at night. It is no wonder students misbehave or fall asleep in class. There is a great deal of stress placed on Korean children by society and by their parents; the kids must be smart and excel in school. In Canada this pressure exists but is lesser, and our children are not sent to school all day and evening. In Canada different burdens are often stronger – to be thin, to be popular, to excel in sports. I wonder which pressures are harder on these kids. Is it better for them to be in school until midnight, or to have their hockey parent screaming at them from the stands? I wonder how Dale and I will parent our own children someday.

Last weekend we realized just how much pressure is placed on these kids to excel at school. We met a group of Hagwon English teachers in Jinju and hung out with them for an evening. Just the week before, one of their students had committed suicide after he'd received a bad grade in school. Dale and I were shocked.

So I didn't get too upset this week when one of my students shot another at close range with his umbrella. The shooter was sitting in the desk behind the victim and they must have been having words. The shooter pointed his umbrella at the victim, ejected his weapon, striking the boy in his eye. The injured turned around in his seat, grabbed his eye, and began to cry. I disarmed the boy with the umbrella and examined the other boy's eye. It appeared fine. By this time the victim is softly crying, as is the girl sitting next to the shooter. I have no idea what her problem is. Perhaps it was her umbrella and she thought I was not going to give it back. Perhaps the victim was her boyfriend. I don't know. I went on with my lesson and pretty soon everyone was laughing and happy again.

This past Tuesday was my second day teaching at Hwagae Elementary School. I was prepared. I'd made signs displaying various instructions, "Please sit down," "Please be quiet," "If you listen, we'll play a game." With Mr. Kim's help I wrote the instructions in both Korean and English so the kids would understand and also learn the commands in English. I went through the English sections of the textbook, and wrote down what I thought were the main points from the first lesson.

Unfortunately, my second day of teaching at the elementary school was also White Day. This is like a second Valentine's Day. The idea is that on March 14 people give presents to those they had received gifts from on Valentine's Day. At Hwagae Elementary School the teachers and children ignored the rules about who should give and receive presents, and everyone gave *everyone* else candy on Tuesday – male, female, teacher, student, it didn't matter. And, while they gave each other candy, they also ate each other's candy. By the time I arrived for my first class at eleven a.m., the children were on a schoolwide sugar high.

The kids were hyper beyond belief. They jumped around the classroom, they yelled, they screamed, they threw various school supplies, and they ate more candy. Despite the craziness, I enjoyed my day. It was chaotic and frustrating at times, but the kids responded to the signs I'd made, and I somehow had more control over the classes.

My smartest and most well-behaved class that day was grade five, and again the teacher remained to help me with instructions and translating. The grades three, four, and six teachers took off as soon as they saw me nearing their classroom. Being on my own with twenty-five sugary elementary kids was daunting, but I came up with ways to woo them into learning.

I learned the grade threes love "Head and Shoulders, Knees and Toes." I learned the grade fours love drawing. And I learned the grade sixes know the continents and like matching countries with continents. I had some wonderful moments throughout the day.

There were also a few not-so-wonderful moments. I had to sit one boy at the front of the class so I could keep my eye on him. If he wasn't being watched he was jumping off his chair, throwing items around the room, and making the girl next to him cry. I didn't know it was because of him that she was crying. All the other girls in the class suddenly started chanting, "Teacher, Teacher, Teacher …" and pointing at the girl who was bawling at her desk. Neither she, nor anyone else, could explain to me why she was crying. Maybe it was because somebody had written on her scribbler. Maybe her appendix was about to explode. I had no idea, so I went searching for another teacher. The kind administration lady was in the hallway. She spoke to the crying girl, who pointed at the boy whom I had moved to the front of the classroom. He had said something hurtful to her. Eventually, she stopped crying. He, however, didn't stop being a challenge.

In that same class I also had a little boy who wouldn't stop playing with his penis. He sat in the front row so it was impossible for me not to notice. Every time I looked his way he slowly, nonchalantly, pulled his hand out of his pants. When I glanced back at him, minutes later, his hand was again deep inside his gray sweatpants. I made a mental note to have Mr. Kim write a sign for me saying, "Please, keep your hands out of your pants in class!"

* * *

As he promised, Mr. Chang is no longer our "servant." Before school started, he'd warned us that once classes began he wouldn't have time to be our "servant" anymore. He is much busier now but most days Dale and I still get our fair share of Chang-time. Often, he'll telephone to the teachers' office for me.

"Bess," – what many people in Hwagae call me – "please come to my office." I walk downstairs quickly, imagining the important task Mr. Chang might need me for.

One day Mr. Chang wanted me to show him and the gym teacher how to in-line skate. I don't know why he thought I was an in-line skating guru but he would not be dissuaded of this delusion. I'd had rollerblades in high school, but I was not confident on skates and used them only a handful of times. Mr. Chang and the gym teacher led me to the hardwood-floored gym and had me put on somebody's in-line skates. I moved around very slowly, and without an ounce of fluidity. They thought I was fantastic! Then they asked if I could show all the children how to play roller hockey. Probably ninety-nine percent of these kids have never worn in-line skates, and I would guess the same percentage have never watched a hockey game. I suggested that maybe I could teach the children floor hockey without in-line skates: have the kids just run on the floor. They thought I was a genius.

They requested that I find the history and rules of floor hockey on the internet. Mr. Lee would translate the rules into Korean and look into purchasing equipment. Each day Mr. Lee asks me to explain various words and phrases from the rules I printed for him: possession, pinnies, faceoff, etc. He seems to enjoy the task and appreciates having something to do.

Despite being the vice principal, Mr. Lee never appears to be very busy. A few times each day I catch him staring off into space or sleeping at his desk. In fact, many of the teachers take daily naps at their desks. They don't try to be discreet about their snooze – some put their head right down on their desks, while others sit spread-eagled in their chair, hang their head back, let their mouth drop open, and snore.

On Monday Mr. Chang called me to his office again. There I was met by Mr. Chang, Mrs. Bark the administration lady, and a travelling salesman. The salesman was selling massage pads to put on the back or seat of your chair. Mr. Chang was considering purchasing some for "teacher wellness" and he wanted my opinion on the product. I wondered why he thought I was some massage product connoisseur. Later Dale suggested that Mr. Chang was showing me off to the travelling salesman ... his pretty white teacher.

I sat in the chair and the travelling salesman turned the pads on. I thought someone must have kidnapped Helga, a three-hundred-pound massage maniac, cut off her fists and forearms, and somehow implanted them into the mechanics of this massage pad. My eyes widened, then nearly popped out of my head, and in true Maritime slang I exclaimed, "HOLY JUMPINS!!!" Helga was unreal. She went up and down and around my back. She got harder but never lighter. I had no idea these massage pads were so realistic. When I could take no more, I asked the travelling salesman to turn it off. My back was numb. I could barely get out of the chair.

They then wanted to lay the massage pad on the seat and have me sit on it. I politely declined, wincing at the notion of Helga pounding on my delicate tailbone. I considered suggesting that Mr. Chang look into purchasing the Massage Pants Dale and I had seen on an infomercial on TV. I really wanted to try them out and wondered how many Helgas were inside. But I kept my mouth shut and escaped back to the teachers' office. My back was stiff for two days.

My latest Mr. Chang encounter happened Wednesday. I was working hard at my desk when he asked me to come to his office. Naively, I always expect Mr. Chang will give me an assignment or lecture when I'm called to his office. Actually, I would prefer if he ragged me out or gave me some work to do. Instead, he invited me to sit down and said, "You can relax. Anytime, come to my office to relax." He handed me two oranges to eat. He turned on his stereo and his office was filled with "If you're going to San Francisco ... Be sure to wear some flowers in your hair ..."

I looked around, searching for a lava lamp. I wouldn't have been at all surprised had he lit a joint, and the thought even crossed my mind that perhaps I was on *Candid Camera*.

No, Mr. Chang was having a lull in his day, and he needed somebody else to be bored with him. He hummed along to the song and when he got to any part he knew, he belted out the lyrics heartily. The song ended and started again. He had it on repeat. I wondered if he would break out his bamboo flute.

Later in the day Mr. Chang was in the teachers' office, still humming the words to "San Francisco." He asked me if I thought it would be fun to change the words.

"How about," he suggested, "if you're going to Hwagae town ... be sure to wear the flowers in the hair ...?"

I told him I thought it was a fantastic idea.

* * *

I only talk to a few staff at Hwagae Middle School: Mr. Chang, Mr. Lee, Mr. Kim, Mrs. Bark, and Mr. Bear (if you can consider our interactions talking). The rest of the teachers greet me in the morning and say goodbye at the end of the day, and that is the limit of their English – or perhaps their confidence.

Mr. Kim speaks to me at random intervals throughout the day. Each time he takes a seething inhale through his teeth, rolls his chair towards me until it's kissing my chair, and then he looks at my computer screen. It drives me nuts! Nosey people irritate me. People invading my personal space irritate me. Sometimes I wonder if he's trying to catch me playing Solitaire or looking at inappropriate websites, neither of which I ever do. I'm always preparing my lessons or, at the very worst, sending an email. I've seen all of the other teachers emailing friends and chatting online at one time or another, so I don't feel bad about it. Moreover, if Mr. Bear and Mr. Lee can sleep, and Mr. Chang can eat oranges while listening to 1960s hippie music, I can send a few emails.

After Mr. Kim has perused my computer screen, he pushes his glasses back on his face, seethes again, and says, "Knowles. Ah, Ms. Knowles, yeh."

More seething.

"Snow, Ms. Knowles."

More seething.

"Snow outside. Yeh. Yeh."

It's been snowing for the past hour but instead of pointing this out to him I smile and say, "Yes, Mr. Kim. It is snowing. Thank you."

He nods his head very quickly, "Yeh, yeh, yeh," and smiles a wide proud smile.

Mrs. Bark is my second favourite person in Hwagae, second to Mr. Bear of course. She is thirty-six, has two elementary school-age sons, and a husband whom she only sees every second weekend as he is an electrician in Seoul. She lives with her sons and her mother-in-law in a nearby town, and is the administration assistant at Hwagae Middle School. As with many people we've met in Korea, Mrs. Bark looks much younger than her thirty-six years. It helps that her hair is streaked with various colours and she is always very fashionably dressed.

At first, Mrs. Bark never spoke to me and rarely came near me. I assumed she couldn't speak English. Dale said it was unfortunate because she seemed to have a fun personality and might be someone I'd like to hang around with. Soon, however, I realized she was merely too embarrassed to speak English to me. As Mrs. Bark and I saw more of each other, she started gaining confidence and initiating short conversations. "You look beautiful today." "Are you happy at house?" "How's Dale?"

Despite our limited conversations, I enjoy having a woman to chat with and I think Mrs. Bark enjoys practising her English with me. Each time I speak with her, she has learned a new phrase or adjective which she'll start our conversation with. It is interesting to see a person's English progress daily.

Recently, Mrs. Bark started insisting that I sit next to her or across from her at lunch. Sometimes I notice she has a piece of paper under the table which she glances at periodically. I would imagine her phrase or word of the day is written on the piece of paper, and she probably reads it and repeats it until she gets it right. I love the anticipation and wondering what her daily question or comment will be. One day it was, "What time do you go to bed?" Another day she said, "My favourite colours are pink, yellow, and green." I wish my students were as interested in English as Mrs. Bark is.

There is a female cook at the elementary school who also practises her English with me. The first day I met her, she was waiting for me in the teachers' office after my last class. It took her a few minutes, but eventually she was able to articulate that she worked in the kitchen. She was delighted when I told her how much I had enjoyed the lunch she'd prepared. Then she started leafing through the library of English she had stored in her head. Conversation becomes very random when a person knows five different topics with no common theme. "You like kimchi?" "Guess my age." "You eyes very beautiful." "You like soju?" "You have babies?"

It is surprising how much Dale and I get asked to guess someone's age. Keep in mind it isn't kids smiling at us, saying, "Guess my age!" It is adults in their thirties and forties. Everyone has been pleased when we've guessed them to be younger than their true age; they are very proud of their youthful appearance, and they want us to know it. We try to play it up as much as possible, especially Dale, with his handsome winning smile, telling forty-six-year-old women that they look twenty-six.

Mr. Chang has told us he is sixty-two, and he dyes his hair. We think he might use a product we saw on an infomercial. I would describe it as mascara for hair. Infomercials for this, and other products, are blasted about every forty-five minutes during movies. They last roughly fifteen minutes, and are very loud with lots of annoying sound effects and seizure-inducing graphics.

Mascara used to get rid of gray streaks in your hair is one of the least bizarre products we've seen. I am still baffled, but mildly curious, about the Massage Pants. The A B Power is like an Ab Roller but built slightly different and is demonstrated by people using horrible form, lurching their torsos off the ground to get those washboard abs. And then there are those men's underwear. I believe the key selling feature is that the undies are reversible. Yes, reversible underwear! I think their slogan should be, "Two wears, one pair!"

* * *

After my second Tuesday at the elementary school, the lady from the kitchen was in the teachers' office waiting for me again. Just like Mrs. Bark, she had prepared a new string of words and phrases to use in conversation with me. A male teacher came into the office during our chat, pointed at the kitchen lady, and said, "She is very beautiful. Perfect blend of Korean tradition and American looks." The kitchen lady blushed and changed the subject.

There does seem to be an obsession with looks here. Not that there isn't in Canada as well. But in Korea, nobody tries to hide it. Next to the door in each classroom there is a mirror. On the landing of each school's staircase hangs a mirror. In the entrance of the girls' high school, where Dale teaches, there is a massive mirrored wall. You have to walk past it, and around it, to enter and exit the school.

In the middle of teaching, Dale often catches his high school girls gazing at themselves in a mirror at their desk. They adjust their hair, they fix their makeup, they perfect themselves. Each time a teacher leaves our office, they stop at the mirror and primp and adjust themselves as well.

We've noticed that instead of greetings like, "Nice to meet you. Where are you from? How is your family? How are you today?" greetings are almost always accompanied by some reference to appearance. People we've met have been quick to point out when somebody is overweight ... "He is so fat. Why is he so fat?"

When I showed Mr. Lee a picture of me waterskiing last summer he said, "Oh. Hmmm. You were much fatter then. Now you are much slimmer."

Mr. Chang is perhaps the most blatant and inappropriate when it comes to comments concerning appearances. He boasts of how proud he is of his pretty female teachers. I think he couldn't care less whether they are good teachers, let alone smart or skilled.

Dale tells me not to be too bothered by Mr. Chang's comments. "It is why we're here," he says.

Along with our résumés, when we were applying to work in Korea, we were also asked to send a picture of ourselves. I'm not saying we have movie star looks but, it seems by Korean standards, we are both quite handsome. It makes us wonder, had we not sent a picture of a *good-looking* couple, would we have been invited by Mr. Chang?

One day, Mr. Kim asked me to help him with the English lesson he was preparing. The students were to read a text and then answer questions about various themes in the reader. The dialogue in the text, for his highly impressionable middle school students to read, started with, "I'm a little fat. I hope to get thinner soon."

SEVEN

If we go broke in Korea I will blame it on Dale – more specifically, Dale and his jam and toast. I have never before seen anyone put so much jam on one piece of bread. He calls it an "ample amount of jam." I call it reckless disregard of jam application.

I was raised in a household with only two children and enough jam and money to go around. Nonetheless, my mother had us believe otherwise. Jam was to be applied sparingly: a thin film atop your piece of toast; just enough jam so you knew it was there. This rule carried over to all condiments we consumed: margarine, peanut butter, ketchup, everything. I grew up thinking one of two things: either Mom bought hundred-dollar bottles of jam or there was a worldwide condiment shortage. The first theory I was quick to disprove; if Mom didn't have a coupon or if an item wasn't from the crash and dent aisle, she wasn't buying it. Instead, I believed in the second theory. I thought we were one of the lucky families: the ones who were fortunate to have ketchup to dip their first ten french fries. After that first blob of ketchup was gone, however, there was no need to have any more.

To this day Mom's favourite reason for saying no to something is, "There's no need." I don't know how many times I was denied something, and when I asked, "Why not?" Mom replied, "Beth Ann, there's just no need."

For years those words haunted me. I laugh about it now, but I still can't bring myself to indulge in even a teaspoon of jam. Perhaps I need some jam application therapy. Each time I see Dale smother his toast with gobs of jam I cringe. I bite my tongue. I think, "My God! What would Judy say?"

It wasn't until I met Dale that I discovered a bath could be an enjoyable experience. Growing up, we were limited to one inch of water in the tub.

"Beth Ann, there's just no need to waste any more water," Mom would say. My scrawny little body would shiver and shake, and I would be in and out of the tub in under a minute. I used to hate having baths. The first time I saw Dale draw a bath I thought he was crazy. He filled three-quarters of the tub with hot water, and he soaked himself for the better part of an hour. If the water started to cool, he added more hot water. *What a waste of hot water*, I thought. *What a waste of time.*

I was skeptical that our relationship would last. How could I date someone with so little regard for the hot water supply? I spoke to some friends about my concerns with Dale's bath behaviour, and I soon discovered that, in fact, he was the normal one.

It has taken me a while to get used to indulging in a bath, to relax in the tub with the water actually covering me. During my first few attempts I wondered when it would be over. I wondered how anyone could sit there for so long and do nothing. It was so boring. I thought about the dishwasher that needed emptying and the clothes in the washing machine. I couldn't relax and my body felt like it was overheating and I thought that I might pass out. After mere minutes, my indulgent soak would be over.

We don't have a tub in our bathroom in Korea, and for the first couple of weeks we had very little hot water for showering. But recently, through careful trial and error and random button pressing on a control panel in the spare bedroom, we figured out the water system and now have copious amounts of hot water.

Rather than having hot water readily available at the turn of a tap, in many Korean houses you must turn on the hot water heater and then wait for the reservoir of water to heat up. If Dale and I could read Korean, we would have understood the directions on the little hot water panel on the wall. We wouldn't have gone so long having unpleasantly abrupt showers, and we wouldn't have peed in a toilet full of hot water. Actually, we still would have peed in the hot water toilet – we still do. It is one mystery we haven't figured out. I've considered saving the hot toilet water by siphoning it to the kitchen sink for dishes, or just washing my hair in the toilet. If Mom were here, I think she would.

*   *   *

There is snow in the mountains again. We've had a few weeks of warm spring weather, but this morning it is evident that winter is still lingering.

I fell asleep early last night and vaguely remember Dale walking in and out of my dreams, in and out of our bedroom. He was busy at some task, but I was too drowsy to ask him what. When he awoke beside me this morning, he said he hadn't slept well. He had wanted to talk to me but didn't want to wake me, and then he couldn't wait until morning when we could talk again. I fell in love with him a bit more in that moment.

It occurred to me this morning that I never worried about moving to Korea with Dale. I never considered our relationship might strain or suffer. We had been together only five months when we got married. During that next year we bought a house, adopted a dog, and supported each other through some high-stress events. A lot had happened in our short relationship when we decided to move to the other side of the world.

When I told clients at my former work that I was going to teach English in Korea, they asked, "But what about your husband?"

I tried to hide my shock at their question. "He's coming with me of course. He'll teach English too."

How could they think I would go away for a year by myself, leaving Dale behind? Dale got a similar reaction from some of his co-workers.

A friend had marvelled at how brave we were to move away together. She was impressed at how much faith we had in our relationship. I had laughed at her and said, "But we're married!"

It seemed people thought that our relationship would suffer if Dale and I spent all our time together and only had each other for social support; being on the same schedule would make us bored with each other. Maybe some couples need time apart: to appreciate each other more during the times they are together; to fall in love all over again when they reunite.

Dale and I do have the odd argument over jam and toast, but overall Korea seems to have brought us closer together, instead of driving us apart. Throughout the day we email each other many times, and we listen to music or watch movies together in the evening. Each afternoon I walk to the bus stop to meet him. I try to stroll, but I'm always too excited to walk slowly. Yesterday I stood waiting for him at the Hwagae bus stop. As I do every day, I felt the butterflies in my stomach. I couldn't wait for his bus to pull in, to see him step off and say, "Hi, honey," and embrace him and feel his kiss on my forehead.

Sometimes I am late for the bus and I meet Dale somewhere between the bus stop and our house. When we catch sight of each other we wave. I can see his emotions in his wave. If he's in poor spirits he waves like everyone else does: short, fast motions, his arm dropping to his side quickly. More of a "hey" wave than a "Hey! How the hell are ya doing?"

But more often than not, Dale is cheerful and silly. When he's feeling good, his whole body waves – happily, vigorously, almost idiotically. His flailing arm gets his head bobbing side to side and then his torso gets swaying and then I get smiling. I sometimes worry that he'll wave himself off the sidewalk into oncoming traffic, but he seems to be adept at the full body wave.

Dale and I chat before work in the morning and we whisper about life, long after we go to bed at night. We love this extra time we have to spend together, and we enjoy missing each other during our workday.

* * *

When we told my parents we were going to Korea for a year, my mom said, "There's no need to go to Korea! Why would you want to go way over there?"

I couldn't imagine why she didn't understand. She'd thought Dale and I had done too much in our short relationship and should slow down. She also didn't want to be away from me for a year. But Dale and I both love to travel. He's been to Australia and New Zealand, as well as Southeast Asia; I've lived in and travelled around Europe. It seemed a natural progression that eventually we'd travel the world together, creating memories of our adventures as husband and wife, to complement the stories from before we were "we."

Mom came around to our Korea plans sooner or later. She still wasn't thrilled we were leaving and perhaps didn't believe we were going until we were actually gone. I kind of set her up to not believe us, telling her little white "harmless" lies over my lifetime.

During my university years I used to write her letters while she and my father were wintering in Florida. I'd tell her I had rearranged her kitchen cupboards and painted the living room. I would write that the basement had flooded, or I'd forgotten to take down the Christmas tree and it caught on fire, but luckily, I was home and I put the fire out and there's only a small burn hole in the carpet. The house was always intact when my parents returned, but still my mom is never certain if I'm telling her the truth.

Dad, never conveying his emotions, was more interested in the logistics of our year away. Would we both quit our jobs in Canada? What would we do with Keno? Who would take care of our house and our bills?

My only sibling, my sister Carla-Jo, lives with her husband in England. My parents don't get to see very much of her, and wish she and Andy would move back to Nova Scotia. I am the daughter who is always close by, visiting most weekends in the summer, phoning often for recipes and cooking tips. I think my parents assumed once I "settled down" with a husband, I would be in the province forever. Our travel news came as a shock to them.

Dale is part of a very large family, so his parents took the news of us leaving for a year significantly better. While they will certainly miss us, the five boys and sister Sarah still living at home will keep them busy.

I think some family and friends worry that maybe we won't come home. Perhaps Dale and I will fall in love with Korea and stay here forever.

I love Canada though. I love my home, my community, and my province. I gain more of an appreciation for home when I'm abroad. Travelling helps you realize what you want out of your home life. When you see the world, you discover the place where you want to call home. Dale and I have many more places to discover, but we'll always make Nova Scotia our home.

Travelling teaches you many things as well, and I've learned a great deal from each of my experiences abroad. I've learned about people, how to deal with people, and even how to avoid people. Mr. Chang is a difficult person to avoid. Perhaps his former career in the Korean military taught him the ability to sniff people out. It seems he can find Dale and me anywhere.

So, as we'd prefer not to spend all of our free time with Mr. Chang, we've skipped town each weekend.

The weekend following our visit to Mr. Chang's church, Dale and I headed for Hadong. It was the second Saturday of the month, meaning school was in and Mr. Chang would be at school. Thankfully, the contract Dale and I signed said we would only work from Monday to Friday. Saturdays were ours. We snuck to the bus stop and boarded the bus for Hadong. We sat down and I turned to Dale and sang *Hadong gone gone, she been gone so long, she been gone gone gone so long.*

Harmonizing, Dale joined me, *Hadong gone gone, she been gone so long, she been gone gone gone so long.* Mr. Chang would have loved it.

Besides avoiding Mr. Chang, we had other reasons to go to Hadong. Dale needed a haircut and I needed to shop, primarily for toe socks.

Upon entering the schools in Korea, you must take off your outdoor footwear and put on a pair of indoor slippers. I don't know if the idea is to keep the buildings clean or to give your feet a break from your outdoor shoes. My thong sandals have become my slippers. I've worn them all over the great Canadian outdoors, but I don't tell anyone in my school this information.

Our Korean travel book had told me it was customary to wear socks with indoor footwear. I've since discovered socks aren't necessary, and that some parts of our travel book are outdated and inaccurate. Before I realized this, however, I had to come up with a system for wearing socks. You see, it is difficult to wear socks with thong sandals, unless, of course, the socks are worn over the sandals and I figured that definitely wasn't a Korean custom. Instead, I required toe socks – socks that have separate compartments for each of your toes. Metaphorically speaking, toe socks are gloves for your feet. I have seen such socks on an occasional pair of feet in Canada and, more recently, on the feet of the man who installed our Samsung washing machine. Before stepping on our wet bathroom floor, he donned my shower flip-flops, his toe socks allowing for a snug fit around the thong of my flip-flop. This man was a genius. Immediately, I wrote toe socks on my shopping list.

I bought two pairs of toe socks in Hadong. A black and a grey pair. Dale and I walked through the open-air market. We smiled, and said *annyeong haseyo* to the vendors. After getting over the surprise of seeing two foreigners in their market, they smiled back at us, motioned to the wares they were peddling, and launched into rapid-fire Korean. Did they think we knew Korean?

We nodded, smiled, nodded again, and kept walking. Perhaps it is better if we don't speak any Korean.

We brought our Korean travel book along to aid us with translations. When we attempted a word or phrase, the locals looked like they vaguely understood but were also confused. We would come to discover that the author of our travel book had included old translations, phrases that were no longer common. Our translations were pretty much useless. Our Korean travel book was pretty much useless. The next time we go away for a year to a foreign country, we've decided to spend more than thirty seconds deliberating over the selection of travel books at the bookstore.

Eventually, we felt it was time for Dale to have his hair cut. We spied one of those spinning red, white, and blue poles, and headed down the street. As we approached the shop, Mrs. Bark emerged with her husband and son. It was her husband's weekend home and they had taken their son to have his hair cut. After quick introductions, she came back into the barber shop with us to help translate. We'd brought a picture with us – of Dale sporting shorter hair. The hairdressers *ooohed* and *ahhhed* over the picture. The lady who would cut his hair seemed to understand what Dale wanted, and so Mrs. Bark said her goodbyes.

Dale sat in the chair, and I sat in the peanut gallery. There were three hairdressers, some of their family and children, and a few other female clients present. Everyone was quite interested in us. They talked animatedly, and frequently they motioned at us with scissors and fingers. A new lady came into the shop, sat down next to me, and immediately joined the conversation. I heard her say, "Hwagae English Teacher." They knew who we were.

A girl of about twenty sat on the other side of me. She knew a bit of English and tried to communicate some of what was being said. I gathered from her that she was a university student in Jinju, and her hometown is Hwagae. She asked if I could teach her English. It took what seemed like an eternity for her to convey this information to me. I strained so much to understand what she was saying that my head began to pound. Every fifteen seconds she wiped her brow and fanned her face. The room wasn't particularly hot; our conversation must have been tiring for her too. She took some pictures of me with her camera phone. Then I got a few moments of reprieve when some rice desserts were passed around the room. I grabbed a handful, and tried to look busy with my eating.

Meanwhile, the hairdresser was vigorously attacking Dale's head. She'd used scissors, a razor, electric clippers, and a very sharp-looking knife. Hair was flying, scissors were snipping, and I wondered if Dale was as nervous as I was. I had never seen anyone snip that fast. I worried she'd lose a fingertip or Dale would lose the top of his ear.

I avoided any further English tutoring conversation with the young girl. We've learned that it is illegal for Dale and me to work for anyone else while on contract with our respective schools. We would lose our visas and be sent home if it were discovered we were giving private lessons. This was too much for me to attempt to explain to the girl. Instead, I played dumb and pretended I didn't understand what she was asking me.

Finally, the snipping ceased, and Dale and I could leave. It was getting late in the day, so we decided to head back to Hwagae. We started walking along the bus route, hoping to find a bus stop or wave a passing bus down. Eventually we had walked to the edge of town, and there was no sign of a bus or a bus stop. I approached a man putting gas in his car, and with a French accent I said, "Bus terminale?" I figured if I said the words with an accent, he would understand me. I don't know why I thought he'd understand a French accent, but it was the first thing that came to me. I repeated the words a few more times, speaking louder each time, and emphasizing different syllables. He motioned for Dale and me to get into his car.

I said, "Hwagae?"

He nodded.

We got in. Fantastic! This man was going to drive us all the way to Hwagae himself. He pulled onto the road and headed back into Hadong. For a few moments I thought he might be kidnapping us. I checked to see if our doors were unlocked. I closed my eyes and did a visualization practice of me opening the car door, jumping, and tucking into a combat roll. I was ready. I looked at Dale. He did not appear ready. The man drove us to the bus station in Hadong. I was a bit disappointed I wouldn't get to execute my escape maneuvers. We got out of his car and he herded us inside. He ordered two tickets to Hwagae for us, we paid, told him thank you, and he left. I felt guilty for thinking he might kidnap us.

We boarded the bus and sat down. An older gentleman sat in the seat across the aisle from us. He offered us each a piece of gum. *The people are so nice here,* I think.

Dale whispers to me that the man probably thinks I'm a Russian prostitute. In the larger cities in Korea, there are communities of Russian prostitutes and many of them have blonde hair, like I do. I was told that, one day, I might be mistaken for one of these "women of the night."

I assumed Dale was joking, but as I chewed on my gum, I felt a little used.

EIGHT

While Dale was waiting for his bus at the Hadong bus station the following week, he ran into two foreigners. The guy's name was Kimon. He spoke with a British accent, but originated from Greece. Kimon teaches English at a Hagwon in Hadong. Dale had actually heard of him from one of his high school students. Likewise, Kimon had heard about Dale.

Kimon was dropping off his Canadian friend, Jenny, at the bus stop so she could travel back to Jinju where she works at a Hagwon. The three of them chatted for a few minutes, and Kimon and Jenny invited us to Jinju to visit anytime we liked. There is an English teacher community in Jinju, with about seventy-five foreigners. Kimon goes there every weekend so he can socialize with other English speakers.

Dale returned home that evening and told me about Kimon and Jenny. We decided to take them up on their offer that coming weekend.

Friday morning Mr. Chang met Dale at the bus stop. He asked what our plans were for the weekend. Dale told him we were going to Jinju. Mr. Chang said he wanted us to go hiking with him and the other school principals in the area on Saturday. Then on Sunday, he would take us to his church, and then for some more sightseeing – hosted by himself – around

Jinju. Dale told him it sounded nice but we already had plans, so "maybe another time."

I was not at the bus stop with Dale, so was unaware of this conversation.

At about 8:45 that morning I received an email from Dale telling me about his Mr. Chang encounter. Moments after I read the email, Mr. Chang approached my desk and demanded, "I'd like to know your plans for the weekend."

He was trying to catch us in a lie. Unfortunately for Mr. Chang, Dale and I work as a team.

"We're going to Jinju this weekend to visit friends, Mr. Chang," I replied.

"Why don't you go next weekend? I thought you would come climbing mountain with the school principals, and Sunday we go to church, and then I take you around Jinju."

"Sorry, Mr. Chang, we already have plans. Maybe another weekend." I added that last lie, hoping it would satisfy him.

He nodded and left me alone.

Saturday morning Dale and I left for Jinju. It was a warm sunny day, so I decided on capri pants and flip-flops. We brought one backpack along with us, one of our big travel packs as we intended to buy some supplies if we found a large grocery store.

To get to Jinju you take a bus to Hadong and then another on to Jinju. With connections, the trip takes two hours. The bus ride is enjoyable – for a while. We chat, doze in and out, and take in the scenery. Whenever on the bus, I insist on sitting in an aisle seat so I can see the road out the front window. The roads are very twisty and hilly, and the drivers are very aggressive. The car sickness I had as a child seems to be haunting me again. I haven't actually *been* sick, but I've often felt very squeamish, and on the verge of asking another passenger for a grocery bag.

Ever since I was a child, I haven't been able to get too close to grocery bags. I was car sick so many times and had my head dangling inside a plastic bag on so many occasions that today the smell of them turns my stomach.

If you knew my dad you'd know he loves to drive, and loves to arrive. He drives as fast as he can on the shortest route possible, in order to arrive yesterday. The route he used to take us to the cottage we named "The Hilly Road." It was somewhat like a roller coaster, and I was sick ninety-five percent of the time on this road. There was a flatter road he could easily have taken, but it was a couple of kilometres longer, so absolutely wasn't an option. My parents always seemed to forget that I got car sick, and they always sat me in the backseat. It never failed, though – a mile or two down The Hilly Road, and I was either moved to the front seat, handed a grocery bag, or already outside of the car being cleaned up.

My only fond memory of the drives to and from the cottage were the ice creams. If I was lucky, we'd stop for ice cream after The Hilly Road. But often, by the time we reached it, I had already eaten a Neapolitan ice cream which, after a few dips and twists, I would throw up.

Another contributing factor to my car sickness was my mother's hand cream. She rubbed a dollop of the cream into her hands prior to each long car trip. I'm sure it smelled nice to most people, and I'm sure it made her hands feel silky smooth, but that hand cream was my nemesis for many years.

We'd pile into the 1983 Chevrolet Caprice Classic, and Dad would turn on the air conditioner. I remember thinking I was going to suffocate. The smell of Mom's hand cream invaded. I could taste it in my mouth, and it turned my mouth dry and pasty. I could also taste the musty air from the air conditioner. I don't think the filters had ever been changed, but Dad insisted on using it anyway. I would sit in silent agony, wishing away my churning stomach, wishing I was in someone else's car.

An hour later I would get my revenge on them all.

"I think I'm going to be sick," I would say.

I can remember the last time I was car sick. I was in grade four and we were driving to Florida during March break. We had two cars going – my family, the Wards, in our car, and my aunt's family, the Estabrooks, in the other car. The two cars would stick together for the trip, stop and have meals and bathroom breaks together, and stay in the same hotel at night. I was sick three times before we reached the United States border. Each time our short caravan would have to pull off the highway, I would be cleaned up, and eventually we'd be on the road again. We weren't making very good time, and I'm sure the Estabrooks regretted coming with us. But then, a miracle happened. I was never sick again. I don't know why, but in a matter of a few hours I grew out of my car sickness troubles. Until now.

The bus drivers in Korea are very smooth and the buses are quite comfortable. The roads, however, are winding and rolling and remind me of The Hilly Road back in Nova Scotia.

Sometimes I find myself staring into space, or at the seat back in front of me. All the seats are covered with material that looks like spandex but feels like vinyl. The pattern reminds me of a bathing suit my great-aunt Queenie would have worn. With a name like Queenie, and knowing she's a great-aunt, it's not difficult to imagine what multi-coloured pattern her bathing suit might have. It would make anyone sick if they were to look at it while riding in a bus on a winding road. My insides were already churning when I realized that I was staring at Aunt Queenie's bathing suit. I made myself look out the front window until my stomach recovered.

Arriving in Jinju, we recognized much of it from being there with Mr. Chang. It's a small city, and with the wide Nam River splitting Jinju in two, it appears relatively easy to navigate. If you can orient yourself to the river, you'll never be lost.

We passed a music store just before we arrived at the bus station and decided that would be our first destination. We've been missing our guitars. We left two at our house in Canada and have decided we should buy one for our stay in Korea. It's nice having a guitar lying around the house. You can go weeks, even months, without playing it but then comes a moment when you're inspired, or you've thought of a new song you want to learn, and you become a guitar player again.

We also needed more hobbies to occupy us at home in Hwagae. We could only do so much emailing, watching movies, and playing cribbage. I only find crib to be fun if there is money on the line. I love winning a dollar or two off my dad or my uncle John. But to me the game is meaningless when you play against your husband, and the dollar (or in our case the 1,000 Korean won) is coming from the same pocket it is going into.

We watch some TV but our channel selection is limited. In Canada we didn't watch a lot of TV and didn't have cable. We have significantly less to do in Korea, so we often surf through the twenty channels. Three of the channels air English movies ninety-five percent of the time. About half of them are classic 1950s flicks which we really enjoy, while the other half are terrible 1980s made-for-TV movies. Even the good movies are hard to watch because they are always interrupted by a lengthy and dreadful infomercial. They are always louder, the acting is horrible, and often they show close-ups of disgusting-looking food or people chewing with their mouths open. We were looking forward to keeping the TV off most nights and jamming on the guitar.

It's funny to shop in a Korean music store. Dale would say "frustrating" as he was doing the shopping; I say funny as I was the audience. None of the guitars were in tune and almost all of them still had paper covering the strings. I chose a handsome mahogany-looking guitar and Dale picked it off the wall. I have no idea if the guitar is actually mahogany, or if guitars are ever made out of mahogany. In fact, I know nothing about purchasing or the quality of guitars. Dale often plays someone else's and says to me, "Hear the difference? The action on this one is really good." I always nod and say, "Oh yeah. Sounds great." I love playing, but I'm not interested in the technical specifications or really anything other than *can I play it?* Some guitars are prettier than others, which is why I chose the "mahogany" one. Dale seemed to think it was pretty too.

We tore the shopkeeper away from the couch at the back

of the store where he was watching Korean game shows. He seemed very disinterested in selling to us. Eventually, he helped Dale get the paper off the strings. Dale started tuning the instrument, which became a long and tedious task, more than he had anticipated. It seemed the strings had been installed but not tuned even slightly. At one point I thought he might give up and walk out. He required food, which I knew before we entered the store and should have done something about.

If Dale's blood sugar is low, I need to get him something to eat, immediately. Otherwise, he becomes a very cranky Dale and can be unpleasant to shop with. I've learned this from the very few grocery-shopping experiences we've shared. He hates grocery shopping on the best of days and I usually do the food shopping by myself. Sometimes, he gets brave, though, and forgets his hatred for it. I lie to him, "Sure. It'll be fun to get groceries together." I start planning my quickest route around the store to be sure he doesn't decide mid-shopping that he's had enough. We've had to leave malls before because Dale is hungry and cranky. To prevent any angry episodes, I try to have a granola bar on hand to give him soon after we enter the store. Then I let him saunter behind me, pretend I don't hear when he suggests that we buy Count Chocula cereal, and I go like hell. I make believe that I'm in one of those contests where you win all the food you can get into your cart in ten minutes. Halfway down the canned goods aisle, I hand him another granola bar. Then I keep one bar in reserve in case there is a long lineup at the checkout or if the cashier forgets the code for sweet potatoes.

Unfortunately, I had no granola bars in the music shop in Jinju. Dale was getting frustrated by the tuning of the instrument, and I worried we wouldn't be buying a guitar. I spoke soothing words of encouragement.

At last, he had the guitar in tune and he played a few songs to see how it sounded. I crossed my fingers that this would be the one. I didn't want to endure another guitar tuning. He said the action was okay, and it had a pretty good sound. I inquired about the price: 150,000 won, about $170 Canadian. The salesman would include a "top-quality" soft guitar case in the price. Dale told him we'd probably be back the next day. If he was purchasing it, he wanted to do so just before we boarded the bus to go back home.

I would have bought it on the spot and walked around the city for two days with it. That's the kind of shopper I am. I have my mom's frugality but also my dad's impulsiveness. I knew the guitar was a good price, and I wanted it then and there. I hate waiting for things.

Dale said, "It will still be there tomorrow."

"Okay. Fine," I replied.

I was testy and needed food at this point too. We bought a sandwich to split between us and walked past the fort Mr. Chang had taken us to, down the street towards our second destination.

When we had been going over contracts and deciding where we wanted to teach in Korea, many recruiters boasted about different cities, saying, "There is Walmart, and Baskin Robbins, and McDonald's and ..." I would interrupt them, and, in my best self-righteous voice, I would state, "I rarely shop at Walmart in Canada, and I don't plan on shopping there in Korea."

I thought of those conversations, as we walked up to the beautiful, big sliding doors of E-Mart, Korea's own Walmart. We were going to be *those people* I had scorned back in Canada: *those people* who couldn't cut it in Korea without their Western luxuries.

I needed a new watch battery and Dale wanted to price video game systems. I was never allowed to have video games when I was growing up, so today I'm horrible at them, and I think they're a waste of time. My mom and I agree on that: "There's no need for video games!" Dale doesn't have one in our house back in Canada, although I'm sure he'd like one. He plays when he's at his friend Eben's, and I think that is completely sufficient. I also don't plan on letting our future children, if we have children, have a game system. I wonder if that rule will stick once kids have arrived.

Against my better judgment, I agreed that a game system would be a good purchase for our stay in Korea. We only have one computer and both of us hate having someone reading over our shoulder, so one of us is often left to our own amusements. I spend a great deal of time on the computer, documenting our Korean adventures. I try to do as much writing as I can early in the morning, while Dale is sleeping or when he's at school and I'm home. Sometimes, though, I get inspired at about 7:17 p.m. and it is during those times I'd love for Dale to be playing NBA Jam, instead of searching the web for pictures of people surfing.

We figured that game systems would be cheaper in Korea, since they are manufactured in Asia. This was not the case. We struggled with E-Mart salespeople for ten minutes to find out the prices and left once we learned how expensive the systems were. Perhaps we'll find one second-hand.

I went to the jewelry counter to pick up my watch. They had installed a new battery, and had shined and cleaned it, even buffing away a scratch in the watch face. We paid about five dollars Canadian for the service, and the sales lady let us use the E-Mart phone to call Kimon.

Dale and I have decided not to invest in a cellular phone in Korea. The cost of purchasing one, and using it, is minimal. However, we'd rather spend the money in some other way. If we lived in a city like Jinju, we would probably opt for a cell phone instead of a landline, as it is convenient for contacting people when you're on the go. But living in Hwagae, we get very few calls. And if we did have a cell phone, it would be easier for Mr. Chang to find us.

As it is, our home phone is on a party line with the principal of the elementary school. Therefore, we don't answer the phone when school is in session. We usually know in advance if our parents are phoning from Canada or one of our Canadian friends in Korea is phoning. If we're not expecting a call, we don't answer.

Mr. Chang phones at night, maybe to invite us to volley-ball or badminton, maybe to invite us to his house to share a can of Spam, "the good meat," as he calls it.

We assume it's him calling and don't answer the phone. If he mentions it later, we tell him we unplugged the phone during the day so we wouldn't have to listen to it ring for the elementary school principal and we'd forgotten to plug it back in.

It's unfortunate that our Korean party line isn't like the party line we used to have at our cottage. If the call was for our family, the phone rang in two-ring intervals. If it was for the other cottage that we shared the line with, it rang in single-ring intervals. That way, we always knew if it was for us. I wonder if they still have party lines in Canada.

Mr. Chang usually lets the phone ring about thirty times. Dale and I sit, holding our breath, tensely listening for the ringing to cease. Finally, there is silence. For twenty seconds we relax. Then he tries one more time, again letting the phone ring and ring and ring. If you'd been to our house in Hwagae, you'd know it might take us, at the most, three rings to answer. Maybe if I had a broken leg (and I was outside at the clothesline) it might take me ten rings to reach the phone. Mr. Chang is relentless.

At the E-Mart, on the jewelry counter phone, we called Kimon and he told us he was on his way to Jinju University to play basketball with some buddies. We thanked the jewelry lady and left the store to search for a cab.

Dale was excited to play basketball. I sulked as I had worn flip-flops and not brought sneakers with me.

A ten-minute taxi ride cost us about five dollars Canadian, and Kimon was waiting for us on the sidewalk when we arrived. It was so nice to be around English speakers again for a little while. Conversations were easy. We met tall Tim, curly-haired Dave, and "blonde guy," whose name escapes me. I watched from the sidelines, vowing that I'd never travel again without sneakers. It was good, though, to see Dale hanging out with "the boys"; they seemed like guys he'd chum around with back home.

After an hour I noticed the air cooling, the clouds becoming more prevalent, and goosebumps forming where my capri pants exposed my legs. My bum was numb when I moved it from the cold cement to sit on our backpack. The boys finished their game, and we were invited to join them and their friends for supper.

I was happy just to be inside when we arrived at the restaurant. I was starting to realize that Korean weather can be as unpredictable as Nova Scotian weather: one minute sunny and 15 degrees Celsius, the next minute snowing and five below. I'll pack smarter the next time we go away for a weekend.

Much of the little restaurant was occupied by the twelve of us. All of our new acquaintances were from Canada, most from Ontario, and all were Hagwon English teachers in Jinju.

Our meal of chicken and cabbage in red pepper sauce was cooked on a grill in the middle of our table. We had no plates, only chopsticks. If I were a germaphobe I would struggle to eat in a Korean restaurant. Everyone eats from the same dishes. I agree that isn't so odd. What's different is you use your own chopsticks to retrieve the food. You put the food in your mouth using those same chopsticks. Then you pick up another piece of food and put it into your mouth, all with the same chopsticks, without ever washing the chopsticks in between bites. And sometimes one eater's chopsticks kiss another eater's chopsticks during the food retrieval.

Anyone with sharing issues, as I sometimes have, learns very quickly that no dish or plate of food has an owner in Korea; everything on the table belongs to everyone at the table. I like having my own plate, with my own portion of food, that I have ordered myself. I see nothing wrong with that. Dale says I'm a control freak. I tell him he's just lucky he had so many siblings; he had to learn to share. I never had to share – my older sister, Carla-Jo, always did.

Dinner was amazing, super spicy but incredibly delicious. After, we went to a bar for some nightlife. Other friends joined us throughout the evening. Some Americans were amongst the group, and one guy who went to school with Dale's friend from home. As is common when travelling, especially with Canadians, we all played the name game, "Oh, you went to school at Dal? You must know so-and-so ..."

"You're from Nova Scotia? Well, my cousin's veterinarian's stepsister went to summer camp in Cape Breton when she was five. Do you know Susie?"

I find it so strange to be on a foreign continent and run into someone I know or who knows someone I know. It makes the world seem so much smaller, like nothing is ever very far from home. I like how there is instant camaraderie between Canadians when we meet in a foreign country. It's like we're all on the same team – being Canadian makes us automatic friends. As well, it's nice meeting people who are going through similar experiences. Everyone we met in Jinju taught different age groups and had been in Korea for varying lengths of time. It felt so good to swap teaching stories and share cultural adventures.

Dale and I slept on a mattress on Jenny's kitchen floor that night. We don't mind camping at other people's houses at all. In Canada we used to take our air mattress everywhere with us, in case an evening turned into a night.

We were grateful to have a place to crash in Jinju. They invited us back, and there are so many reasons to come back: for friends and conversation, for the nightlife, for the opportunity to play sports, for the great shopping, and for the freedom from Mr. Chang. Actually, he was there, somewhere, possibly searching for us so he could take us to church again. Knowing this did create a little fear for Dale and me – the thought that Mr. Chang could be lurking around any corner.

The Jinju boys invited me to play on their soccer team the next day. I would have loved to play, to run with the boys, to prove myself to ... I'm not sure who.

I guess I felt a bit like I had to prove something after quitting volleyball in Hwagae. I'd never quit a sport before. Dale encouraged me to buy cleats and shin pads, but the game wasn't until the afternoon and I didn't want to wait around Jinju all day. Besides, our heads were sore from the party the night before, and we both wanted to get back to Hwagae where we could nap and recover.

Dale and I left Jenny's apartment early and caught a cab to E-Mart. Our new friends had told us about the huge grocery section in the basement of the store. We hadn't noticed that section on Saturday, and we wanted to see if they sold any food we couldn't buy in Hwagae. I also wanted to buy more toe socks. The morning wind in Jinju called for hats and mittens. It was freezing and I was wearing flip-flops. Besides my feet being cold, they were sore from wearing thong flip-flops which hadn't quite been broken in yet. I knew Dale was thinking *I told you so,* so I didn't complain.

Dale was not in a shopping mood, and I knew that even a granola bar would not bring him around. I quickly found a pair of gray toe socks and we headed downstairs to the grocery store. I was losing Dale by now. I could see the look of desperation on his face. *Don't make me shop,* his eyes cried out to me. I sent him to sit in the food court while I combed the store.

What I wanted most was kidney beans. They are a big part of our diet in Canada, and since the only meat we've found to buy in Hwagae comes in a can, we'd like our protein to come from beans. We've eaten them in many Korean restaurants, but I haven't found a can of kidney beans in any grocery stores. Logic tells me there must be kidney beans for sale somewhere in Korea. Every restaurant and household can't have its own personal beanstalk. I searched and searched the shelves and aisles of E-Mart, but found no kidney beans. I'm starting to think the Koreans are holding out on us; maybe the entire country has heard of Dale's post-bean flatulence episodes, and they've hidden the beans. Maybe everyone does grow their own kidney beans. I will be looking through our neighbours' backyards in Hwagae when we get home. I *will* find kidney beans!

I joined Dale, who was sitting in front of the McDonald's counter in the food court. We dined on Western fast food for the first time in Korea. Dale tried to order two Quarter Pounders but instead we got pork burgers ... we think. My chocolate milkshake was vanilla, but delicious, and the fries tasted distinctly McDonald's.

We left E-Mart feeling heavy and bloated. Once outside, I put on my toe socks. They were wonderfully warm. We looked down at my new socks and speculated on how much my feet looked like Muppet feet. My feet and toes were gray cotton and each toe was outlined by my toe socks. I had to keep wiggling my toes to prove to myself that, in fact, they really were my feet. When my feet weren't moving, I definitely looked half-Muppet. Perhaps if the teaching gig doesn't work out, I could be a stunt double on Korean *Sesame Street* or some such program (for those rare times when a puppet's legs and feet are shown running or walking). The only difference I could see between my feet and those of a Muppet was that I had ten big gray toes and I think Muppets only have six or eight toes – I'm not sure, though.

Then I wondered why toe socks had spots for all of my toes – why not just my big toe? It must be difficult to sew socks with little compartments for ten little toes – very tedious and time-consuming. Why did the inventor of toe socks jump right to gloves for your feet? Why didn't he/she start with feet mittens? Now there's a better idea: mittens for your feet; socks with compartments for your two big toes, still allowing for wear with thong flip-flops. Easier to sew and just as warm. Perhaps instead of being Oscar the Grouch's stunt double, I will invent Feet Mittens. Feet Mitten sales will surpass toe sock sales tenfold. Our future is looking brighter.

We headed to the guitar shop, purchased our new guitar and case, and boarded the bus for home.

We had a half-hour wait in Hadong. It was too cold to

stand waiting for our next bus, so we headed for Tous Les Jours, a French-named bakery where we often get our chocolate fix. As we trekked down the street, we heard, "Hello!" behind us. We turned to find Mr. Chang and another teacher from my middle school getting out of a car. The two men looked as though they'd been hiking. Mr. Chang was a cowboy – he wore jeans, a ball hat, and a bandana tied around his neck.

He asked us, "Where have you been?"

It was hard to tell exactly how he intended this question to come out, because his emphasis wasn't in the usual places. Was he asking in a friendly way? Like, "Where have you been this weekend? What have you been up to?" Or was he demanding? "Where have you been? I've been looking all over for you, and I called your house and let it ring *thirty* times but you didn't answer so I came to your house *ten* times, and banged on the door and you *still* weren't there!"

We told him we'd been to Jinju and were on our way back to Hwagae. They wanted to drive us, but luckily, we had bought our bus tickets already. They looked disappointed, but drove off without us.

At Tous Les Jours we dined on sweets and mini pizzas, which had pieces of hotdog as a topping, and then we made our way through the windswept streets back to the bus stop.

The wind was even stronger when we reached Hwagae. I never understand how it can be so windy in Hwagae. Our village is tightly protected on all sides by high mountains, but the wind prevails. It sweeps down the valley and hits your face, no matter which direction you are facing.

When we got off the bus, Dale and I saw a large restaurant sign had blown off a building. It lay atop a car, crushing its roof and windshield.

The wind was personified. It was angry, and relentless. It scared me.

NINE

Over the next week the wind persisted. I got used to the gusts and grew to enjoy listening to the howling as Dale and I cuddled in bed. It was like the wind was breathing spring into Hwagae. Our valley started to come alive. In Korean, Hwagae means blossoming flower and the area we live in is famous for blossoming plants – apricots, cherries, pears, and more. People come from all over Korea to view the birth of spring in Hwagae.

Since Dale and I arrived here, we've enjoyed the magnificence of the scenery, the power of the mountains, and the drama of the valleys. But the landscape has been muted by the death of winter, brown and gray and drab. During the last week of March, our surroundings were slowly decorated with the hues of a Korean spring. Vibrancy was born along the mountainside and down through the valley floor. Even the restaurants and small motels that comprise our village were painted and beautified in anticipation for spring and summer visitors.

Hwagae is known for its cherry tree road. In the spring, more than six kilometres of cherry trees create a canopy over the road that my two schools are on. People refer to the road as the "Scenic Road of Korea" or the "Wedding Road," and it is said that couples who hold hands walking down the road will have a happy life together. We had heard a lot about the cherry trees of Hwagae and the annual Cherry Blossom Festival, but we were still astounded when April brought out the vibrant blossoms all along the valley. The sight was truly breathtaking.

Very quickly we learned just how famous "cherry tree tunnel" was, as April also brought onlookers from far and wide. Our typically quiet neighbourhood erupted with bumper-to-bumper traffic, moving at a snail's pace, and pedestrians strolling and stopping everywhere to take photos.

Even new businesses appeared. Little tents popped up along the route from our house to Hwagae. They sold food and drink to the crowds of tourists who had come to witness spring in Gyeongsangnam-do. While walking home from town, Dale and I discovered one tent (run by an elderly lady) that sold delicious traditional Korean food, as well as rice wine known as *dongdongju*. This alcoholic beverage, made from rice fermented in large clay pots, was served to us in a bowl with a ladle to spoon it into our own smaller bowls. The flavour was very distinct, not like anything we'd ever tasted before, and the appearance took some getting used to as it was a milky white liquid. But we liked it and it was very inexpensive.

We had been served what we thought was the same thing at the Hwagae Market once before, but that had been called *makgeolli*. The main difference between the two drinks is that *dongdongju* is fermented for less time and isn't strained during the process, so often there are pieces of rice floating in it.

Mr. Bear too got into the spirit of spring. He came to school that week with a fresh haircut. It was shorter and neater, but it was still Mr. Bear's trademark shag: straight, chin length except for his bangs, and flipping under at the bottom as if he curled it in the morning. He is the only man I know who can wear bangs and get away with it.

At lunch I gave him the thumbs-up, pointing to his hair and making scissor motions with my hands. He nodded and smiled. When he smiles his whole face squishes up. His eyes disappear, his eyebrows become his eyes, and his lips become an extension of his nose. Then, with a tone of great pomp and importance, he exclaimed, "Hairrrr Cutyyy!"

Another day, when I sat next to Mr. Bear at lunchtime, he elbowed me in the side and said, "switchy, oppositey," pointing to his tray and my tray. When I looked at both of our trays, I saw the rice and soup on his tray were in fact in the opposite divots than they were on my tray. He found it quite amusing. The next time I sat next to him at lunch, our soup and rice were again opposite, and again he pointed it out. Two other teachers came and sat across from us. They sat down, looked at each other's trays, said something in Korean, and pointed and laughed. I knew they too had discovered the very funny reality that their rice and soup were in opposite divots, and I chuckled along with the group.

Adding an "ee" sound to the end of words is one of the common pronunciation errors we often hear and try to correct with our students. Mr. Bear always calls it "lunchy," teachers talk to me about the "homeworky," and Mr. Chang often brings up the "Frenchys" and the "Japanys" when he tells us stories of his military service.

Like my sister who has unintentionally developed a bit of a British accent since moving to England, Dale and I have unwittingly adopted some of these bad English habits. We catch ourselves saying "lunchy" and "Marchy" and "catchy." And sometimes we notice each other adding *the* when we shouldn't, as we hear our students and co-workers do.

"Dale, how was the lunch?"

"The lunch was good, Beth Ann. We had the rice and the kimchi."

*   *   *

The next weekend saw us heading to Daejeon to visit Dale's university friend, Candace. We didn't get any inquiries from Mr. Chang about our plans for the weekend, and we were both a little disappointed that perhaps he was over us.

Candace is a Cape Bretoner, and as is typical of a Cape Bretoner, she is a lot of fun and has a great personality. She and Dale attended Acadia University in Wolfville, Nova Scotia. She worked a few jobs in Nova Scotia after graduating, but eventually the travel bug bit her too. Candace found an English teaching job at a Hagwon school in Daejeon (a city north of Hwagae). Shortly after she arrived in Korea, around September of 2005, I began emailing her to find out about the job and the life of an English teacher. She replied that she loved Korea and teaching English was a great experience as well. The Hagwon paid for her flight to Korea and would also pay to fly her home, they provide her with an apartment, her working hours are great, compensation is fantastic, and she earns an extra month's pay if she finishes her contract. It sounded like it was right for us too.

We liked the benefits Candace described, and we both wanted to try our hand at teaching. We'd considered going back to school to become teachers, but were uncertain if we'd like the profession. A year of teaching English in Korea would help us decide if teaching was the path that we might later take.

We decided on Korea early in December of that year. Candace had recommended the website eslcafe.com to search for jobs. I applied to probably fifty different recruiting agencies, and I think every one of them called us back ... at least once! By the end of December, we were unplugging our phone at night so we wouldn't be woken by giggling recruiters stationed in Korea (and unaware of the time difference). They were always giggling. We found it annoying and wondered what was so funny. Once in Korea, we discovered the giggling is out of nervousness, and perhaps lack of confidence in their own English abilities.

I think it was early in January when we received the phone call from Joshua. His real name is Korean but he, like all of the recruiters, used an English name when communicating with us. Joshua told us about the two public school positions in Hwagae and Hadong. The working hours would be better than in most Hagwons – only twenty hours a week teaching, plus five hours of preparation time. Our pay would be great for first-time teachers, and if we taught more than twenty hours a week, we would be paid overtime. All of the other benefits were offered too: flights paid for, fifty percent of our health insurance covered, housing provided, and a bonus month's pay upon completion of the contract. By the end of January, we had signed our contracts and were in the process of applying for our visas.

We quit our jobs and went on a week-long vacation to Aruba where Dale was the best man in his friend Craig's wedding. Dale went on a four-day ski trip to Quebec with his buddies, we prepared our house, packed our things, said goodbye to Keno, our family, and friends, and were off to Korea before the end of February. It was a whirlwind month.

Now, just a month later, we were aboard a bus heading towards Daejeon to visit Candace.

Our journey was longer that weekend. After Jinju we had to take another two-hour bus ride to Daejeon. While waiting in Jinju for the Daejeon bus, we wandered away from the station and found ourselves in what appeared to be the strip club area of town. It was mid-morning, so it was too early for these streets to be bustling. Still, I couldn't help but think people might be getting the wrong impression about us – me with my long blonde Russian prostitute hair and Dale with his cheesy moustache. Yes, the night before Dale had decided it was getting too warm for his winter beard. He shaved it off but kept his 'stache for the weekend, thinking Candace might get a kick out of it. Very few men can wear a moustache and still look sexy and handsome. Dale is not one of them. Dale is no Tom Selleck. Dale looks like a porn star.

We cracked jokes about how we might appear to the Koreans as we made our way through these disreputable streets of Jinju – the Russian prostitute and her porn star husband (or worse, pimp). My laughter was of the nervous type though. As usual, I was worrying. I was wondering if we were going to be picked up by police for questioning or approached by some "customers" of the night. Eagerly, we made our way back to a more virtuous area without incident. I knew we were away from the dark side of town when we came across a Baskin Robbins.

I was going to be one of "those people" again. I couldn't pass it by ... ice cream is probably my favourite food. I knew if I truly wanted to live the Korean experience, I should buy myself a rice cake dessert. But I wanted a treat, and I can't consider anything with rice in the name to be a treat. So into the store we went. We both indulged in a wonderfully chocolatey, rich, and creamy ice cream, our first in Korea. I waited a few minutes before I pointed out to Dale that he had some ice cream in his 'stache.

We boarded the bus for the final leg of our journey. On the ride, between discussing the pros and cons of Dale's moustache, we practise our Korean. *Hangul* is the Korean word for Korean. Dale and I have started to learn how to read *Hangul*. It helps, especially when travelling, as the city names are written in *Hangul*. There might be fifteen ticket counters in a bus station, but only one sells tickets to Hadong. Then, if you've been skilled enough to find the right counter and purchase your ticket, you have to find your bus from a lineup of thirty different buses, all with city names written in *Hangul* displayed in the front window.

Some of the bus station staff can speak a bit of English or at least understand our destination when we say it. However, some Korean words have only slight differences in their pronunciation. Dale and I, being new to *Hangul*, don't always use the precise pronunciation, which has led to some confusion.

Once when trying to get to Hadong by bus, we approached the ticket counter and I said to the lady, "Hadong." And I held two fingers up, indicating we'd like two tickets.

She just stared back at us.

I said again, "Hadong."

This time I emphasized the Ha.

She still doesn't get it, so I try again, and instead accentuate the dong.

There's a limited number of ways one can say a two-syllable word. Eventually, Dale joined my effort, and both of us had our noses pressed up against the glass of the booth, yelling "Hadong" at the poor ticket lady.

Then, suddenly, she smiles.

"Aaaaah. Hadong!" she says, exactly like the first five, and last thirteen, times I said it!

And Dale and I say, "Yes. Hadong."

Korean words, like English, are comprised of letters/sounds represented by symbols. There are fourteen consonants and ten vowels. Sometimes a syllable is comprised of two letters beside each other. At other times the letters can be stacked on top of each other, creating the syllable. For example, this is Korean for Hadong: 하동

h = ㅎ a = ㅏ d = ㄷ o = ㅗ ng = ㅇ

You can see the *h* and the *a* sound are beside each other, creating the syllable *ha* (하), while the *d*, *o*, and *ng* sounds are stacked, creating the syllable *dong* (동).

It actually didn't take us too long to memorize the letters and be able to read Korean aloud. We don't know what we're saying, but we can read it. And knowing how to read the street names and town names has made travelling on our own much easier and less stressful.

About five hours after we left our house in Hwagae, we arrived in Daejeon. It is an enormous city of nearly one and a half million people, far too big to learn to navigate in one weekend. We phoned Candace, found out approximately where she lived, and hailed a taxi. Cabs are so much cheaper here. The ride would have cost us thirty or forty dollars in Nova Scotia, but we paid about half that amount.

While waiting for Candace where our taxi let us out, we grabbed a snack in a convenience store, and then mused over Dale's moustache until we spotted Candace and another girl approaching. It was great to see a familiar face. We each hugged, and she introduced us to her friend, Sarah.

"I know you," Sarah said, pointing to me.

"Hmmm." I looked hard at Sarah, but didn't think I knew her. "Where are you from?"

"Dartmouth."

She looked about my age, so I asked her, "What high school did you go to?"

"Dartmouth High," she replied.

"Hey, I went there too!" I said excitedly. "What year did you graduate?"

"1999," she replied. That would put her in grade ten when I was in grade twelve. She went on, "And I have a sister who is two years older, Katherine."

"Yes!" I said. "I know Katherine! I went to school with her since grade eight."

Coincidentally, I had just said to Dale, "It would be cool if we ran into somebody we know from Canada in Daejeon."

Candace had told us there was a large English teacher population in the city, and many were Canadian. Dale and I had both fallen silent, imagining who we might meet from home.

Sarah was my person from home. I didn't know her well, and perhaps I'd never spoken to her before, but I did eventually remember going to school with her. In high school her hair had been long and extremely curly. Now her hair was still long but she straightened it, giving her a very different look. As soon as I thought of her with the crazy curly hair, I remembered her.

I definitely remembered her sister, Katherine. She had been in many of my classes throughout junior high and high school.

"I remember when Katherine brought beer to band class in grade nine," I told Sarah.

"Yeah. That sounds like Kat," Sarah said, smiling.

It's funny, the things I remember. I can never remember the year I graduated from university, but I can still remember the day Katherine brought alcohol to school. In fact, I remember it vividly.

It was lunchtime band class. Everyone had already eaten and made their way from the lunch room to the band room. Katherine lived close to the school and had gone home for lunch. When she returned for band, she brought a Gatorade bottle filled with beer. She quietly told the reed section what she had in the bottle. Of course, the news spread around the room quickly. Being in the woodwind section, I got the news well before the drummers at the back.

I was shocked and thought Katherine was stupid for doing that. At first, I didn't understand what would ever possess someone to bring alcohol to band class. *Aren't we supposed to be playing instruments?* I had thought.

In grade nine you could find my picture in the dictionary, next to the definition of Goodie-Two-Shoes. I never did anything wrong. I was terrified of getting in trouble at school or home, and I hated disappointing anyone. Katherine was a badass, and it was confusing to me.

I watched the reaction light up the room. I saw the attention Katherine attracted, my classmates crowding around her, some taking a swig. Suddenly, I got it. Katherine was "cool." Katherine had been accepted. For a few moments I had wished I was Katherine, the one with the beer getting all the attention.

Along with being a Goodie-Two-Shoes, I was a bit of a geek in junior high. I used to carry my pen, pencil, and highlighter in my pants pocket so I would be ready for class as soon as I sat at my desk. I didn't waste my valuable learning time by rummaging through a book bag and pencil case to find writing supplies.

I didn't know I was a Goodie-Two-Shoes and a geek, because I was also quite naive. I'd had one boyfriend, one disgusting French kiss, and I didn't plan on kissing any boys again if that was what it was going to be like. Sex was something I'd heard about, but never thought about, and didn't really understand. Our Health teacher, Mr. Johnston, once gave us each a scrap of paper. He told us to write any "sex-related" questions on it that we didn't want to ask out loud in the class. My question was: *If a girl swallows sperm will she get pregnant?*

I assumed everyone would write a question, but when Mr. Johnston opened the papers there were very few. Thinking back, he had probably noticed who had written each question. I hope not. If he had, he would have known which question was mine, and he might have thought I was having oral sex! I was doing nothing of the sort, though. At the time, I didn't even know there was such a thing as oral sex. I had been thinking more along the lines about a girl drinking a cup of sperm. I don't remember why I thought a girl would ever drink a cup of sperm ... maybe there was some in her orange juice by mistake. I hadn't really thought the question through, I guess. Mr. Johnston answered my question without bringing any attention to me. I was grateful.

I was a keener, a geek, very innocent, and I tended to blend into the background. For once I wanted to be Katherine with the big curly blonde hair, and a Gatorade bottle full of beer.

I did eventually pass that awkward teenage stage. I grew up, learned about sex and many other things, kissed a few boys, found the right boy to kiss, married him, and twelve years after that band class, was chatting about Katherine's beer escapades with her sister Sarah on a sidewalk in South Korea.

* * *

Candace lives in an apartment building owned by her Hagwon. The other Hagwon teachers, including Sarah, live in the building as well. Candace shares her dwelling with her dog, Casey. Besides looking forward to our visit with Candace, Dale and I had been anxiously anticipating our visit with Casey. We missed Keno terribly and really wanted a furry friend to play with. Casey is a tiny, white, cute-as-a button Maltese. Even his bark is tiny, more of a "yip" than anything. If we never left Candace's apartment all weekend, we would have enjoyed ourselves immensely, just playing with the dog.

Dogs add so much to a situation. Sometimes I wonder what we'd talk about if there wasn't a dog around. They seem to fill any awkward voids in a conversation. Dale and I talk for Keno all the time. We pretend we know what he's thinking, and we say it in our best dog voice. If we're right, Keno has a pretty good sense of humour.

We even make up Keno dialogue in Korea. Just the other day Mom emailed us some Keno and Gunner stories. Gunner is my parents' dog, the yapping Shih Tzu that Dale loathes. Gunner is allowed on the couch, but Keno isn't. It seems a double standard, but Keno is a shedder and we'd rather keep his hair on the floor as much as possible. We have many comfortable dog beds placed around the house for Keno to lounge about on, so we don't feel it unfair that he's not allowed on the furniture. But Mom wrote that when Gunner recently jumped up on the furniture, Keno lifted his head from his dog bed, looked at Gunner, then looked at Mom with great disgust in his eyes.

Dale's Keno dialogue went something like: "What?! Is it 'cause I'm not purebred? Because I'm a mutt? That's it. That's it, isn't it? It's 'cause I'm just a mongrel," then, muttering under his breath "Stupid Gunner. Stupid couch. I don't need that couch anyways. You just wait, Gunner! You'll get yours."

Later that day, Mom told us Keno had Gunner's leash in his mouth and was leading him around the yard. Perhaps he had concocted an evil plan of doom for little Gunner. We'll never know, though. My dad foiled any scheme when he saw the two dogs and took them inside.

We played with Casey, caught up on Candace's life for a few hours, and then went out for dinner. The restaurant was fancy compared to others we'd dined at since arriving in Korea. As we've grown accustomed to, we took our shoes off before entering the eating area. This restaurant had a special shelf for its patrons' footwear. We placed ours amongst the thirty-odd other pairs of shoes and went to eat.

The restaurant was busy, a tribute to the excellent food. We cooked different kinds of meat and fish on our tabletop grill, and ate various types of kimchi and other side dishes that Korean meals are famous for. At one point we counted the number of plates on the table, and our total came close to fifty. When we got up to leave, we found our shoes had been taken off the shelf and lined up for each of us by a doorman/host gentleman. I was amazed. There must have been forty pairs of shoes there by now. How did he know which shoes were ours? Was he some kind of footwear psychic? The man didn't speak English and looked like he was taking his job very seriously, so I didn't bother him with my questions. His secret remains a mystery I think about while I lie awake at night, just before I dream about the bat returning to our air conditioner.

We went to another restaurant for kiwi *soju*. Up until this point, I have not enjoyed *soju*. This colourless Korean hard liquor contains, on average, twenty-four percent alcohol. Korean people drink it straight. I've tried it that way and have great difficulty swallowing it … it's like sipping on vodka.

Candace, however, had discovered the wonderful world of kiwi *soju*. They take some kiwis and they take some *soju*, and they mix them together with ice in a blender. The result is a delicious drink that tastes nothing like *soju*, and also provides a healthy dose of vitamins (as well as fibre), something our bowels would thank us for later.

With a few pitchers of kiwi *sojus* under our belts, we were ready to go dancing. Candace took us to a place owned by two Canadians. It had a pool table and foosball table, and about twenty people milling around. The night before had been St. Patrick's Day, and Candace told us the bar had been packed with Canadians drinking green beer. All the partiers must have still been recovering the next night, as the populace of the bar never exceeded twenty people.

We met another guy from Halifax, who incidentally was friends with someone Dale had worked with back home. He was African-Canadian, and taught English and basketball in Seoul. He'd been here for a few years and I wondered about his experiences. Our impression so far was there was still a great deal of blatant racism in Korea. Mr. Chang had used the N-word and also made stereotypical comments about Black people. Our friends in Jinju had told us that many Koreans are racist towards Black people and other minorities.

A teacher we knew was put in charge of hiring more teachers for her Hagwon. When she showed her director the résumés and pictures of a few candidates who were well qualified, he said no, because they weren't white.

* * *

Sunday morning found us sleeping in. I got up to use the washroom, and Casey greeted me in the kitchen so I brought him back to bed with us. I felt like a horrible cheating jerk. We'd never let Keno up on our bed at home, and now, after only knowing Casey one day, Dale and I were sleeping with him.

We rose just before noon and met some of Candace's friends for lunch.

At about three p.m., Dale and I found ourselves again shopping where we always tried not to shop, where we prided ourselves on not shopping, a big-box store. It wasn't E-Mart this time – it was Costco. I admit we did it because of the peer pressure; everyone else was doing it. Candace was doing it. Sarah was doing it. Even Sarah's boyfriend, who seemed very socially responsible, was doing it. As we approached the doors, we saw hordes of people doing it too – already inside, or getting out of taxis and entering the store. I let myself be comforted by the fact that Dale and I weren't alone in our need to shop at this giant chain store.

It was wonderful. Two warehouse levels of anything I could ever want. So different from the few little stores in Hwagae, which had to jam a whole lot of stuff into a tiny space.

We found huge bath towels for twelve dollars Canadian, and bought three. I found my brand of face wash, an eight-pack of canned kidney beans, a double box of GoLean cereal, and even a three-pack of Canadian maple syrup. Each item I found got me more excited.

The kidney beans proved what I'd suspected all along: there were no magic beanstalks hidden all over the country. I would have bought forty-eight cans instead of eight, but we still had to transport our purchases back to Hwagae, so I settled for eight. I was surprised to see the GoLean cereal. We used to eat it in Canada, but I didn't think they'd sell it here. Even Dale got excited over the cereal. We were growing sick of jam and white bread toast for breakfast. And jam is so expensive here, and, as I've already mentioned, Dale likes "ample" amounts of jam on his toast so we go through bottles very quickly.

I planned on giving a bottle of maple syrup to Mr. Bear, Mr. Lee, and Mr. Chang, in appreciation for the hospitality they'd shown us since we arrived in Korea. The bottles said "Made in Canada," and the only Korean on them was a price sticker that I would later use nail polish remover to take off. I didn't plan on telling them we bought the maple syrup at Costco in Daejeon.

* * *

On Monday I asked Mr. Chang what he had done on the weekend. He told me he'd been to Seoul, to his cousin's wedding.

Aha! I thought. That's why he didn't question us on our weekend plans. He had plans of his own and didn't need us for entertainment.

I gave our maple syrup gifts to Misters Chang, Bear, and Lee on Wednesday. I thanked them for being so kind to us. Then I briefly told them how Canadians might consume maple syrup – on top of pancakes, by dipping bread in it, or by drizzling some over ice cream. I explained it's like the maple water they drink, except much of the water has been boiled from it, leaving behind a very sweet, concentrated syrup.

Later that afternoon, Mr. Lee came to my desk with his bottle of maple syrup. He put the bottle to his lips, tipped his head back, and drank. My mouth dropped open.

"Mr. Lee! You're not supposed to *drink* it!" I exclaimed.

"Ahhh. Yes –" he wasn't listening to me "– this is much sweeter than our tree water. I mixed water in with it and then I drank it."

"You drank *all* of it?" I tried to hide my disbelief.

"Yes. Is very good. Good for the health," he said as he patted his chest. He would notice later that day how his "health" felt … probably rather jittery and anxious. I figured he'd crash from his sugar high around suppertime.

"How can I thank you enough for this gesture?" he asked.

"Oh, it's nothing!" I replied, rather perplexed.

In Canada, a person might be thrown in jail for watering down maple syrup. It would be sacrilegious. I didn't tell this to Mr. Lee.

"I'm just glad you enjoyed it," I replied.

TEN

The alarm clock rang at six this morning. The alarm rings at six every weekday morning. As I am a control freak, I won't let an alarm tell me it's time to get out of bed. So I hit snooze. The snooze on our alarm clock lasts four minutes. I hit it ten times before I get out of bed around 6:40. I walk to the kitchen and turn on the kettle. I head to the washroom. I head back to the kitchen and mix soy milk into cereal. Hot water with instant coffee. I stir. I return to the bedroom with the food. I tell Dale, "Time to wake up, honey. Here's your breakfast." Dale rolls over, blinks a few times, and says, "Oh. Wow! What a surprise! Thank you so much."

Each school day starts like this for us. I have become what Mr. Chang calls *a good Korean wife* and I *prepare the breakfast for the husband*. I do it for two reasons. First, I'm always out of bed before Dale, and if I don't get him going, he will probably miss his bus. Second, I feel a slight bit guilty that Dale must catch the bus before 7:30, while I don't have to be to school until ten.

While Dale eats his breakfast, I read him the emails we've received through the night. It is one of our favourite times of the day, hearing about life in Canada or England or wherever our friends and family might be. There is almost always one email from my mom. I get worried when there isn't. Her emails don't tell us anything earth-shattering or shocking, but each message contains a simple narrative that we love.

Hi. 3:30 PM. Just came out on the deck to e-mail in the sun. It's cool and I've got a turtleneck and fleece on. I made some meat-balls and sauce to take to the supper. They are in the oven baking. I also have brown bread in the machine and I made a pan of no-bake squares.

Many people wait until exciting things happen before they email. We like to hear about the ordinary, because that is what we're missing the most.

Most mornings, there are messages from other family and friends. We get news about births and deaths, and we talk about how our world will be different when we return home. There will be new family members to meet, and we will remember the family we've lost. Happy or sad, we love getting a little taste of home in our morning emails. I feel depressed if I turn on the computer in the morning and there is nothing in our inbox.

After breakfast and emails, and sometimes a frantic shower, Dale gets dressed in his best teacher clothes. Once the first day of school was over, he chose not to wear a tie to work. Perhaps the tying of the tie was too much for him. He has, however, begun tucking his shirt into his pants ... I never thought I'd see this day.

Every morning there is a frenzied search for keys, wallets, schoolwork, belts, and sometimes umbrellas. I put my jogging clothes on and try to organize the chaos.

We walk to the bus stop together. Dale boards his bus at about 7:17, and I head off for my morning jog.

The "school bus" Dale rides to school isn't a typical Canadian school bus. It doesn't have that funny school bus smell, it doesn't have bench seats, and it isn't yellow. The "school bus" is actually a large comfortable touring bus, fully equipped with seatbelts, reclining seats, and a TV. The ride takes about twenty-five minutes. At first Dale sat by himself – the students who boarded the bus were too shy to sit with him, so they just stared from a distance. After a week, one of the high school boys mustered up enough courage. He began sitting beside Dale, saying nothing more than "hello" and occasionally smiling up at Dale.

Then Dale and June Man discovered each other. June Man is one of Dale's male students who lives in our town. His mother runs a small grocery store, and his father has a garage.

I met June Man when I was invited to go hiking with Hwagae's Hagwon staff and students. On the Monday following my first encounter with June, he sat next to Dale on the bus and told him all about meeting me that weekend. Dale has so many students that he doesn't know them all by face or name yet. Until June Man sat with him and struck up a conversation, Dale didn't know he existed. Now I would say Dale and June Man are buddies. They sit together every day on the bus. Many mornings June Man has a word or phrase that he asks Dale to explain. Then the next morning he will use that word or phrase in their conversation. June Man's English is improving, and Dale has someone to chat with – a mutually beneficial relationship.

The bus drops everyone off between the boys' and girls' high schools. Then Dale spends his day with one of two factions: screaming girls or hormonal boys.

Mondays and Tuesdays, he teaches the high school girls. There isn't a girl (or female teacher) in the school who isn't enamoured by him. They scream, "I love you!" as he walks past them in the hall. They write, *I love you* on paper, and hold it against the glass of the teachers' office door.

High school in Korea is broken into grades one, two, and three: grades ten, eleven, and twelve respectively in Canada. Dale teaches only grade one and two girls. One of the grade three students is the daughter of a female teacher. One day, Dale was asked to come into the hallway where he found the daughter, a few of her friends, and the mother/teacher observing from a distance. The daughter handed Dale a package with a note. He opened the gift. It was about twenty packets of powdered Vitamin C. Dale read the note. *Hello! My name is Soo-Yeon in third grade. Teacher! You looks great tall and handsome ... I want to get along with you. Bye-bye. Have a good lunch.*

Dale wasn't quite sure what to make of the note, the gift, the girl, or her mother who appeared to have orchestrated the entire event. How did she want to "get along" with him?

He thanked her and returned to the safety of the teachers' office.

* * *

One day I did not have to work. It was my school's birthday, which meant there were no classes. I thought it was a weird custom, but I didn't question it. It was a Monday, so Dale was teaching at the girls' school. We'd decided that I would attend his last class of the day, so after lunch I headed to Hadong on the bus.

Before going to his school, I went to the Hadong bank to wire money to our Canadian bank account. Our Korean bank accounts are with the Agricultural Bank of Korea. There is a small branch in Hwagae, but we couldn't wire money from that location, only from the larger branch in Hadong. I had asked my Mr. Lee to write down my transaction in *Hangul*, so I only needed to pass the paper to the bank teller and wait. The process took about twenty minutes. I leaned on the counter and looked around the bank.

It had the same sterile hushed atmosphere as our banks back in Canada. The first difference I noticed, however, was that all the employees stared at me. I stared and smiled back until they looked away. I also noticed that the Agricultural Bank, unlike the banks in Canada, sold bags of fertilizer and other farming needs. Nobody tried to sell me RRSPs, but

I feared I would be roped into purchasing some top-grade manure.

Once I completed my banking transactions, I walked the ten-minute route to Dale's school. I arrived during a class so there were no girls in the hallway. I made my way to the teachers' office and was greeted, seated, and given an energy drink.

Minutes later, the bell rang, and the hallways filled with girls. I caught sight of Dale pushing his way through the throngs of teenagers. He stepped into the teachers' office, and closed the door behind him. Some of the girls were watching him through the glass. I saw their eyes follow him as he walked towards me. And then they caught sight of me. The screams were deafening. News of my presence spread around the school in about fifteen seconds. Within a minute there were more than twenty screaming girls banging on the office windows and waving frantically at me. None of the teachers reacted to this. They didn't quiet the girls, they didn't send them away, they just watched with amused expressions on their faces. *My God!* I thought. *What is happening?*

Dale looked at me, an amused expression on his face as well.

"I think they like you," he managed over the screaming.

I smiled, waved, and we made our way to his class.

Mr. Kim, an English teacher at the school, accompanied us. I would describe his English as pretty good. He speaks and understands better than Mr. Kim from my school, but he isn't yet fluent. During Dale's classes, his Mr. Kim paces up and down the aisles with his hands clasped behind his back and controls the chaos. The girls always have many questions for Dale, but can't always communicate them. Mr. Kim translates … sometimes. Occasionally a girl will say something in Korean, the class will laugh, Mr. Kim will smile and shake his head, and will say to Dale, "You don't want to know!" One can only imagine what these teenage girls are saying.

Mr. Kim stepped into the classroom first, then Dale, then me. When the girls saw me, another round of screaming lit up the school. Dale told them we'd have a discussion class, their favourite, as long as they kept asking questions. If they weren't participating, he would teach a lesson, their least favourite.

Their line of questioning went like this: How did Dale and I meet? When did Dale and I meet?

I answered, "At a party in September, 2004."

Dale was writing the answer on the chalkboard for them to see the sentence structure. He finished writing and turned to the class to address the next question. I looked at the chalkboard and noticed that he wrote Sept. 6th. He was close, but a couple of days off. Knowing the girls would get a kick out of it, I erased the 6th and wrote 4th. They squealed and went into fits of laughter.

Then they asked me why I love Dale. I told them how wonderful he is, and they all started rubbing their arms saying, "Chicken." At first I thought they were calling me chicken, but then Mr. Kim explained that "chicken skin" is what we call goosebumps.

Next question: *Who is the prettiest girl in the classroom?* I wasn't playing that game and answered everyone is pretty. They were disappointed with my answer, but saw they wouldn't get anywhere by asking me things like that.

Back to relationship questions: *Where did Dale propose? How did he propose? What did I say? How many times did he propose?* I thought the last question was odd. We later found out that in Korea a man will propose to his girlfriend many times before she will accept. It is common to decline eight or ten times.

They asked me if we had any babies yet, and when I told them Keno is my baby, they asked why we didn't have babies.

Each time I answered a question the girls screamed, swooned, giggled, or cheered. They also took pictures of me with their camera phones. They didn't ask if they could take a picture of me, nor did they try to be subtle about it. Eventually, Dale told them to put their phones away.

One girl started pointing at me and telling Mr. Kim something. He came over to me and asked, "Do you know movie actress Uma Thurman?"

I said I did.

"This girl thinks you looks like Uma Thurman."

I thanked the girl. I've gotten this comparison a few times in Canada – probably because of my big eyes and pointy chin. We're also both blonde and suffer from RBF (resting bitch face). So if you see me, and you think I'm cranky, I'm not. That is just my face.

*   *   *

On Wednesday, Thursday, and Friday, Dale teaches high school boys. While he finds the girls to be slightly more advanced in their English skills, he prefers classes with the boys ... less screaming.

I got a chance to visit the boys' school and sit in on one of Dale's classes when I had a Friday afternoon off.

When I walked into the school, I saw a young man on his knees in the hallway outside a classroom, his arms extended in the air over his head. This was one of the first times I saw student punishments. Sometimes the students are given a chair to hold over their head, while they are kneeling on the floor. If the student's arms get tired and they lower the chair to rest on their head, a teacher might come along and bring their arm down hard on the seat of the chair, jarring it against the student's head. The boy I saw had no chair. When he spotted me, he started frantically whispering into the classroom, glancing again down the hallway at me, pointing, and whispering more. By the time I reached the classroom, everyone inside knew I was coming.

Everyone waved. One boy yelled, "I love you!"

I heard, "Mrs. Knowles!" and "Beautiful!"

It would appear that high school boys are just as shy as high school girls.

I met Dale, and together we ate lunch in the school cafeteria. Thankfully, we ate while classes were still in session. I wasn't looking forward to a few hundred males watching me. I hadn't experienced that since my last trip with the Canadian military in Bosnia, walking into the mess hall of a camp with four hundred soldiers, six of whom might be female.

The class I observed at the boys' school was quite different. When I entered the room, I got some hoots and hollers. One boy made a heart shape with his arms over his head and he yelled, "I love you!" He didn't even belong in that class. Dale shooed him away, shut the doors, and the room became quiet. The boys were shy.

Dale ended up teaching them a lecture, as they wouldn't ask any questions. The lecture was painful. It was like pulling teeth trying to get any of the boys to volunteer information or ideas. It was a completely different world to the girls' school. After the class, Dale told me they are never that quiet.

Dale really likes the teachers at the girls' school. They often give him baked goods to bring home, someone always drives him to the bus station after school, and they are all very nice. While the teachers at the boys' high school are very pleasant, I found that environment to be less warm and fuzzy.

There are two Korean English teachers at the boys' high school: Mr. Lee is a jolly older man, whose English is comparable to Mr. Kim's from the girls' high school. Ms. Ko is a tiny mousy-looking woman of twenty-seven who is fluent in English.

Dale has her translate things we need to ask or say to Korean people in our everyday lives. He was dropping film off for developing one day in Hadong and realized before he headed out that he didn't know what to say to the clerk. He had a number of questions and requests. He didn't want doubles. Would there be a choice between glossy or matte finish? How much time would developing the film take? He wrote down what he wanted to say, and Ms. Ko translated for him so he could just present the paper to the store clerk.

As at my schools, the teachers at Dale's spend a great deal of time at school, but they don't actually seem to do much work while they are there. Many of them nap at their desk during the day. Dale's Mr. Kim does bicep curls with a weight Dale says is hardly worth lifting. And there is a balcony off the teachers' office, where they go to practise their golf swing.

One day Dale finished teaching a class and returned to the teachers' office to find a putting green had been set up and the teachers were practising. Another day he found them all huddled around a TV, watching Korea play in the World Baseball Championships. That same day at my middle school, a big screen TV was moved into the teachers' office, so we too could watch the game, instead of doing work.

* * *

Dale finishes school late in the afternoon, usually. Sometimes he's done early, but he doesn't know that in advance. Our teaching schedules are constantly being altered. Sometimes our classes are cancelled; sometimes they are moved to another time slot. They usually inform us of any changes just before the class – never the day before, or even a few hours before. If we say, "Oh, I wish somebody had told me earlier," we are told, "But I just told you!" We have learned to be flexible.

Dale takes public transportation back to Hwagae. His school pays him about $120 a month for his transportation costs. We come out on top, as he takes the school bus in the morning and the public bus costs only about $1.70 per ride.

Dale would take the school bus home at night, but it doesn't run until 9:30 or ten p.m., as many kids stay at school to study. June is one of the kids who remains late at school. When he returns to Hwagae at ten, he then goes to the

Hagwon until midnight. Then its home to do more studying and homework until two a.m. Lately, Dale tells me June is struggling to stay awake on the bus in the morning.

We've both noticed the energy levels in our schools dissipating. Not in the elementary school, as those kids still have a somewhat playful childhood, but the middle and high school students are waning. Many fall asleep in class. We let them. They're kids. If they're so tired they're falling asleep in class, they need the sleep.

When I was high school age, I had energy to spare during the day. I wouldn't have been able to fall asleep in class if I tried. By third-year university I started to struggle to stay awake at times, but I've never reached the state our students are in.

Many are sick with colds and flu, and the lack of sleep shows around their eyes. The kids study for close to fifteen hours a day and are given very little play or exercise time – what they do get comes from gym class. There are no organized sports or teams for the students. The teachers, however, always have at least one volleyball match a week; often they play against the staff of other schools. While the teachers play, the kids are in the school studying.

ELEVEN

After I say goodbye to Dale in the morning, I start the timer on my watch and head down the valley. I love jogging here. When we first arrived, I thought I would hate it. There are so many mountains and steep hills. I have an aversion to running up hills. My legs don't like it, and I have a mental block against it. I usually plan my routes to include as few inclines as possible. The roads in Hwagae have been carved along the valley, though. Very few go up into the mountains, so my jogging routes are relatively flat with some gentle slopes.

I haven't had such scenery to gaze at while running since I was in Bosnia. It really is breathtaking here. The flowering bushes and trees are blooming and growing greener, and the valley looks ever more incredible since the day we arrived.

Two years ago, I ran a marathon, half marathon, and seven triathlons all in a space of five months. By the end of my last race, I was tired of the hours spent training. But I still had the mindset that I *had* to train ... had to bike, had to run, had to swim. If I was going for a run it had to be an hour long, or it wasn't a good run. If I missed a day of exercising, I lamented over it all day. I started to resent exercising. I think working in a gym had a lot to do with it.

Since moving to Korea I've regained an appreciation for

exercise. I've grown to love running again, and I've realized that if I'm not training for an event, I don't need to run like a maniac. I've developed two running routes: one for twenty-five minutes and another for forty. If I head out on my shorter run, I run down one side of the valley, cross the first bridge I come to, and run back down the other side. On my forty-minute session I do the same thing, but go to the next bridge. While running I think about lots of things, like what kind of budget does Korea have for bridge-building? There are bridges everywhere! Within a three-kilometre radius of our house alone there are six bridges. Some are right beside each other. Most are concrete and plain but are still expansive.

When we first arrived in Hwagae we felt the size and number of bridges was overkill. The little river, barely more than a brook, that ran beneath them surely didn't require such big bridges. We'd even attended an event on the floor of the valley, adjacent to the river – fair tents and a huge stage had been set up, and there was a concert followed by an incredible fireworks show. Such a concert was only possible certain times of the year and late spring was not one of those times. Once the snow and ice from the mountains started thawing, the little brook trickling through the valley spread across the entire valley floor. Almost overnight that little brook became a wild, wide river. It ran with incredible speed and power toward Hwagae village, where it flowed into the Seomjin River. We could hear its roar from inside our house, like we lived beside a waterfall. The need for the huge bridges became apparent.

Near Hwagae's centre is the most elaborate of the bridges, the Namdo Bridge that spans the Seomjin River. The meaning of Seomjin is "toad ferry," which I find quite endearing. This river is always fuller than the one that runs past our house, but its water level also fluctuates with the season. The Namdo Bridge is quite extravagant with two huge arches, one blue and one red, that intersect at their apex. Along both sides of the bridge is a brick pedestrian path, as well as a wider observation deck. At night there are coloured lights shining on the bridge and the arches. The lights change and move, and create rainbows up and down the arches. It's quite an attraction for such a small town.

As I ran this morning, the air reminded me of a May long weekend morning at my family's cottage in Tidnish, just outside Amherst, Nova Scotia. On the May long weekend, the early morning air is still cool but smells of spring, and it is damp from the salty Northumberland Strait. In Tidnish, my morning runs are always quiet and peaceful. Normally, it's the same in Hwagae, with the only noises being a few cars on the road and some roosters announcing daybreak.

Today, however, there was some idiot driving around in his truck screaming things on a loudspeaker. It was only 7:20 a.m., too early for the Mobile Market. I ran down one side of the river and he drove slowly, in the same direction, along the other side. He was my pace car, and his disruptive bellowing followed me through the valley.

"Blah blah blah blah blah!" his intonation rose and then fell, and each phrase ended with "*Hamnida.*" Adding "*hamnida*" to the end of a sentence makes the sentence more formal and polite. Over and over again the man in the truck said the same thing with the inflection in the same spot every time, a slew of words I didn't understand followed by "*hamnida.*" I crossed the bridge and headed towards the guy so I could pass him, and we'd be headed in the opposite direction. When I met the truck, it didn't appear to be selling anything. I couldn't imagine what he might be yelling. I shook my head and kept on running.

I've met only one other runner since we arrived in Hwagae. It was on a warm morning and I was dressed down to shorts and a t-shirt. He jogged towards me wearing a full tracksuit zippered up to his chin, a winter hat, and gloves. Even the few joggers we see in other cities always wear gloves – no matter how hot it is. On a really hot day they wear shorts, a t-shirt, and gloves.

When I get back to our house, I sometimes do a couple sets of cheater chin-ups in the elementary school playground. I grab hold of a horizontal bar on the swing set, extend my legs in front of me, keep my feet on the ground, and lift.

The playground at the elementary school is quite old and was not planned or built with safety in mind. All of the equipment has rusted and the paint has mostly chipped off. There is one swing set that is supposed to have two swings on it. One swing is missing, and the other has been wound tightly around the top crossbar since we arrived here, so nobody can use it. There is a climbing contraption that is nine rungs high. It resembles a large metal cube, with another smaller cube on top. The cubes are sectioned into many smaller cubes inside by metal bars and rungs. If a child fell from the top, there are about thirty rungs for them to hit their head, smash their teeth, or cut themselves with rusty metal. Besides that, there are four other metal pieces of equipment. One is a teeter-totter that teeters side to side as well as up and down. Another is a small rocking device that, at one time, would have had two seats on it but now just has metal bars to sit on. My tailbone shudders just looking at it. My most hated apparatus is a metal rocking horse that is in desperate need of a good oiling. It squeaks a horrible sound, like something out of a bad horror movie. The squeaking echoes up into our house and tortures my mind every morning.

What Dale and I find the most mind-boggling is that each classroom in the elementary school has a big-screen TV hooked up to a computer with internet. There is also a computer lab with another big-screen TV and about thirty computers – but there isn't enough money to give the kids a safe, enjoyable playground.

Kids in Korea are growing up quite differently than kids in Canada. There are many things I disagree with when it comes to student life and expectations in Korea, but one of the things I really like is that students are in charge of cleaning the school each day. In fact, there is no janitorial staff, only a maintenance man. At the end of the school day all of the kids buzz about and clean their classrooms, hallways, and even the teachers' office. At first I thought it was a great idea and thought students in Canada could benefit from such work as well – perhaps there would be less destruction, littering, and graffiti if students were responsible for cleaning their school at the end of the day. Now, I still feel Canadian students should clean their schools, but I wish Korean children didn't.

I see my students cleaning the offices, while the teachers play volleyball, sit on massage chairs, or nap at their desks. Then the children have to go to Hagwons to study for the evening. On weekends, if they're not in school on Saturday, many help out at their parent's businesses. I think they could use a little break.

If there are kids already in the schoolyard when I finish my run, I pass on the chin-ups and escape inside our house. I turn on the hot water, and sometimes do Pilates or check emails again, while I wait for the water to warm up.

By the time I got back from running this morning, there was already an email from Dale in the inbox. He wrote that today is a "yellow dust day" and he urged me to shower and brush my teeth as soon as I got back from running. Yellow dust plagues Korea during the spring. It blows from arid lands in China, and collects pollutants such as heavy metals like cadmium, lead, aluminum, and copper as it travels south. When the wind is blowing from the north, the dust settles over Korea and causes many health problems. Maybe that's what the guy was yelling from his truck this morning, "Yellow dust day! It's a yellow dust day, if you please!"

When we first arrived here, we noticed many Koreans wore masks over their nose and mouth. We asked why and were never given a straight answer: "Maybe to protect them from the sun." "Maybe because they have sickness." We thought perhaps face masks became popular here during the SARS outbreaks, and people were still worried about infections. Nobody thought to warn us about yellow dust.

Dale read about it in *The Korean Times*, a newspaper for English speakers. The article warned people to stay inside on days when yellow dust levels were high, to wear long sleeves when outside, and wash any exposed skin and brush your teeth when you return inside. The dust and pollutants can enter your body through pores in your skin, your mouth, and your eyes.

I find it hard to follow the safety guidelines. I never know if it's a yellow dust day until after my run, and it's too warm to wear long pants and shirts when running. I've had a number of Korean women grab my bare arms and speak rapidly to me in Korean. I thought maybe they were remarking on the fact it wasn't summer yet, and I was wearing short sleeves, but now I'm starting to think they might have been warning me about yellow dust on my exposed skin.

I brushed my teeth and had a shower as Dale suggested. Our showers have progressed significantly since the cold dribble we suffered through in February. The hot water was our first discovery. But due to the low water pressure, we still had to either lean into the cold bathroom wall in order to get wet or always hold the nozzle in our hand.

There is a shower curtain rod hanging in our bathroom. There is no curtain hanging from it, as there is no specific shower or tub – water goes everywhere regardless. For the first month we used the rod only to hang our socks and unmentionables to dry, instead of hanging them on the clothesline outside. One day I tried draping the detachable shower nozzle over the rod. The water sprayed up first and then down, and with gravity providing more pressure, a fairly effective shower could be enjoyed away from the cool ceramic tiles of the wall. It was wonderful. Because of the new shower discovery, I had to change my shower regime.

Showering is like breathing to me. I don't have to think about it. I always start by washing my face, then my hair, then I take the bar of soap in one hand and wash this and that, and at the exact same point I always switch the soap to the other hand and wash that and this. When I'm finished, I towel off in the exact same manner every day. I do this all without thinking. If I do think about what I am doing, I am suddenly lost. Everything becomes awkward and forced, until I find my way back to my normal routine again.

This morning as I washed my hair I was so deep in thought, probably coming up with a solution to some world problem, I found myself washing my hair with the bar of soap. I was so thrown off when I realized what I was doing that I forgot all the problems I had solved. Perhaps I'll recall them later. I rinsed the bar of soap out of my hair, which by the way is much harder to rinse out than shampoo. I found my way back into my normal routine, finished my shower, and towelled off.

I got dressed in my teacher clothes. The teachers at both of my schools dress considerably more casually than Dale's teachers. If it's a volleyball day, many put on their tracksuits before lunch. I often wear jeans and flip-flops to school, as I brought a limited selection of dressier clothes. When we were packing to come here, I asked our recruiter if we'd be expected to wear formal work clothing. He said we wouldn't, so I didn't bring much. Nobody has told us our clothing is inappropriate, and since people haven't been shy to make other comments about our appearance, we think we must be dressing all right.

After I eat my breakfast, I brush my teeth again and put on my makeup, which has regressed back to only a bit of lip gloss.

When I can tolerate the incessant squeaking of the metal rocking horse from the playground no more, I pack my bag. Along with my school supplies I pack fruit, as lunch isn't until 12:30 and I'm always starving by then. Coffee is the only fluid my teachers drink, or that is provided at the school, so I fill up my water bottle. Another quick bathroom break, and I'm out the door.

Today is Monday, so I cross the elementary schoolyard and head down the hill towards Hwagae Middle School. The kids still yell, "Hello!" at me at least seventy times a day. If I don't say anything back, they scream it louder and louder until they get a response from me. One sweet-looking girl hides around the corner of the school, and jumps out and screams, "Hello!" at the top of her lungs as I approach. It scares the bejeepers out of me every time, and I want to strangle her. Then she gives me a cute little smile, so I ignore it for another day, thinking maybe she won't do it tomorrow. But she does. She always does.

TWELVE

I love teaching at the middle school. The students are well behaved – most of the time – and many can understand me enough that I can joke and have fun with them. I'm starting to learn many of their Korean names. All our Hagwon teacher friends gave their students English names to make it easier when teaching. I was asked to use my students' Korean names. At first, I got a lot of giggles at my pronunciation but lately I'm starting to get them right.

In Korea the family name is said first. The second name said would be their first name in Canada, and the last name said would be their Canadian middle name. When I say my students' names, I use the second two names. For example, one of my favourite students is Kim John Gun. His family name is Kim and I call him John Gun. It's actually spelt something like Jeon Kyun but it sounds like John Gun. I more easily remember the names that have an interesting or catchy sound. There's Ji Ho, Jin A, June Bom, Ki Ho, Won Ki, Jay Hok, Chang Su, Rang Gyu, and Sang Il. I remember Sang Il because he is my most challenging student at the school, the only one who acts immature and disrespectful.

Out of the names I listed only one is a female, Jin A. Her name sounds like the English "Gina," so it's easy to remember and she's also my best female student.

The only student I call by her full name is Jo Jang Gin. It's such a fun name to say, especially quickly, and I can't help repeating it. She is very quiet, and conservative in appearance. She doesn't have many friends, so I try to give her attention by having fun with her name in class and telling her, "I love your name!"

She smiles, casts her eyes downward, giggles quietly, and covers her mouth.

*   *   *

The contracts we signed before coming to Korea were for teaching twenty classes a week, and being at school another five hours a week to prepare for classes. We've had to put our foot down many times because our Korean teachers expected us to be at school from 8:30 to five o'clock, as they are, and work every second Saturday. We chose our contract because of the low number of teaching hours and the fact that we wouldn't be teaching on Saturdays. A few meetings with Mr. Chang straightened everyone out, and my Korean colleagues now understand that we are on a special contract, and will work the hours we are scheduled to work – not sit around school doing bicep curls or sleeping when we're not working.

Every week, Dale and I have worked many more hours doing class preparations than the five we are paid for. Dale mostly does it because his daily classes are spread out over the day, and he stays at school between classes. I do it because part of my teaching job is creating a textbook, because, as you'll remember, I am teaching math in English.

Mr. Chang gave me a math textbook when we first got here and said I was to use that to produce an English-Math textbook. I haven't even gotten through the first chapter, Addition, yet.

I quickly realized I would have to start with the basic number system first. My students were great with one through ten, but numbers after that were a bit foggy. If they saw 73 written on a paper, they would understand the value of the number, but they didn't know how to say (or spell) seventy-three. So I started by teaching how to say and spell numbers. I give them information sheets, exercises, tests that don't count towards anything – but which tell me if they're getting it or not – and play games with them. Next, I taught about time: days, months, dates, and how to say quarter after, half past, and so on. I used the same format as my lessons on numbers: information, exercise/review, test, game. It seems to work well for them.

I haven't taught twenty hours per week since I started teaching. My middle school is so disorganized when it comes to schedules that the most I've taught was nineteen, but usually I'm around sixteen.

There are six different classes at the middle school: two grade ones, two grade twos, and two grade threes (grades seven, eight, and nine in Canada). I teach each class twice a week, which totals twelve classes. I teach four classes a week at the elementary school, bringing the total to sixteen.

Recently, I started teaching English Conversation Club three afternoons a week. It's a group of about twenty-five middle school students, from various grades, who want to better their English. Then, once a month during a school assembly, I am to run a "Speech Contest" where three of my club members give an English speech they've written. There is never a winner or loser during the Speech Contest, so it really isn't a contest, but Mr. Kim insists on calling it that.

It's about 9:15 when I arrive at school. The first class starts at this time, so I know I've avoided the morning teachers' meeting. I used to go earlier, thinking I would get something out of the meeting, but nobody bothered to translate anything for me, so I always just sat there catching up on emails. Now I don't bother going.

My first class is at ten, my 3-1 class. Mr. Kim has told me he's teaching with me today. Our contract states that the Korean and foreign teacher are supposed to teach together. Mr. Kim, however, never attends my classes. I don't know what he does while I'm teaching or why he chooses not to come to class, but I do know he would benefit from listening in on my lessons. Mr. Kim teaching English to Koreans is like the equivalent of me teaching French to Canadians. I am far from bilingual. Oddly enough, Mr. Kim's major in university was German. How he landed an English teaching position is still a mystery to me.

Before class, Mr. Kim tells me Mr. Bear will be video-taping us as we do this "team teaching."

I say, "Okay, what are we teaching?"

He says, "English proverbs."

He tells me I will help with pronunciation, and he wants me to come up with a proverb related to work, and a sentence showing the meaning of "get along with."

The proverb I thought of was *The early bird gets the worm*, and my sentence was *My brother and I always fight; we don't get along with each other.*

The "Greensleeves" bell rang at ten, and Mr. Kim and I walked together to the 3-1 classroom. He started in Korean and then introduced me in English. I have been teaching these kids twice a week for a month and a half, and didn't feel I needed an introduction, but perhaps Mr. Kim wanted to show off his English. Then it took him about five minutes to get his PowerPoint presentation set up.

Mr. Bear had arrived in the classroom and was video-taping random things. I could see Mr. Kim was nervous as his hands were shaking, and he was seething twice as much as usual. Finally, his presentation was ready. It was terrible. I think he likely just learned how to create PowerPoint presentations, as he made use of *every* tool possible. There was music, sound effects, things flying across the screen, the whole shebang. It was way too much for these kids to handle.

He started with proverbs. The words "English Proverbs" slid onto the screen from the right side, along with the Korean translation. Each word appeared one at a time, accompanied by zooming sound effects. As the words came to a stop there was a popping sound.

Mr. Kim said, "Repit af meh. OK. Englishy Pravebs."

And all the students did repeat after Mr. Kim, with the same mispronunciations. I wondered if that was my cue to jump in and help. I decided to wait until Mr. Kim handed the floor to me. I didn't want to make him more nervous than he already was.

Then, with the same sound effects, Mr. Kim's proverb appeared on the screen. It read, "He who sows, so shall he reap."

I said it a few times in my head until I got it. *Way to pick an easy proverb, Mr. Kim. These kids aren't going to have a clue what you're talking about,* I thought. But he rushed them through it, repeating after him many times, each time mispronouncing a word or two. The kids repeated like robots, and he praised them for it.

The next exercise was word pronunciation. A few sentences appeared on the screen, and the students had to repeat after him before he chose a few words to concentrate on. One was toothache.

Mr. Kim said, "Repit af me. Toosake."

And all of the kids said, "Toosake."

Finally, after a few sentences, Mr. Kim asked me to pronounce some sentences and words. I made sure to include toothache in my examples. He let me say two sentences and four words, before he took over from me. The kids were looking at me and trying not to laugh, and I was doing the same. They all know Mr. Kim's English is terrible, and they are wondering the same thing – *Why is he teaching English?*

I haven't seen the video yet, but if Mr. Bear recorded me at all it would show the confused disbelief I was experiencing at the time. It would have been more productive had I stayed in the teachers' office.

The class dragged on. Mr. Kim pronounced plenty as *plen*, and said *sin* when he meant to say think, thing, or things. As well, he taught the kids to say, "Why do you so late?" I wanted to scream.

As we neared the end of the forty-five-minute class, a slide entitled "Formative Test" appeared on the screen. What the hell?

The next screen had what appeared to be the innards of a clock. He passed out a paper that also said Formative Test, set the PowerPoint clock to three minutes, and began playing classical music. It was "Flight of the Bumblebee" or something equally spontaneous. The kids giggled during the dramatic portions and tried to stay focused on their Formative Test. The bell rang before Mr. Kim could go over the answers. He had the class clap for me, and he thanked me for my troubles.

Back in the teachers' office, he told me he was nervous because of Mr. Bear videotaping him, and he thanked me once more. I hoped I'd never have to "team teach" again.

Between classes I have a ten-minute break and I usually spend this time jotting down what I did with my last class or checking my emails. Today I couldn't wait to email Dale my latest Mr. Kim story.

* * *

My second class on Monday, 3-2, is probably my favourite class. Many of the best English students in the school seem to be in this group, which allows me to converse more freely. As well, John Gun is in this class. While his English isn't great, he compensates with enthusiasm. Dale and I both noticed John Gun during the first assembly at my school in March. He's very thin, has big ears, and reminds us of Dewey, the youngest brother on *Malcolm in the Middle*. He stands out even more in class because he's so loud. Many of my middle school students are shy, and I can barely hear them when they speak in class. Most of the girls also cover their mouths when they talk, so I can't even attempt to read their lips. John Gun, however, is extremely loud and charismatic. I love having him in class.

There are also two girls in this class who haven't said a word since the first day I taught them. Along with Ji Ho (the boy known for being the best-looking), June Bom, Jin A, and Jay Hok are also in this class.

Today, I did a lesson on Time and taught the kids to say, "Yesterday was … today is … tomorrow will be …" As we neared the end of class, I finished up my Time lesson and opened the floor for a discussion on any English topic. I do this every class because I'm bored with teaching math, and the kids are bored with learning it. Sometimes I have to coax discussion out of them, but not usually with the 3-2 class. Today was no exception.

Jay Hok started the questioning off with some personal questions – how Dale and I had met, and when we got married. I told them about eloping on a beach in the Dominican.

John Gun, with a questioning tone, said, "Nudie beach?"

I said no, but told them it was topless. John Gun seemed disappointed.

They asked what topless was. I thought for a second this might not be an appropriate topic, but then I thought, *At least they're learning English.* So I explained "topless." John Gun's enthusiasm returned.

Soon they exhausted relationship questions, and their attention started waning. Then Jay Hok raised his hand and said, "Mrs. Knowles, what is your blood type?"

Those who understood "blood type" perked up. I thought it an odd question but again, it was in English, so I explained what "blood type" means. If charades were an Olympic event, I'd be a gold medalist. The kids were quite amused by my theatrics of stabbing myself and blood gushing from the wound. They understood, though. I told them my blood type and they all oohed and ahhed. Then I surveyed the class. Everyone looked around with great interest to see who raised their hand to each blood type. Do kids in Canada know their blood type? Would they care what a classmate's blood type was?

The bell rang and I returned to the teachers' office. I don't teach during the next class, so I prepare for my afternoon classes or my elementary school lessons. Sometimes I read world and Canadian news on the internet.

Working on my computer I am reminded why the teachers spent hours on the first day of school changing desks. It was so the more senior teachers could have the better computer systems, while the rookies got the sloppy leftovers. My computer is the worst in our office. I didn't realize this until one day when Mr. Kim let me use his. It was considerably faster than mine. I guess one does need a fast computer when creating such stellar PowerPoint presentations.

Fortunately, Mr. Bear has managed to reinstall the Word program for me so I now have the English version. Dale does not. None of his colleagues have been able to do this for him so everything on his computer is in Korean and he has to rely on memory to figure out which commands and tools are where. I refrain from complaining about my computer woes to Dale.

THIRTEEN

Lunchtime continues to be at 12:30 yet, without fail, every day, one of the teachers *still* comes over to my desk and says, "Time for lunch!" or "Lunchy time." Lately, I've been barely managing a smile back at them, thinking, *Gee thanks. I almost forgot that the bell that rings at 12:30, every day, means it's time to eat lunch! Just like every freakin' day since I've been here!*

The students let the teachers go through the lunch line first. I pick up the metal tray with the five divots, a spoon, and a set of chopsticks. I serve myself rice, and then the students, who are on lunch-serving duty, slop or plop the rest of the meal onto my tray. Ninety percent of the time I hate the soup, or rather the hot liquid mingling with a few pieces of seaweed. I always have a few bites because I'm sure it's good for me. I try to eat all my kimchi but sometimes it's too spicy or it doesn't look appealing.

Some days radish kimchi is on the menu. I *love* radish kimchi. It's sweet and crisp and *mashisoyo* (Korean for delicious). There is always a protein component to lunch. Sometimes it's tofu, sometimes breaded meat, sometimes fish (with all of the bones and eyeballs still intact), and sometimes it's hotdogs. The day they first served us small hotdog pieces

I just stared at my tray in disbelief and waited for someone to call it "the good meat."

"I can't believe we're eating hotdogs!" I thought out loud.

I didn't realize I had said it, until Mrs. Bark tapped my tray with her chopsticks and said, "No hotdogs. Sausages!" She seemed enthusiastic and excited over the fact.

"Nope," I replied, "these are definitely hotdogs."

At least once a week someone will compliment my chopstick abilities. I have to admit, I am getting pretty good. I can pick up a piece of meat, dip it in sauce, then pick up some rice, all in the same chopsticksful. I'm still working on cutting with my chopsticks. My colleagues can hold their chopsticks in one hand and tear apart meat or kimchi. To cut things up, I use my chopsticks like a knife and fork, one in each hand. If one of the teachers is watching me, as they usually are, and they think it's taking me too long to cut something, they'll reach across the table, with their own chopsticks that were just in their own mouth, and tear it up for me. And sometimes if I've finished off my meat and another teacher thinks I need more, they'll pick up some meat off their own tray and plunk it down on mine, and then wait for me to eat it.

This is hard for me to stomach, literally. I'm the kind of girl who, when her friends bought a bucket of ice cream to share for her birthday, was appalled (and more than a little disgusted) when the friends wanted to eat right from the container. I promptly fetched four bowls from the kitchen so we could all have our own equal portions and keep our bodily fluids to ourselves.

Today's lunch was one of my favourites: rice that you put in a separate metal bowl with curried vegetables and meat on top. Mr. Bear instructed me to "Mixy!" the concoction, and then he started eating … with his spoon! I was just getting used to chopsticks being my lifeline to nutrition. Were they just testing me this whole time? Could I use a spoon to eat more than my soup, all the time? Would they mind if I brought a steak knife to use as well?

Korea is incredibly rich with culture and traditions, and the people are so proud to share them with us. I've never been anywhere that was so different, where most aspects of one's life have a specific traditional method. From bowing when meeting someone, to handing someone money using two hands. From a beautifully choreographed way of making and serving green tea, to never pouring one's own glass of *soju*. Even when pouring someone else a glass of *soju*, if they are older than you, you must put one hand to your heart to show them respect.

I try really hard to follow all of the customs we've been taught, but sometimes I wonder if some of these customs are as rigidly followed as we've been made to believe. Dale had read that it is very impolite to make any gestures towards your nose at the dinner table. For me, the problem with this is Korean food is very spicy, and my nose gets running when I eat spicy food. I can't imagine snorting and sniffing is a desirable alternative, so I spent a lot of time going to the bathroom to relieve my nose during meals when we first arrived here.

Then recently I noticed a roll of toilet paper on the table in the cafeteria. I eyed Mr. Bear breaking off a long piece of toilet paper and dabbing at his nose. I expected people to fall off their chairs at this insolence. Was it because he was older than all of us and so can do no wrong? Was it the way he did it? Maybe blowing one's nose is rude, but dabbing is okay? Did yellow dust season have something to do with it, and maybe that was what the man in the truck was shouting over the loudspeaker that morning: "Yellow dust season! Nose touching is acceptable table etiquette from today, until you hear me yelling that it isn't!"

At lunch today, I chatted a little with Mrs. Bark and as I was finishing up my rice Mr. Chang asked me, "How is your husband Adam?"

"What?" I replied.

"Your husband, Adam. Working hard in the fields."

What the hell!

"Are you talking about my husband Dale, Mr. Chang?"

"Yes. Adam is the symbol for man," Mr. Chang enlightened me.

"Dale is at school in Hadong, of course," I replied, not amused by whatever this conversation was.

Mr. Chang nodded. "Men work very hard."

I can't let the sexism go. "Yes, and so do women." I got up and was gathering my tray and cutlery.

"No. Women stay home and take care of the house," he told me.

Again I thought, *what the hell!*

"Not in Canada!" I shot back, and left.

Mr. Chang's "humour" has been wearing on me lately. Most of the English he learned was years ago, during his work alongside the U.S. military. Perhaps he doesn't realize that the racist and sexist jokes he heard are not appropriate, especially in non-military company – or any company, in fact.

I dumped the leftovers from my tray into the big, disgusting bin of uneaten food. We've recently heard that food waste is composted. Whether it's true or not, I don't know, but after seeing the hundreds of partially empty side plates in restaurants, I really hope it is.

Mr. Chang's comments were fresh in my head, as I walked across the schoolyard and mounted the hill to our house. I continue to make this trek at noon every day. It's a tough decision, though; either I stay at school and squat or I walk the gauntlet of screaming kids in the elementary schoolyard to use the toilet in our house. I almost always choose the latter and suffer the consequence of another fifty "Hellos!"

Today was as typical as any. I heard about thirty Hellos! and twenty *Annyeong haseyos!* Some of the kids swarmed around me as I walked, some grabbed my arm, and some ran away in fits of hysterical laughter when I said, "Hello" back to them. That sweet little devil of a girl jumped out to welcome me with an ear-piercing, "HELLO!" and a couple of kids banged on our door after I had safely locked myself inside. They bang on the door the whole time I'm in the house.

I had put a load of laundry in the washing machine this morning, and it was ready to be hung out. I loaded it in the basket and went outside, shooing the kids off our lawn. As I hang the clothes, they're still yelling at me from the playground below. A couple of little ones are riding the metal horse contraption. The horrific squeaking echoes through the valley. By the time I have the clothes hung, I'm bordering on insanity. Back into the house for another bit of reprieve: *Why don't I just squat?!*

I brush my teeth, take a few deep breaths, and I venture back across the schoolyard again. The exact same kids scream, "Hello!" but nobody grabs me or swarms around me. Thankfully, they've become preoccupied with skipping or Hula-Hooping.

I haven't given up on squatting completely. Sometimes it's unavoidable, and it's really not so bad if you get it right. Getting it right, for me, involves squatting as low as I possibly can (so there's less chance for error), getting my pants out of the way as much as possible, not squatting on a day when my legs are tired or sore, and always bringing toilet paper. I still haven't found toilet paper in any squatters. I guess everyone knows to always bring it with them, but it's something that slips my mind on occasion and, as a result, I have had to "drip dry" a few times. Just like peeing in the woods, I guess. You don't flush your toilet paper in Hwagae and many rural areas. Instead, it is put into a little garbage can in the bathroom stall. The can never has a lid but is always filled with used toilet paper. Because of this, most of the bathrooms smell like outhouses.

Luckily, I haven't had to use a squatter for a number two yet. Dale has – teaching in Hadong, he doesn't have the option of running home at lunch. He says it makes you go a lot quicker, when your legs are shaking, muscles nearing failure, as you hover in a deep squat. I don't think I've ever squatted like that in my life, so my inflexible body does not do it well. People here use it almost as a resting position. We see people squatting while working in the fields, while waiting for the bus, while selling things at the market; even elderly people seem to have no trouble squatting. When I would kneel or sit cross-legged, people here will squat.

Dale says many of the teachers take toilet paper, a newspaper, and a pack of cigarettes with them to the bathroom. As they squat, they read and smoke. Quite impressive really.

Last Friday I had to pee so badly I couldn't wait for the lunch break. I went to the bathroom, walked to the far end, and opened the last stall, one I hadn't been in before. I couldn't believe my eyes. There sat a perfect North American toilet! What caused me even more disbelief was that stacked upon the toilet and filling the stall around it were buckets and mops and piles of bathroom cleaning supplies. It was completely inaccessible. The one sit-down toilet was being used as a broom closet. Who was in charge of this atrocity?

Dejectedly, I opened door two, knowing what I would find. I assumed the position above the squatter. To my right I noticed a small box attached to the wall at about eye level – eye level while squatting, that is. There was a button in the middle, which said *Etiquette Bell*. It looked kind of like an intercom you'd find in a house, and I desperately wanted to press the button. What wonderful events would pressing the etiquette bell trigger?

Just then, I heard someone else enter the washroom and open stall number one. Before they would have had time to even get their belt undone, I started to hear toilet flushing sounds, and other sounds I couldn't identify. There was something funny about what I was hearing – there was an echo to it, and it sounded more like the gushing sound of a North American toilet flushing than the soft whooshing sound the squatters make when they empty. Then it dawned on me. The etiquette bell, when activated, fills the bathroom with bathroom noises, so nobody can hear you tinkle or toot. *Brilliant!* I thought as I heartily pressed my etiquette bell.

Dale hasn't found an etiquette bell in the squatters at his schools. He hasn't found toilet paper either, and he sometimes has trouble finding soap.

When I told him about the etiquette bell on Friday, he told me he'd used this strange soap to wash his hands with that day. In his defence, the item was sitting in the soap dish and it did have a familiar smell. As well, living with me Dale has used many strange-looking and -smelling soaps. He's never quite sure what is soap and what isn't. He once tried to wash his hands with rocks at a friend's house, as he thought the rocks were a decorative soap. The soap he used on Friday didn't smell quite like normal hand soap, but it did smell lemony fresh. It didn't create much of a lather in his hands, but Dale ignored that fact, and used it three times throughout the day to wash his hands. Towards the end of the day, he used the urinal and noticed the soap he'd been using all day was sitting in the bottom of the urinal. It took him a second to realize. Then he quickly found a bottle of liquid soap or detergent – he didn't know (nor did he care) which it was – and scrubbed any remnants of urinal cake from his hands. I never imagined that one of the main dramas of our year in Korea would be our trips to the bathroom.

* * *

I only have one class on Monday afternoon, grade one (grade seven in Canada). Despite being at the lowest English level in the school, they try the hardest, and stay focused throughout the class. When it is quiz time, I give every grade the same quiz, as I've been teaching them the same materials. My grade ones score just as well as the other grades. Technically, their English is as advanced as their older schoolmates, but they aren't as good at applying it verbally yet.

Mrs. Kang, the other Korean English teacher, came to my class today. I've learned that she is quite proficient in English. She also seems to be one of the hipper teachers, and we can have normal conversations, unlike the awkward ones Mr. Kim and I have.

Mrs. Ryui is a math teacher and since I'm teaching math in English, she attends some of my classes as well. She's not as good as Mrs. Kang at expressing herself in English, but she understands a lot of what I say and can translate things for the class.

I prefer teaching with Mrs. Ryui, as she only steps in when I ask her to. Mrs. Kang tends to take over at times. Today I was playing a number game with my class. The entire class stands up, and one by one I get them to either spell or say a number. If a student gets an answer wrong, they sit down. Last one standing gets a prize – a candy.

While I always encourage the students, and give them the opportunity to think and respond, Mrs. Kang seemed eager for them to fail. I don't think she was being mean on purpose; I don't know if she realizes how shy the kids are, and how hard it is for some of them to stand up and attempt an answer in front of their classmates. If a student hesitated when answering, Mrs. Kang raised her hand in the air, fingers extended, and lowered one finger at a time counting down. Then, if the student didn't answer, Mrs. Kang placed her arms across her chest in an X shape and made a buzzer noise. "*AAAAAANN!* Sit down!" She smiled and giggled each time she got to be the buzzer.

She often laughs at the kids when they mispronounce words as well. I was reviewing the continents with one class. They knew each of the land masses, which I was impressed with, but their pronunciation was off. I looked over at Mrs. Kang and saw she was going through fits of laughter at every mispronounced word. The kids were noticing her too and were getting quieter and quieter. Without thinking what I was doing, I gave her a dirty look and shook my head slightly. She seemed to get more serious. It is not surprising that when the kids attempt to speak English, they often cover their mouths and lower their heads.

When the class finished, and the number game was over, I awarded two lucky winners with a candy which they received graciously. They bowed, held one hand out with their palm facing up, and held that hand's wrist with the other hand. That is the Korean way of accepting a gift.

Dale is pretty good with Korean customs, while I am better with the language. Together, we make a fairly polite foreigner in Korea.

Bowing, like many customs, varies based on age. If somebody is older than me, even by a year, I am required to show them more respect, and bow lower to them than they do to me.

Mr. Chang uses age to his advantage all the time. As he's in his sixties, he's older than all the staff of my two schools, as well as the staff in Dale's schools. Dale's two principals and vice principals speak very little English, so when Dale had concerns about our contract, he went to Mr. Chang to translate. Instead of just translating what Dale said, Mr. Chang enforced his superpower of age.

"I told her" – the principal is a man but Mr. Chang often mixes up the pronouns – "just follow the contract. I am older than she so she listen to me," Mr. Chang said proudly, like his age was a special skill he possessed.

"So Mr. Chin understands that I can leave during my free time?" Dale asked, unsure if Mr. Chang had actually explained this to Mr. Chin or just berated the poor man for not being as old as Mr. Chang.

"Yes, I told her ..."

"Him," I interrupted.

"Yeah, yeah. I told him. Just follow contract. He will because I am older than him."

Since then, Dale has chosen not to ask Mr. Chang for help with discussions with his own vice principal. Instead, he wrote a very polite, professional letter explaining our views on some aspects of our contract, and had Ms. Ko translate it for him. Ms. Ko is not a good translator for him in a verbal debate or discussion with his VP, because she is too shy and afraid to be involved in anything that smells of conflict. However, the letter she translated for Dale seemed to go over very well with Mr. Chin and there have been no further contract problems.

*   *   *

I left my third and final class for the day and returned to the teachers' office to pack up, remembering to take my elementary school files, as I wouldn't be coming to the middle school at all the next day.

I opened the door of the teachers' office, gave a quick bow-ish head nod, said, "See you Wednesday. *Annyeonghi gyeseyo*," a goodbye with the beautiful meaning "peacefully exist," and made my way downstairs. I pulled my outdoor shoes out of my cubbyhole by the front door, number 17, put them on, placed my indoor shoes into the cubbyhole, and I was out the door.

I have to walk past Mr. Chang's office when I leave the school. Often he's hanging out the window smoking, and more often than not he feels the need to say something to me. One day I was heading home to use the washroom at lunch. Between puffs on his cigarette he said, "Where are you going?"

"To my house."

"Why don't you take a boy?" was Mr. Chang's response, his usual sly grin evident on his face.

I stopped, confused. "Umm. No, that's okay."

He nodded and took another puff. I turned and walked away.

Luckily, today Mr. Chang was nowhere to be found as I left school. I didn't have to listen to any more of his random, creepy, sexist banter. I did, however, have to deal with the kids in the elementary schoolyard one more time. They seem more subdued in the afternoon. Perhaps they are too tired from screaming at me in the morning and at lunch. They settle for one, pleasantly normal, "Hello" as they run past me and down the hill to catch their ride home.

Dale doesn't get to the bus station in Hwagae until five on Mondays, so I have some time to kill before I walk to meet him. I clean up the house, send some emails, and log more of our Korean adventures. Then I make a pot of rice. Rice has become a staple part of our diet in Korea. It isn't because it's inexpensive and convenient, or that we want to immerse ourselves even further into the Korean culture. It is because we just like rice a lot. Dale and I don't ever seem to get tired of it. We add our own twists, and fry it up with vegetables and spicy Korean sauces. Each time it tastes a little different than the last but each time it turns out delicious. Years later our Korean rice mixture would still be a favourite dish in our household.

FOURTEEN

At about 4:30 p.m., I leave home to walk to town. Every day, some of my middle school students are at various intervals along the road stretching to Hwagae's town centre. They always ask me where I'm going, and every day I tell them, "To get Dale."

Most of the kids are heading to the Hagwon, and some are going to catch their bus home. It is their time to be kids. They stroll, they joke, they fight, they cause very little mischief. They are really good kids. They begin their walk with a stop at the "old lady's store." That's what Dale and I call it. The woman who runs the store looks about a hundred and five years old. Her store, which is the front room of her tiny house, is situated directly between the middle school and the elementary school.

The middle school was built in the valley while the elementary school is above it, partway up the mountain. The old lady's store is built into the side of the mountain between. So to get from one school to the other, I (and anyone else headed that way) walk up the narrow cement steps that abut the side of her house. I always feel a little awkward "cutting through" so close to her, through her tiny little yard and walk-through that is cluttered with various pots and bowls and plastic chairs. Each day, the "old lady" sells incredible amounts of chips, chocolate bars, ice cream sandwiches, and candy to the kids from the two schools. The kids emerge from her store with handfuls of junk food.

Dale and I buy *soju* and Joe Louis-like cakes from her. The first time we went to her store to buy water, she seemed to not want to sell it to us. We had disturbed her, I guess. She was lying in a room at the back of the store, watching a Korean soap opera. The room was up half a level, putting the floor at waist height, and it was partially obstructed by a sliding door. When we came in, she very slowly crawled over pillows to the sliding door, not turning the TV off or lowering the volume. We grabbed the biggest jug of water she had, and she shook her head and spoke sternly to us in Korean. We awkwardly looked at each other, bowed a bit lower, smiled, and Dale held out the money using two hands as is customary. She shook her head again and seemed annoyed, and her tone and flailing arms suggested she was chastising us for something. Dale stepped forward, and she reluctantly took his money, crawled over to a little tin to retrieve his change, and we left.

We felt a bit bad about this interaction. She really did not seem to like us or want to have us in her store. But when we got home, we realized what she was trying to tell us. We opened the bottle of water and the smell of *soju* wafted out at us. What were we going to do with this giant jug of *soju*? Why would anyone buy this much *soju*? How did she know we were trying to buy water? Perhaps she is Mr. Chang's supplier of *soju* and this was meant for him? We had a lot of questions.

It took a while for the "old lady" to warm up to us. She would serve us, but there were no smiles. We didn't shop there often because she sold mainly junk food and, as we came to find out, she didn't even carry water. But at some point, she seemed to come around to us. It might have been the kids telling her we were okay, or it might have been when Dale brought her a flower from a bouquet we'd been given. Ever since then she gives us a big smile when we shop in her store or cut through her yard.

*   *   *

Sometimes, I reach the bus stop early, so I wander across one of the downtown bridges to the market and buy some snacks. Everything we buy at the market is cheaper now than it was when we' first arrived. We speak some Korean to the vendors, tell them how *mashisoyo* their wares are, and the prices drop. Our favourite snack is green chip-like things. They are shaped like elbows, are very crunchy, are coloured green with green tea, and come out of a big metal machine in the market. They taste nothing like green tea, however; they have a kind of plain taste but have a crunch we both enjoy.

Sometimes I run to meet Dale. If I don't have much time, I run the most direct route. One day I ran past about ten of my middle school boys, and they decided to run with me. There I was in my tights and turtleneck, running the streets of Hwagae in a pack of boys all wearing their school uniforms and carrying backpacks. I wished Dale had been early that day and could have seen us barrelling along.

Other days, when I have more time, I cross the bridge near our house and run to town along the other side of the valley. I was running this route one day shortly after I'd given the maple syrup gifts. It was also the day the middle school had basketball nets installed in the gym.

I had gone to Mr. Kim (the gym teacher) earlier in the day and handed him a piece of paper with five o'clock written on it. I mimed shooting and dribbling a basketball and pointed to myself – "Me. Dale. Play basketball. Five o'clock." – and I pointed back at the time. He nodded. I wanted to make sure the gym would be open, so Dale and I could play. Mr. Kim the gym teacher is possibly the youngest teacher at my school. I would guess that he's around my age, maybe a couple of years older. He can't speak a word of English, but he is movie-star gorgeous. Even Dale admits Mr. Kim is the best-looking male we've met here. He could be a model. I like him because he breaks a lot of male Korean customs. Anytime food is served, all the male teachers sit and wait while the female teachers pour drinks, peel fruit, pass out plates, and cut things up. Mr. Kim the gym teacher always helps out. As well, when we sit down to a meal, he always sits with the female teachers. I don't blame him. The female teachers are fun and a lot more liberal.

I had emailed Dale to say we could play basketball as soon as he got home, and we were both excited to get on the court. I ran through town towards the bus stop and heard, "Bess-uh! Bess-uh!" coming from across the street. *Bess-uh* is what almost all the Koreans I know call me. There is no *th* sound in the Korean language, so Beth is difficult to say. And the extra *uh* at the end is kind of like when a *y* sound is added to lunch … Bess-uh … lunchy. I've learned to respond to "Bess-uh."

I looked over and saw Mr. Chang hanging out the window of a restaurant. The window hadn't been open when I was coming up the street, and the windowpane was completely opaque, so I have no idea how he knew I was running by.

"Hi, Mr. Chang," I said, jogging on the spot. He waved me to cross the street and join him. "I'm just going to get Dale, and we're playing basketball."

I had told him this at school, earlier in the day.

He nodded, "Mr. Bear wants to buy you the good meat."

"Oh, that's very nice of him."

Mr. Chang nodded. I figured Mr. Bear felt he needed to buy us a gift, after we gave him the bottle of maple syrup.

"I called your house," Mr. Chang said.

"I was running," I said, pointing out the obvious, "to meet Dale."

Mr. Chang nodded again. "You must wait here. Mr. Bear will buy you the meat."

My understanding was that Mr. Bear wanted to take us to the grocery store and buy us some meat to put in our freezer.

"Where is Mr. Bear now?" I asked.

"He went to find you. I said to him, 'Maybe they play the basketball?'"

I had told him that Dale and I would play basketball when Dale returned to Hwagae at five. As it was still only 4:55, I wasn't sure why he'd told Mr. Bear we'd be at the school. I looked down the street and saw Dale's bus pulling in.

"There he is," I told Mr. Chang. "I'll go get him."

I ran across the street and met Dale as he stepped off the bus. I quickly explained that Mr. Bear wanted to buy us some meat, and Mr. Chang wanted us to wait for Mr. Bear at a restaurant across the street. Dale always takes things in stride. I didn't want to wait around and was eager to get on the basketball court.

"That's nice of Mr. Bear," Dale said. "We'll let him buy us some meat, hurry straight home to put it in the fridge, and then run down to the gym for ball."

We crossed the street and joined Mr. Chang at the window he was still hanging out of. He and Dale exchanged pleasantries.

"I call Mr. Bear and he is coming this way now. Please, please come inside. Wait here."

"No, thank you, Mr. Chang. I was just running, and I'm too sweaty to come into the restaurant," I tried.

"But you must. Please. Come inside," he insisted.

Reluctantly, we obliged. We each grabbed a square mat and sat on the floor across the table from Mr. Chang. He seemed pleased. I looked around as Dale and I chatted about our day. The restaurant had eight foot-high tables arranged in four rows of two. At one end of the room was a window, the same one Mr. Chang hailed me from. The other end was a mirrored wall, which made the small room appear much larger than it was. Each table had a grill set into the tabletop, for cooking meat yourself. The only things hanging from the white walls were menus and price lists, containing about ten items, and a large twelve-month calendar poster. The calendar caught our attention, as the background picture was a few naked women facing away from the camera, their bodies painted in beautiful colours and patterns.

We had met the restaurant owners as we entered: a man and woman in their thirties, both dressed in athletic shirts made of those highly advertised materials that claim to "wick away the moisture." Dale thinks he learned a thing or two about fabrics from his salesman days in the sportswear industry, and he always tells me there is no fabric that can "wick away sweat." The shirts appear to be working for the restaurant owners, though, as I watch them buzz around arranging plates on trays, seemingly cool and comfortable.

Minutes later, Mr. Bear and Ms. Kim, the young teacher from my middle school, came through the sliding glass doors of the restaurant. We all said hello, and bowed, and before Dale and I could stand up the female owner was coming towards our table with a huge plate of raw meat. We had misunderstood. Dale and I spoke to each other quickly and quietly to ensure Mr. Chang wouldn't overhear us.

We both had understood from Mr. Chang saying, "Mr. Bear wants to buy you the good meat" that Mr. Bear would buy us meat from a grocery store. We didn't realize he wanted to take us out for dinner. But now we knew why Mr. Chang was at the restaurant and wanted us to come in to sit down. It still confused me, though. Mr. Chang had known all day that we were going to play basketball after school. He hadn't mentioned anything about dinner plans to me. Why wouldn't he have said something to me? Or why not plan it for the next day, so he wouldn't have Mr. Bear driving around looking for us, and he wouldn't be pulling us off the street and bus? What really got me is that Mr. Chang had already ordered a meal for five people. He was sure living up to the name "King," which he'd jokingly (but not so jokingly) called himself on an earlier day. Dale and I wanted no part in being his "prince and princess." I felt uncomfortable.

"I don't want to stay," Dale said quietly to me. He was feeling the same way I was.

"I know, me neither," I replied. "It's very nice, but we had plans. I'm all sweaty too."

"We can't be forced into eating with them. They have to understand that we have a life, and things to do of our own. I want to play basketball right now."

"Me too."

"Well, let's tell them thank you but we already had plans," Dale suggested.

"Okay."

"This is very nice of Mr. Bear," Dale started, "but we had plans to play basketball."

"You can play the basketball after we eat the food," Mr. Chang said, very sure of himself.

"Thank you, but we can't play after eating, Mr. Chang," I said. "Also, the badminton club is playing in the gym later. We won't have time to play if we eat now."

"There is room. I tell them to make room for you."

I didn't want Mr. Chang bossing around and pissing off the badminton club so Dale and I could play basketball later in the evening.

"Just taste!" Mr. Chang demanded, with one of his famous lines. A line I'd heard so many times while dining with him at restaurants and at school. A line he uses when he wants me to eat or drink something I've already told him "no" to.

Dale was getting up, and I followed his lead.

"Again, thank you, Mr. Chang," he said, "but we were on our way to the gym. Can you please tell Mr. Bear it was very kind of him to invite us, but we already had plans."

We smiled. We bowed, and we shuffled out of the restaurant, leaving Mr. Chang, Mr. Bear, and Ms. Kim lining one side of a table full of food. We both felt bad about turning Mr. Bear's gesture down, but we felt we needed to prove a point. We were tired of getting roped into things we didn't want to do, or hadn't planned on doing.

FIFTEEN

On Wednesday of the previous week Mr. Kim the English teacher told me early in the day the teachers would be going to the Apricot Festival in the afternoon. He asked if Dale would like to join us. I asked what time we'd be leaving and where the festival was. Mr. Kim thought it was near Hadong, and we'd be going around three in the afternoon. I emailed Dale, and he thought he would like to come. By early afternoon, our departure time had been moved back to four p.m. – so the teachers would have time to play volleyball. I was stupid not to expect this delay, as many of them had been wearing their tracksuits all day, in anticipation for the game.

Mr. Lee approached me shortly after lunch to ask if I could play volleyball that day. I told him no. He asked why. I explained the same thing I had to Mr. Chang a few weeks earlier. He wouldn't drop it. Finally, I said, "But Dale and I are both coming to the Apricot Festival with the teachers. We'll meet you here at four o'clock." Mr. Lee was not satisfied with my response, I'm sure, but I was tired of repeating myself. Tired of explaining that being one of the pylons for the two hitters to smoke the ball at was not my idea of fun. And that while he might be "King" to all the other teachers, Mr. Chang is not *my* King. I left to go home and relax with Dale.

Back at the house, we discussed what an apricot festival might involve: parades, people dressed up like dancing apricots, samples of delicious apricot products. Of course we hoped for the latter, and we also hoped we wouldn't have to spend too much time at the festival.

We walked to the school at four p.m., and the teachers were emerging from the gym in their tracksuits and "work gloves" that many wear to play volleyball. I was happy to see that Mr. Kim the English teacher had worn sneakers, sporty pants, and an athletic shirt. Until that day, he'd played in his suit and dress shoes.

Mrs. Bark drove us in her car. The interior of her car reflected her personality – pink seat cushions, pink steering wheel cover, fluffy pink covers on the gear shift and emergency brake. Even a pink frilly thing outlining her rearview mirror. We arrived at the festival to find cars and people all over the road, trying to park and maneuver between parked cars. There were vendors selling various meats on a stick, vendors selling barbecued corn, and vendors blaring horrible dance music. Mrs. Bark found a place to park, and we waited for the rest of our group. A phone call came to her on her cell phone, and she motioned that we were to cross the street and start up a very steep mountainside.

A Korean man and his wife approached us as we crossed the street.

"Hello, where are you from?" he asked jovially.

"We're from Canada," Dale replied. "Where are you from?"

Dale always liked to ask that back; it never failed to confuse people.

"I am from Korea," the man said, surprised by the question. He gave us each a candy. The one he handed me, he'd already unwrapped and was holding in his bare hand.

"It's nice to meet you," we told the couple as we put the candies in our mouths, not wanting to be impolite.

We followed Mrs. Bark up the hillside and found garbage cans to spit the ginseng candies into. We have not acquired a taste for ginseng products yet. Cars and people went up and down the hillside as we climbed. Mrs. Bark was wearing high-heeled shoes, but she was always puffing just beside me.

We met many couples "coupling" as we climbed the hill. "Coupling" is when couples wear the exact same clothing: the same jeans with Mickey Mouse cartoons below the front pocket; the same pink shirt that says Get the Job; and the same white ball hat. We see couples "coupling" everywhere we go. Dale read that "coupling" has even extended into the world of plastic surgery. Couples are going under the knife together so they can acquire the same nose, the same chin lift, perhaps even the same Hollywood starlet collagen lip injections.

Eventually, halfway up the hillside, we met up with the rest of the teachers who had all driven their cars up, perhaps passing us as they scaled the hill. Dale, Mrs. Bark, and I were all in a lather by the time we reached our colleagues. Once there, we still had to wait for Mr. Chang and Mr. Bear. I wondered what was taking them so long.

Finally, I saw Mr. Bear's truck approaching with a freshly showered and primped Mr. Chang, dressed in his best suit, in the passenger seat. He'd made everyone else wait while he went home to shower after the volleyball game. His dyed black hair was combed just perfectly, and his eyes had a hint of red, indicating he had a sip of *soju* or two at some point. Anytime Mr. Chang has even a sip of alcohol, the whites of his eyes turn red. He looks evil when he's like this. However, as he insisted that first morning we spent time with him back in February, as he offered us a glass of wine at nine a.m., he is "not a drunkard." Dale had said sometime later that day that a person who claims to *not be a drunkard*, especially if they proclaim this within hours of meeting you, probably *is* a drunkard.

The Apricot Festival involved us eating apricot-flavoured ice cream (my favourite part, of course) and walking through paths along a hillside of blossoming apricot trees. We also had our picture taken at least a hundred times. None of the teachers took any photos of the beautiful scenery, which was what I was so taken with. Instead, they had various groups of teachers pose and give the peace sign, over and over again. I probably made them feel bad by not taking very many pictures of them. I focused my lens on the orchards of blossoming apricot trees and fields of kimchi pots.

Any time Dale and I slowed down to look at or enjoy something, we were hurried on to another spot where we had to wait for other people.

I was taking a picture of a thick bamboo forest when Dale, Mr. Kim, Mr. Kim the gym teacher, and I smelled something bad. Dale, the comedian that he is, said, "Oops, I'm sorry!" Mr. Kim the gym teacher didn't understand a word of Dale's fart joke. My Mr. Kim, however, got the joke and, to my surprise, chuckled away with Dale and me. Nothing like a good fart joke to bring nations together.

Eventually, we all congregated in a parking lot, and Dale and I were told we were going out for supper as a group. I'm sure both of our faces fell. We couldn't say no, because we'd have to get someone to drive us home, and then that person would miss dinner. So we went along. The restaurant was located on a wide, beautiful river, and we arrived as the sun was lowering over the mountains. The scene was beautiful. It reminded us of the water we've driven along so many times on our way to Martinique Beach, a favourite spot of ours back in Nova Scotia.

It was a raw fish restaurant. Dale and I are both adventurous when it comes to food, but neither of us enjoy raw fish. I wasn't actually very hungry, so I ate the rice as well as some items from the many side dishes. Mr. Chang must have noticed this, as he kept insisting that I eat some of the raw fish.

"Just taste!" he said.

"No, thank you. I'm fine," I replied.

"But you must. Just taste. It's very good for the health. Full of protein."

So is cooked fish, I thought.

I didn't try any of the raw fish. Soon, however, there was a special order of cooked squid served in front of me on the table. I usually love squid, and despite not being hungry, I thought I had better eat some to please Mr. Chang. Dale picked up one of the squid, which still had the head intact. He squeezed the head, and a substance oozed out of it – *brains?* I paused midair with my chopsticks. I could not eat that. I picked up one of the squid arms and slowly munched on it, not able to get the vision of oozing brains out of my head. Mrs. Bark had gone home and picked up her two little boys and brought them to dinner. I was very thankful for their company, as the youngest one loved the squid heads and oozing brains. He gobbled most of it up, while I turned to my bowl of soup. I stirred it a bit, and what looked like a large rotting fish head floated to the top.

I thought then of the sketch on *Sesame Street,* when a Muppet goes to the restaurant and orders soup, and then discovers a fly in his soup. I wanted to alert the server. I wanted to frantically wave my arms, jump back in disgust, and tell her, "There's a rotting fish head in my soup!" But I looked down the line of teachers slurping, munching, and chomping, thoroughly enjoying their fish heads, raw fish constituents, and whatever else was within a chopstick's reach of them on the table, and I quietly ate some more rice.

I could see from Mr. Chang's eyes that he was drinking his fair share of *soju.* He made his first inappropriate sexual joke to Dale at supper that night. I wasn't paying attention and didn't hear the joke. Dale didn't appreciate it, and didn't want Mr. Chang to think they were old pals who share distasteful jokes and keep them from me. Dale turned to me and whispered, "Don't ask why but just shake your head and pretend I just told you something awful." I did as suggested.

Mr. Chang continued being candid. At one point he said, "TV is my partner."

Dale tried to delve further into the relationship of Mr. Chang and the lovely, elegant woman he'd introduced as his wife in church that February morning.

"*My* partner is my wife, Mr. Chang," Dale said.

Mr. Chang looked sideways at us with his red eyes and said, "I'm Mr. Lonely."

Dale left it at that.

Finally, dinner finished, and we shuffled out to the parking lot to decide who was driving with whom. We were relieved; we'd still be home by eight o'clock and have some time free of our work life.

Then Mr. Chang announced we were going to a Nori Bang. Our faces and hearts dropped this time. I knew this day would come. I'd heard how popular Nori Bangs are in Korea, and I knew we'd be dragged, possibly kicking and screaming, to one eventually. In Korean, *bang* means room and *nori bang* means singing room. Basically, a Nori Bang is a bar with a number of rooms you can rent for a specified amount of time. In each room is a karaoke machine, lots of flashing lights, and a massive sound system. Reluctantly, Dale and I joined Mr. Chang in the school's van, chauffeured by the school maintenance man who was not drinking alcohol. We drove to the Nori Bang, which was in Hadong, and everyone regrouped in one of the singing rooms. Bottles of beer were served, as well as trays of crunchy snacks and fresh fruit. Fruit is often served in bars in Korea, and while I love fruit, I find it odd to eat healthy food while drinking beer.

Soon after we arrived, we realized Mr. Bear had not joined the group. *Smart man*, we thought. If we had known Mr. Bear wasn't going to the Nori Bang, we would have asked for a drive home.

Our experience at the Nori Bang was as horrible as I had anticipated. Dale and I decided beforehand, though, that if we were going to have to suffer through multiple Korean ballads, my fellow teachers were also going to have to suffer through horrific Canadian karaoke. The singing performances started immediately, with Mr. Chang doing his favourite English song, "I'm Sailing," by Rod Stewart. Dale and I found a spot on the room's couch, drank beer to help make the night more enjoyable, and leafed through the songbook trying to find a number for us. I noticed the other female teachers barely touched any alcohol, while the male teachers downed it heartily. In Korea it is less acceptable for women to display signs of drunkenness in public. Men, on the other hand, can get as rowdy and idiotic as they want. It is also taboo for a Korean woman to smoke in public. Often, when I use public washrooms, there are women sneaking a smoke in the stalls.

The singing went on for two hours. It was incredibly loud, lights were flashing the entire time, and there was a big-screen TV that displayed the words to the songs as well as people dancing to music different than what we were hearing. Dale and I did three songs together. I was losing my voice from a cold that week, so my singing was even more horrible than normal, but I belted out the tunes anyway. The teachers shuffled and danced around the singers. Sometimes, Mr. Cheoi, the social studies teacher, would grab onto one of the female teachers and dance with her. We both found him to be a bit inappropriate, and definitely drunk. The female teachers awkwardly smiled, and went along with whatever the male teachers asked of them.

Our first song was "I'm Sorry Miss Jackson," by Outkast. We'd both forgotten the lengthy rap component of the song. I left that part to Dale, while I just sang the chorus over and over. The karaoke words on the screen were never on the screen when we were supposed to be singing them, and the music was sped up. Our performance was both atrocious and unpleasant – but we felt the need for more. Our next choice was "Brown Eyed Girl," by Van Morrison, a song we couldn't get wrong. We did, however, as again the music was faster than expected. Nonetheless, the teachers clapped along and danced around us. They were so enthusiastic towards us that I even wondered if perhaps we were good. We finished off our performance with "Cotton Fields," by CCR, and once again we kept screwing up the timing.

Soon after, we were in a cab with a very drunk Mr. Chang and young Ms. Kim. Mr. Chang kept saying that the song "Cotton Fields" reminded him of "old Black joke." He desperately wanted to share this "joke" with us, but we insisted that racist jokes are not appropriate. He was disappointed.

The next morning, some of the teachers asked me, "Aren't you hungover?"

Their tone, whether intended or not, was accusing.

I told them, "No, of course not. Are you?"

I really wasn't, but even if I was, I wasn't going to let them think I was.

Other teachers accused, "Aren't you tired?"

Again I said, "No, of course not."

I wondered if I should mention how tone and intonation can affect meaning, but I didn't.

SIXTEEN

We've had many outings with teachers from our schools recently. The first was a couple of weeks ago, when Dale's Mr. Kim invited us to his house for supper. We were both quite excited to be going to a Korean house besides Mr. Chang's and have a home-cooked Korean meal.

I met Dale in Hadong the day of our dinner engagement, and we walked with Mr. Kim to the Hagwon where his wife is a teacher. We were served green tea, and once she was ready, we left for a scenic drive to Namhae Island, about forty-five minutes away. Unfortunately, the day was rainy, so we didn't get out of the car during the trip. But my heart warmed when we reached the coast. I didn't realize until I saw the open sea how much I missed the Atlantic Ocean at home.

Our house in Nova Scotia is only a few minutes' drive to open ocean and beautiful beaches. Typically, I see the beach or walk on it at least three times a week, even during the winter. Glimpsing the blue waters leading to the Korea Strait made me miss our summers back home: running on the beach with Keno, Dale trying to get me over my fear of bigger waves and surfing. I think Dale felt homesick when he saw the coast as well.

Mr. Kim pointed out a few tourist attractions along our drive, and we chatted with them about differences between Canada and Korea. We arrived back at their home in Hadong before darkness fell, so we had a few minutes to enjoy their lovely view from the wide-paned windows in their apartment. Mrs. Kim served us a rice mixture, with a side of kimchi and *pajeon*. Dale and I love *pajeon*. We're not sure exactly what it is, but Koreans sometimes call it "Korean pizza." It looks like an omelet, but instead of egg there is a dough base, and mixed with the dough are various vegetables and often squid. Then the mixture is fried up and served with a soy sauce-based dipping sauce.

Still getting accustomed to Korea's large annual consumption of kimchi, I asked Mr. Kim if young kids eat kimchi. He said they did. I asked how old children are before their parents feed them kimchi. He said about four years old.

Mrs. Kim pointed to what looked like a washing machine in their kitchen. She said, "Kimchi refrigerator."

I thought maybe I hadn't heard her correctly.

"I'm sorry, did you say kimchi refrigerator?"

"Yes," Mrs. Kim replied. She led us to the machine and opened the lid, and indeed it was filled to the brim with bags and containers of kimchi. She explained that living in an apartment building, they cannot store their kimchi in big pots on their driveway or lawn, as people who live in houses do. Since the majority of Koreans are now living in apartment buildings, they have kimchi refrigerators to store this food staple. When I ask my students what their favourite food is, ninety percent of them say kimchi. At this point, I don't mind kimchi. I've been acquiring a taste for it as it's served with every lunch and whenever we eat in a restaurant. It hasn't yet reached *favourite food* status for me, though.

Our Korean colleagues swear by the health benefits of kimchi. It is claimed to contain a high content of vitamins A, B, and C, can help lower cholesterol and body weight, and can help prevent yeast infections and cancer. According to an item in *The Korea Times* entitled "Kimchi Makes International Health Cut" by Kim Tae-Jong, "The origin of kimchi dates back to at least the 13th century when the first written record of it appeared in a book by the scholar Lee Kyo-bo. He wrote, 'Kimchi preserved in soybean paste tastes good in the summer, whereas kimchi pickled in brine is served as a side dish during the winter.' Since then, the taste of kimchi has evolved over the years, but the introduction of red pepper into Korea in the 1900s gave kimchi the spicy personality it is known for today."

Kimchi is made by fermenting cabbage with spices. The mixture is kept in large barrel-like pots for preservation all year round, or in your kimchi fridge if you live in an apartment. I read a newspaper article recently that debated whether kimchi is all it's cracked up to be. The sources in the article (who did not want to be named out of fear of ridicule from their fellow Koreans) explained how kimchi is very high in salt and can lead to digestive cancers. They attributed the cancer cases more to the overconsumption of kimchi, rather than to kimchi itself. An average Korean consumes over thirty kilograms of kimchi per year.

Mr. and Mrs. Kim drove us home shortly after supper, and Mrs. Kim gave us a large bag, full of her best kimchi. We put it in our own refrigerator when we got home. It stayed there about a week. When we couldn't drink another sip of kimchi-tasting milk, and could stand the garlic smell in our fridge no longer, we threw it out. Secretly I feared we would be arrested that week – be awoken one night to "Dale and Beth Ann Knowles, you are under arrest for throwing the sacred food of Korea to the curb." We would be dragged from our beds, thrown in a cell, then tried in court for crimes against Korea … felony against kimchi. No arrests or summons occurred.

* * *

Our second evening involving Korean colleagues happened when we invited Mr. Chang to dinner at our house. He had been asking us if we could teach extra classes and summer school, and since it was difficult for the three of us to meet during school hours, we figured we could have him over for a business supper.

We deliberated a long time over what we'd serve him. Dale wanted to make something that tasted disgusting and watch Mr. Chang choke it down: a bit of revenge for all the things he made us "just taste!" and all of the situations he forced us into. The problem was, we had to eat the meal as well. We decided upon Western Sandwiches – something I am great at making – a very non-typical Korean meal that would appall Mr. Chang; something that we could make together, to show Mr. Chang that Dale and I have an equal relationship and share responsibilities.

On many occasions, Mr. Chang has asked me to complete some type of domestic duty: "Bess-uh, can you cut the fruit?" "Bess-uh, can you pour the tea?" He's offering *us* tea, but he wants *me* to make it, the traditional Korean way, and serve it? He's offering us fruit, but he wants me to peel, cut, and serve it? The morning he invited us to his house for breakfast, he had me cook the eggs. Time after time he asked me to cut fruit and pour drinks but never once did he ask Dale. Eventually, I realized he was asking me because I was female, and he felt it was my duty to do these things. I didn't like that.

On one occasion, when we were out for supper with Mr. Chang, Dale had poured water for me in my glass, and Mr. Chang had honestly asked, "Dale, why are you so nice to your wife?" I can't remember Dale's exact response, as we were both taken aback, but he said something like, "Because she deserves it."

I guess we wanted to accomplish more than just business talks with Mr. Chang, when we invited him to dinner. We wanted to change his views on sexism, to teach him about women's liberation. We wanted him to understand that nobody should "wear the pants" in a relationship. We wanted a lot.

I asked him shortly after lunch if he would be available to come for supper that night. He looked surprised, and then asked if Mr. Lee could come along. I'm sure I looked surprised.

I said, "No. Maybe we'll have Mr. Lee over another time."

He seemed disappointed. He asked what time, and if he could bring anything. I told him around 6:30 p.m. and just bring himself.

Six-thirty came, and Dale and I were just finishing the house tidying and starting on the cooking. If he was going to nosily inspect every room like he had before, we wanted to make sure the house was in satisfactory order.

He knocked on the door on time, and I answered. He had brought a bottle of Pear Schnapps and a flat of eggs. We thanked him for the gift, and I immediately used some of his eggs to make the omelet part of the Western Sandwiches. Dale opened the Pear Schnapps and poured us each a glass.

"Did somebody give this to you, Mr. Chang?" Dale was suspicious that Mr. Chang was regifting.

"Yes, it was gift," Mr. Chang responded, not at all embarrassed by his gesture. He'd given us regifted food items, from his office fridge and his house, before.

Dale was on toast and I was on omelet. Mr. Chang sat and leafed through some of our photo albums, and only spoke when we asked him a question.

We sat down to dinner, and he said, "This is food for breakfast?"

"Yes," I replied, "usually we eat Western Sandwiches for breakfast, but sometimes we eat them for supper as well. We wanted to eat something from home tonight."

Mr. Chang nodded and ate. Eventually, he said, "Don't you eat the rice?"

This time Dale responded, "Usually we do eat rice for supper. Tonight, we wanted to make something different. It's really good, isn't it, Beth Ann?"

I agreed, and Mr. Chang said, "Yes, delicious."

He was barely finished his last bite when he got up and said, "Thank you for the dinner. I must go."

He moved quicker than I had ever seen, and had his shoes and jacket on before we could properly offer him coffee or dessert.

Dale said, "We were hoping to talk to you about the extra classes you had asked us to teach, and also about the schedule for summer school."

Mr. Chang had the door open. "Ah. Yeah yeah. I will find out for you the summer school schedule. I will talk about the extra classes to you tomorrow. Thank you. See you later."

And with that, he was gone. Dale and I looked at each other, a little flabbergasted, and a little frustrated. We weren't sure if we'd accomplished anything during our supper date with Mr. Chang.

* * *

Our latest evening out with teachers from my school came on Mr. Bear's birthday. It may have been the last, and most momentous, social event we have spent with my colleagues. Earlier in the day, Mr. Bear had invited us to join the teachers and his wife for a celebratory birthday dinner.

To completely understand what happened that night, you must first know what happened during the day.

Friday of that week would be green tea harvesting day in Hwagae. That meant the middle school had a holiday, so the students could help with the harvest. Which also meant I had the day off. Surprisingly, Mr. Kim had informed me of the holiday weeks in advance, and Dale and I had made special plans. I would go to Hadong in the afternoon, attend his last class of the day, and we'd quickly catch the 3:10 p.m. bus to Busan to visit friends for the weekend, and go car shopping.

Mr. Kim mentioned sometime on Wednesday, two days

before my day off, that the teachers would all be going to a workshop on Friday. Immediately, I went to Mr. Chang to sort things out.

"Mr. Chang," I started. I had gone to his office after I finished my lunch, and I could smell that he'd just finished smoking a cigarette. "Mr. Kim told me that Friday the teachers are going to a workshop. I understood that Friday was a holiday, and I've already made other plans."

"Yes, the teachers are going to Sacheon to international teachers' workshop. You will help me to purchase the books," Mr. Chang replied.

"Where is Sacheon again?" I remembered it as being where Mr. Kim had taken us to get our alien registration cards, but I couldn't remember where exactly it was.

"Ahh. Near Jinju."

"When will we be back?"

"Maybe in the afternoon. After we eat the lunchy."

I could tell that, as usual, there were no finite plans, no exact timings for me to go by.

"Well, Mr. Chang. As I had thought Friday was a holiday, I had planned to go to Dale's school to teach with him on Friday afternoon. And immediately after we were going to head to Busan."

"Ahh. Yes, you had the plans. So you will not come with us on Friday?" he asked.

"If you need me to help you choose books, I can attend the workshop, but I'd rather not go out for lunch. Would it be out of the way for somebody to drop me off at Dale's school after the workshop?"

"You don't want the lunchy?"

"No, I'd rather not. I had planned to eat at Dale's school with him. Would this be okay?"

"Ahhh, I see. Okay. Someone will drive you to Hadong. May I ask why you go to Busan?" I figured he was worried we might be planning on leaving him – of taking a job at another school or a Hagwon and disappearing from his life forever.

"We have friends in Busan. Friends from Canada. We are going to visit them, and maybe look for a car to buy," I replied.

"Ahh yes."

I left Mr. Chang's office and went about the rest of my day.

Just before six that evening, Dale and I left to walk to dinner. The sky had turned an eerie yellow that afternoon, and there was a dangerous wind blowing; it warned to stay inside where everything was safe, but we walked on. Leaves whipped through the air, and everything was wild about Hwagae.

We stopped by a small bakery and purchased a cake for Mr. Bear. The baker packed the cake, along with sparklers and noisemakers, in a decorative box. We met Mrs. Bark just outside the restaurant. It was a place we'd eaten at once before with Mr. Chang. Last time, however, there wasn't a whole pig hanging from its ankles at the entrance to the restaurant. *Pork for supper*, I guessed. What further disturbed me about the pig corpse was the spray-painted price along its back.

We showed Mrs. Bark the cake we'd bought and put it off to the side until after dinner. The rest of the teachers arrived over the next few minutes, and we all assembled on the floor around a long series of tables, pushed together for our large party. Dale sat at one end of the table, I was two people down from him, and Mr. Chang was further down my side of the table. Mr. Chang's eyes were already red from alcohol when he arrived at the restaurant. He looked wild like the evening outside. Mr. Bear and his wife sat far from me on the other side of the tables. She was a very elegant and classy lady, probably in her fifties.

I noticed Mrs. Bark say something in Korean to Mrs. Kang, and then saw her point at the cake Dale and I had bought. Before I could react, the cake was produced, the sparklers lit, the horns blown, and we were singing *Chukka Hamnida*, Korea's version of "Happy Birthday."

The first pieces of meat hadn't even finished cooking, and already the cake was out. Dale and I, dumbfounded, looked at each other and sang along. As it turned out, it was better that the cake was brought out at that time. Dale and I never made it through dinner.

Between sips of *soju*, Mr. Chang said, "Mr. Knowles, be happy! I know about your secret plans for weekend."

Immediately annoyed, I jumped right in, "Our plans are not a secret, Mr. Chang."

He ignored me and continued to talk to Dale. "I know about your secret plans, Mr. Knowles. Be happy."

He was so annoying! "It's not a secret!" I said again, more firmly this time.

"Be happy," he repeated.

Dale and I looked at each other with a "what the —" expression.

The pieces of pork sizzled on the grills in front of us, and everyone chatted and picked away at the kimchi and other side dishes. Just as the first round of pork was cooked, Mr. Chang raised his glass to Dale and said, "Busan is famous for men's suits. They have the special tailors for the men's suits."

I still had no clue what Mr. Chang was talking about or where he was going with this. I hadn't yet noticed the sly look in his eyes and the mean smirk on his lips.

But Dale was now onto him. He replied, "No, I don't need any suits."

"No. Special suit for men. One size fits all. You know what I mean," Mr. Chang said.

Still confused I looked at Dale and was surprised to see how pissed off he looked.

"No, Mr. Chang, I don't know what you mean!" Dale said firmly.

Mr. Chang repeated, "Special tailor for men. One size fits all. You know what I mean."

Dale looked at me and with anger in his voice he said, "He's talking about prostitution."

I said, "Oh!"

Mr. Chang said, "No, no."

I looked at Mr. Chang then and saw his crafty smile. He looked at me, and then back at Dale, covered his mouth so I couldn't tell what he was saying, and then mouthed something to Dale.

Then he said again, "You know what I mean."

Again, Dale said, "No I don't. Please tell me."

Mr. Chang didn't respond. Dale looked to me. "I think we'll leave. Is that okay?"

"Of course," I replied.

We rose, and the table fell silent. Mr. Chang asked, "Where are you going?"

"We are leaving," Dale replied decisively.

"Why?"

Dale used Chang's methods. "I think you know."

"Is it because of me?" Mr. Chang asked.

"Yes," Dale replied matter-of-factly.

We smiled, and said goodbye to the table of people. We wished Mr. Bear *Happy Birthday* again, and, in Korean, Dale told Mrs. Bear how beautiful she was and how nice it was to meet her, which had the silenced table swooning. We told the confused-looking restaurant owner *mashisoyo, kamsahamnida,* (delicious, thank you), nodded, bowed low, and we were gone.

The adrenalin was pumping through my veins, and my legs were shaky as we headed towards home. I'd never done anything like that before. We reviewed our actions on the way home and concluded we'd done the right thing. We didn't need to listen to Mr. Chang imply that Dale was going to Busan to get a prostitute, whether he was joking or not. Mr. Chang needed to learn that his off-colour jokes were not appreciated or welcomed, not by us anyway. We've been told that it is customary to laugh at the jokes of elders, no matter if they are funny or tasteless. But I think it's okay that we don't abide by all Korean customs.

Dale worried about how I would be treated at school after that night. I didn't think about it much. I was happy we now had a great excuse not to dine out with Mr. Chang again. We went to bed that night, excited about the point we'd made. Perhaps the teachers didn't understand exactly what had happened, but they knew Mr. Chang had insulted us. We hoped Mr. Chang felt like the jerk he had been.

At 7:10 the next morning the phone rang. We knew it was him. Dale answered, *"Annyeong haseyo."*

Mr. Chang said, "Yeah. I would like to speak to Dale."

Whose male voice did he think answered the phone?

"This is Dale. Hello, Mr. Chang."

Mr. Chang started to explain that many Westerners go to Busan to have suits made. Dale cut him off, "No, Mr. Chang. That's not what you meant, and don't try to pretend otherwise. We are familiar with the expressions you used, and you covered your mouth so Beth Ann couldn't hear what you were saying."

Mr. Chang didn't stick up for himself – he knew. He asked Dale to forgive him for his "bad habits." Dale said he would. He asked Dale to ask me the same, and again Dale said he would. Then Mr. Chang said he wanted to "have good relations with us."

Dale said, "Yes, Mr. Chang. We will have a professional relationship." He stressed the "professional" part. Mr. Chang sounded depressed when Dale hung up the phone.

I walked Dale to the bus and went running. Mr. Chang and I had about one hundred different conversations in my head during my run: imagining the stupid or inappropriate things he'd say to me; preparing myself with good comebacks for different scenarios. I couldn't anticipate how he'd act around me.

Shortly after nine I went to school and headed straight for my desk in the teachers' office. There were only a few teachers there and they all acted normally towards me, extending a cordial morning hello.

When Mr. Lee came into the office, I went to him and asked if he could apologize to Mr. Bear for us leaving his party. Mr. Lee told me there had been a misunderstanding with Mr. Chang. I didn't let him finish.

"No, Mr. Lee. There was no misunderstanding. Mr. Chang said some inappropriate things that offended Dale and me and we're not going to pretend otherwise. Mr. Chang has already phoned us this morning to apologize."

Mr. Lee didn't defend Mr. Chang any longer. He told me Mr. Bear was quite happy we had joined him for the celebration, and he wanted to thank us for the cake we'd given him. I went back to my desk. I had no classes to teach that day, as our school was supposed to be going on a picnic in Hadong. However, the weather was still very windy and cool, and the picnic was moved into the gymnasium. I hadn't been asked to participate or been given any tasks, so I caught up on emails at my desk.

Soon, Mrs. Kang came and sat next to me. She told me how worried and sad she'd been the night before and didn't understand what had happened. I told her Mr. Chang had made a very rude comment to Dale, and we felt we should leave. I told her Mr. Chang had apologized, and she shouldn't worry, and I thanked her for her thoughts.

Mr. Chang never came to the teachers' office once that day, unusual for him but usual under the circumstances, I guessed.

Lunchtime arrived and I headed to the cafeteria. A few of the students' mothers had prepared an incredible lunch for us: fantastic rice dishes, duck sizzling in sweet and spicy sauces on tabletop grills, even hotdogs carved in the shape of flowers. Mr. Chang didn't look up when I entered the room. I had hoped he would. I had hoped we would have some interaction, good or bad, just so I wouldn't have to anticipate it any longer. But he didn't. I sat amongst the female teachers and anytime I looked down my side of the long table towards Mr. Chang, his whole body was facing away from me.

Before I went home for the day, I asked Mr. Lee what time we'd be leaving for the teachers' workshop the next day. He told me if I didn't want to go, I didn't have to.

"I was asked to go. Of course I will go," I told him.

We left at nine the next morning. I went with Mr. Bear and Ms. Kim on the ninety-minute drive, almost to Jinju. It was then I realized that, contrary to what Mr. Chang had told me, it *would* be out of someone's way to drive me back to Hadong after the workshop.

Of course, the event was nothing like what I had expected or been told. We were visiting a school for international students. There was no workshop, no other teachers there. I wasn't sure we were even supposed to be there, as nobody greeted us and there really didn't seem to be anyone around. Eventually, a man met us, and gave a twenty-minute briefing, all in Korean, and then we toured the school. My colleagues took pictures of everything – the map of the building on the wall, the plant in the hallway, every little thing. There was no book fair, and I was not asked to assist in choosing books. We did spend about five minutes in their library, looking at books, but Mr. Chang didn't even look sideways at me.

After about an hour, we were shuffled back outside. Mrs. Kang came to me and said she would drive me back to Hadong and asked, "Would you like to go now?"

I said, "Are we finished? Is anything else happening?"

For the first time, Mr. Chang turned to me and said, "What about after the lunch?"

It wasn't a warm invitation, not that I would have accepted had he said it any kinder.

"I am eating lunch at Dale's school as we discussed."

"You won't eat the lunch first?" he asked again, as if we'd never discussed the event before.

"No. Mrs. Kang said she would drive me to Hadong."

Mr. Chang said no more. Mrs. Kang and I set off in her car. At first, I felt bad that she wouldn't be able to go to lunch with the other teachers, as Hadong was far from Namhae where they were planning on going to eat. I explained to her that Mr. Chang had told me it wouldn't be out of the way for me to be "dropped off" in Hadong, and I was sorry she had to miss lunch.

She said she didn't mind at all and that she enjoyed spending time with me. It occurred to me then that she might grow tired of all of the socializing Mr. Chang forces on teachers; she was probably grateful for the excuse to pass up lunch. Then Mrs. Kang, not in so many words, said Mr. Chang likes telling people what to do. I nodded in agreement.

SEVENTEEN

We now know what a *waygook* is. *Waygooks* are strange-looking creatures, imported from faraway lands to live in Korea. *Waygooks* are poked and prodded, force-fed, sometimes pointed and laughed at, and often glared at. When a *waygook* isn't looking, Koreans sometimes take pictures of them.

In Hwagae, *waygook* sightings are very rare, and might be a little like the wild animal sightings my mom reports from home: "Saw one bear crossing the road today. Your father saw two deer on his walk this morning."

Waygooks are wild and strange anomalies. Dale and I are *waygooks*.

We had heard the word many times. We heard it from the kids who pointed and laughed at us, and said, "Hello! Hello! Hello! Hello! Hello!" We heard it from the young couple walking down the street in front of us, as they glanced behind them, stealing glimpses of us while they whispered.

Eventually, we learned that "*waygook*" means foreigner.

Sometimes being a *waygook* gets us special treatment, free snacks, and positive attention. But, on numerous occasions, we've felt discriminated against because we are *waygooks*.

People cut in front of us in lineups, and clerks push us to the side if a Korean interrupts to ask the clerk a question. One man stepped in front of us at a cash register, put his purchases on the counter, then left to look for other things in the store. The clerk then refused to serve us, while we all waited for that man to return. We left our purchases, unpurchased, on the counter. We know other *waygooks* who were denied membership at their local tennis club, because they weren't Korean, and we've walked past nightclubs with "No Foreigners" signs posted at the entrance.

We've seen advertisements for English lessons that will take away your "foreigner phobia" and we wonder what is so scary about us. Foreigners have lived in Korea for many years, eating rice, using chopsticks, squatting in the bathrooms. Korean billboards are littered with advertisements featuring foreigners. And all the latest Hollywood movies, starring people of various nationalities, are shown here and are viewed by millions of Koreans. Foreigners are not a new concept to Korea, but it still seems like we are.

I try to imagine the kind of treatment a Korean would receive in North America. I'd like to think they'd feel accepted and welcomed, and that help would be given with smiles and open arms. But I know that wouldn't always be the case. North America is no better, nor is Europe or Africa or Australia or anywhere. It seems there's a bit of "foreigner phobia" in all of us.

I have travelled to more than fifteen countries, and at no time have I been asked to have my picture taken with other people. Many times I've been asked to take pictures *for* other people, but never *with* other people.

Never before have I been lying on a quiet beach, greatly enjoying the solitude of reading a book, and been interrupted by two males asking if each of them could have their picture taken with me. As I smile half-heartedly for the camera, the young Korean man's arm around my shoulder, his girlfriend snapping the photos, I wonder if I'm the highlight of his trip to the beach. I'm not being egotistical. By no means do I think my presence should be the highlight of anybody's trip to the beach, unless of course I am attacked by a shark while walking on water and licking my elbow. Yes, that would make me something special. It would warrant a photo with me. But what is so fascinating about a blonde girl reading a book on the beach?

Sometimes being a *waygook* in Korea is about survival. Not that we are enduring any physical hardships, but mentally and emotionally life can be draining. We are surviving as *waygooks*.

Dale has survived screaming girls and pubescent boys, while I have survived crying girls and grade six boys (the worst kind of boy). But we still love it. We love being at the front of a classroom. We love when our charades and elaborate pictures on the chalkboard get absorbed into our students' minds, and an understanding, "Ahhhhh!" rings throughout our classroom. We love helping them "get it."

And the forty minutes of hell I spend each week, pulling my hair out at the insolence of those grade six boys, does seem worth it when I lay my head on my pillow at night. It forces me to remember back to my grade six days, to the things the boys in my class did to our teacher or to (God help her) a substitute teacher, who had the great misfortune of teaching our class. I can still see one of them spitting in her coffee while she was lecturing another, the decoy, in the hallway. I remember the rest of the class cringing quietly at our desks, as we watched her sip her coffee throughout the morning, too afraid of the wrath we'd endure from our classmates if we told her the truth.

I see the same fear and guile on the faces of my Korean grade six class – years, continents, and cultures apart, grade six is still the same. The bad boys are still bad and bold, the good boys are still scared and thus cross over to the bad side, and the girls still act impressed by everything the bad and good boys do.

I get to babysit, to search the classroom for that incessant whistling sound that seems to be everywhere but nowhere. To intercept notes being thrown across the room. To speak twenty times to the kid who won't turn around in his seat and keeps rocking his desk noisily, until I'm ready to face the consequences of throwing him and his desk out the second-storey window.

The traditional Korean disciplinary measures don't work for me. When I tried raising my voice or made them kneel on the floor, they just smirked up at me and said some Korean pleasantries (I'm sure!) which sent the rest of the class into fits of laughter and gave more boys the motivation to act out. And I wasn't going to hit them – not with a back scratcher, or a wooden stick, or my hand – as some teachers do. Instead, I started kicking them out of class. I put their school bag and their books on the floor in the hallway, and I led them out. It was then that I saw the fear in their eyes and knew I would see results. They were terrified of a Korean teacher, or, worse, the principal, finding them in the hallway. Then they would receive a punishment they would regret. Slowly the classroom dynamic started to change. It's never perfect but it's better.

Sometimes I can't really blame the kids for their inattention and restlessness in the classroom. The students are at such varying levels of English comprehension that I can't cater to everyone at once. Some kids know "Hello" and anything I say to them during the rest of the class is lost. So I have become less strict. If the kids are quietly being inattentive, I ignore them. If they are sleeping or reading a comic book, I let it go. If they start disrupting the kids who are interested and want to learn, then I act.

For the most part, the kids here are more innocent than at home in Canada. In some ways, the whole country is more innocent. It reminds me of what I would imagine life was like when my parents or grandparents were children. Corner stores don't have security cameras, shopkeepers keep their change in their pocket, doors are left unlocked, and neighbourhoods just seem to be safer.

*   *   *

Our small town of Hwagae is lacking many things – a big grocery store, a clothing store, library, etc. However, the one thing Hwagae does boast is a staggering number of fish restaurants. On the sidewalk in front of each restaurant is a large fish tank full of fish, lobster, crabs, or eels, to lure customers in ... pun intended.

Sometimes the lid of a tank is left off, and a brave fish attempts an escape. I witnessed such an escape endeavour one day as I walked to meet Dale at the bus stop. To my horror, the fish leapt from the tank a few metres in front of me and land- ed on the ground, flopping at my feet. I wanted to aid in his break-out but we were too far from the river to make it, even if I ran like hell and did rescue breathing along the way. And he was too big to put in a glass of water, and come to think of it, there was no way I was touching him anyway – maybe if he had knocked himself out from the fall, but not flopping around like he was. So I went into the restaurant and frantically tried to make fish gestures to the owner inside. When she scowled at me and remained on the couch at the back of the restau- rant, watching a Korean game show, I just started waving her out of the store. Eventually, I piqued her curiosity enough and she emerged with a scowl.

I turned and continued walking toward the bus stop, not wanting to witness his reincarceration. As I continued walking, I thought of the point of this whole fish story, which I'm just getting to now. Such a thing wouldn't happen at home. Restau- rants couldn't keep fish tanks outdoors. The first time some Canadian punks saw an outdoor fish tank, they would find a way to smash the glass out of it.

In Canada, bus shelters have the glass shot out of them frequently. In some areas, if we go for a walk after dark, we risk being robbed or beaten up. Our cars are kicked or keyed in our driveways. Graffiti dots our buildings and monuments. As strange as Korea sometimes feels to us, it's nice that people here can trust each other. It's nice that compared to North America, crime seems to be almost non-existent here. Maybe that's why many Koreans don't like us *waygooks*. Maybe they hear about the delinquency of some Westerners, and they think we're all like that.

Dale and I find comfort in seeing that the coolest kids in Korea are the smart ones. The cool kids have baskets and bells on the front of their bikes. They hold their parents' hand in public, even if they are in high school. Kids of all ages are into Hula-Hoops, and skipping, and some kids even run behind rolling tire rims, pushing them along with a stick. University students don't go to the beach to get wasted. They go to the beach to build sandcastles and bury their friends, to flirt with each other away from the watchful eye of their parents, and to use throwing each other in the water as an excuse for physical contact.

Korea is a place of much innocence and naivety. Many Koreans believe there are no Korean homosexuals. In a country of more than forty million people, this is definitely not true. When we first arrived and started teaching, we thought the majority of the country was homosexual. Everywhere we went we saw men holding hands or walking three-by-three down the street with their arms linked. Our students were all over each other – boys always with their arms around each other in class, rubbing each other's backs, holding and caressing each other's hand or leg. After a while, we learned that touching is a sign of great affection and respect, in a nonsexual way.

Sometimes the touching, however, goes beyond what we'd imagine could be construed as respectful or affectionate. A popular practice of Japanese and Korean children is to put one's palms together, point the joined index fingers while folding the other fingers, then sticking the index fingers in an unsuspecting victim's buttocks. There is no actual penetration, from what we've seen, as the suspect is wearing pants, but still! I fear for the Korean boy who moves to Canada and tries to make friends by poking kids in the bum.

*   *   *

The social aspect of being the only foreign teacher amongst many Korean teachers has its ups and downs. On those days when you just don't feel like talking, you can remain in your own world, as much of the time our colleagues don't speak to us. But on those days when you just want to have a good old-fashioned gossip session or swap some classroom war stories, the teachers' office can be a lonely place. Some days pass when I say "good morning" as I enter the office, and not another word for the rest of the day. Many days I make an effort to strike up a conversation, but it seems the teachers only want to converse if they've initiated the interaction – it's as if they want to prep themselves before engaging in a chat with me.

"How are you today, Mr. Kim? Good?" I say to the gym teacher, giving him a questioning thumbs-up.

"No," he replies.

"Oh," I say, standing awkwardly by his desk waiting for a bit of an explanation ... a "how are you" in return, anything. But "no" is all I get. I sit at my desk across from him, and we both go about our work, without a word spoken for the rest of the day.

Some lunch hours lure my fellow teachers from their English silence. They point to their bowl of rice mixed with some vegetables and say, "What do you call this in Canada?"

"Rice," I say.

As limited as some of their English skills are, they all seem to know that "rice" is the English word for it, and they are not satisfied with my answer.

"Ummmm. Rice and vegetables?" It is the best I can come up with.

"Ahhh!" Mr. Bear repeats me enthusiastically to the teachers around him and they all seem pleased.

The vice principal at the elementary school feels it is his job to teach me Korean table manners.

"Bess-uh," he says, "Korea. Gentleman."

He indicates that I should watch him. He lays his chopsticks down across his tray, then picks up his spoon. Next he lays his spoon down across his tray and picks up his chopsticks.

I sit, my spoonful of soup frozen in mid-air just below my lips, my jaw dropped in disbelief. He points at my tray where, scandalously, I have left my chopsticks lying in my rice, and he makes a disgusted face.

I leave my chopsticks in my rice and continue eating my soup, so he says, "Korea. Gentleman," one more time and shows me again.

I point to the trays of all the other teachers sitting at the table, showing him they've left their soup spoon in their soup or their chopsticks in their rice. Why doesn't he pick on them? I want to explain to him that being of the female sex, I will never be a gentleman, Korean or otherwise. But I know, even with my stellar charade attempts, he would never understand. I continue eating in my own way, hoping his little lesson is over. He's relentless, though. He's tried to bring me over to his side on a number of occasions since, but I'm not budging.

I say, "I'm Canadian, not Korean." I again point out the lack of "gentlemanly" table manners of all the other teachers at the table, and I eat how I want to eat.

* * *

I've silently become more irritable lately. Perhaps it's because of the heat and humidity as summer approaches, or perhaps it's because of what heat and humidity makes people do. The combination of the two makes me more than a little crazy.

'I'm a person who becomes very agitated by certain noises. I can't stand listening to a person eat a banana, especially in a quiet room. It grosses me out and I can't get my mind off it while the banana is being eaten. It's all I can think about. Even when it's me eating the banana. I've always had to leave the room when my mom was pouring her homemade mustard pickles from the pot into glass jars. The plopping of the cucumbers and onions mixed with sauce drove me insane. I'm aware my neurotic dislikes of noises can be a bit odd, but I know I'm not the only weird one. Dale can't stand the sound of someone brushing their teeth near him.

For the past few months in Korea, I've been tormented by the sound of cream and sugar being stirred into hundreds of coffees a week. I've never liked the sound of a metal spoon hitting against a ceramic mug while the mug's contents were being stirred. Even worse is the sound of a tiny metal spoon hitting against a ceramic mug. These are the implements my fellow teachers use to make coffee, teeny little metal spoons one might use to feed a baby. Each weekday, I silently suffer, with the high-pitched tinkling of the tiny spoons ringing in my head. And once it's in your head, you can't get it out. You can't ignore it or focus on anything else. It's like when you're falling asleep and your husband says, "Do you hear that?" And you admit you hadn't noticed the slight rattling sound of the window until that moment, but once you hear it you can't unhear it, and you lay awake hearing it for hours while your husband snores beside you.

I've been able to deal with the coffee-making noises until recently. But lately, as the heat and humidity rose, my tolerance fell. And it was with the heat that my teachers began making iced coffees, an even worse torture to my auditory system. I see a teacher going for the freezer, and I cringe. Then the affliction starts ... the tinkling of the tiny metal spoon and the clinking of the ice cubes, against each other and against the ceramic mug. The ice puts me over the edge. Some days I have to plug my ears. Some days I have to leave the room.

* * *

Unlike me, Dale isn't bothered by coffee or iced coffee-making noises, but like me, he does notice that his fellow teachers don't talk to him much either.

As his classes require little preparation, he spends hours searching the internet and often runs out of things to search for. One day, though, he discovered a teachers' lounge at the girls' high school. The room has a big TV with English channels, a treadmill that is covered in dust, and one of those hang-you-upside-down-for-your-health contraptions. Sometimes he passes the time hanging upside down and watching BBC World News.

His lunch hours, like mine, often lead to some type of conversation, though. One day, Dale's Mr. Kim pointed at the fried mystery meat on his tray and asked what it was called in Canada. Dale had already eaten his own serving, had enjoyed it, but wasn't able to distinguish what animal it was from.

"I'm not sure what kind of meat it is, Mr. Kim. What does the animal look like?"

"In Korea we call it eel," Mr. Kim responded.

"Eel?" Dale almost choked on his bite of kimchi. He couldn't really mean eel. "Eel that we see in tanks outside restaurants? They look like snakes?"

"Yes. Eel. What do you call it?" Mr. Kim replied calmly.

"Well, eel, I guess. I had no idea that's what I was eating," Dale said, feeling a bit violated. He had enjoyed the eel when he didn't know it was eel, but he wondered if it would have tasted differently had he known what it really was. Would he have eaten it with the same hungry enthusiasm, or would he have moved it around his tray, nibbling only on a few chopsticksful?

Later that week, Dale's Mr. Kim accompanied a few of the classes on a trip to Jeju-do, a Korean island off the south coast. The island is reportedly very beautiful and is the top destination for Korean honeymooners. The next week when Dale was back at the girls' school, he asked one of his classes about their trip. The girls described the ferry ride to the island, horseback riding, exploring caves, and eating *dong*-fed pig.

"What did you eat?" Dale said.

"*Dong*-fed pig!" one of the braver girls shouted out. The girls started giggling at the surprised, confused, and disgusted expression on Dale's face.

"What is *dong*?" Dale asked, even though he already knew the answer. He hoped *dong* was the Korean word for grain, flax, bran ... anything but what he knew it would be.

Another girl jumped up, went to the chalkboard, and began drawing. The rest of the class was engaged in full laughter by this point. The girl drew a pile of poop with flies buzzing around it. The class erupted into more laughter.

It was at this time that Dale's Mr. Kim jumped in to help in the explanation. "They feed pigs human *dong*."

"What?" Dale asked in disbelief. "And you eat it?"

He faced a classroom full of *Yeses* and *very delicious!*

In the conversations Dale and I have had since, we discussed the health concerns of eating pigs that had fed on human poop. We wondered if restaurants advertised their premium, grade A, human excrement-fed pork. If they did, we wondered how they advertised it ... with pictures of pigs feeding out of toilets on their signs and in their menu? We wondered where they acquire the human excrement. Do they feed the humans anything special, so their feces contain specific nutrients or is of a special consistency? We had so many questions about the *dong*-fed pigs. Later, Dale found out from his Mr. Kim that traditionally the pigs are kept under an outhouse. That was enough for us. We wanted to hear no more about *dong*-fed pigs, and silently we made a pact to never speak of it again. Especially on Fridays when we go to the pork restaurant.

EIGHTEEN

Ever since we walked out on Mr. Bear's birthday dinner, Mr. Chang has left us alone. That small, yet monumental exit was perhaps the best thing we could have done to maintain our sanity until we board the plane out of here next February. The teachers don't seem surprised when we decline dinner invitations, nor do they press the subject further, and Mr. Chang interacts with us on a purely professional level.

Walking out shamed him in front of his peers which, unbeknownst to us, was a pretty significant event. The Korean way would have been to laugh at Mr. Chang's distasteful jokes, as he is senior to us. Then, when he phoned us and gave a lame excuse for his behaviour, the Korean way would have been to, again, laugh it off and pretend to believe him.

At the time, Dale and I weren't aware of the Korean way, but now that we do know, we're not sure if we would have behaved differently.

We did travel to Busan the weekend after the Mr. Chang incident. Contrary to what he implied that we were going to do there, we did purchase a car. We'd been trying to find a vehicle for about a month. We searched foreigner buy and sell websites and newspaper ads. I had my heart set on a RockStar, an SUV we saw for sale, but it was bigger than what we needed and out of our price range.

Dale thought we might buy a motorcycle, and found one advertised through a foreigner website. The person actually had a car and a motorcycle for sale, so Dale responded to the ad.

. The following is the correspondence between Dale and the guy – Randy Q – who was selling the vehicles:

> Hi Randy,
> my wife and I came to korea a few months ago and are
> looking for a vehicle. We are situated about 1 hr.
> south of Jinju but will be in Busan for the weekend
> (april 22 and 23) if you haven't sold your vehicles
> by then we would be interested in taking a look. I
> just have one question, you said they were not used
> through the winter, is there a reason for that?
> thank you
> dale knowles

Reply from Randy Q:

yes there is a reason for me not being there.

the korean booze law is .05–.08% is impaired.
(i was drinking soju with korean corporate bigwigs)
and drove at 3.7 alcohol in my blood)

driving impaired is a criminal offence in korea.
they deported me immediately.
that is why i couldn't start the car or bike.
i wasn't there.

my buddy has the car and bike i his care and selling them
4 me. .... but he is going to thailand tuesday.
not sure 4 how long.
maybe a couple weeks.

cheers

Dale's response to Randy:
> that sucks, (about being deported) I didn't mean to
> pry, I just wanted to
> know if there was some reason regarding the cars ...

> your friend selling the vehicles for you is going to
> Thailand today huh? is
> there anybody he could leave the paperwork and keys
> with, I would like to
> check out the vehicles and likely buy them this
> weekend, I would rather not
> wait a couple of weeks ... anyway, if there is
> anything that can be done
> Great, if not we tried.

> Thanks man

> Dale

Reply from Randy Q:

*it's ok you asked why the car sat. especially if it is
to a guy that says don't let a car sit, and he left it
sit, it would make me wonder!*

*(i didn't add that when i was grabbed i had tried to
stab a guy in with a ball point pen ... lol ... police
gave me a lecture ... pens are for study!!!)
the guy is leaving wednesday, but there is a guy
looking at them on tuesday morning (i told him not to
buy the bike because he never drove one and also can't
shift gears ... AND he will get killed) ...
but he might take both or none ...
at this point though, he took first dibs, and if he
doesn't show, it leaves you the option of wednesday or
waiting 7-14 days ...*

i can keep you posted.

cheers

Dale's answer:
>
> keep me posted,
> I may be able to pop up there on Wednesday afternoon
> and have a look if the
> fella doesn't buy them. I've owned bikes before,
> but am mostly interested
> in the Car (as my wife doesn't drive bikes), but
> would probably take both.
>
> dale

Reply from Randy Q:

> *ok ... i will let you know but i suspect the guy won't*
> *have time wednesday as he is flying out.*
> *he apparently is coming back the 30th*

Reply from Randy Q:

> *guy took the car ... sorry bout that*

Dale responds:
> no worries
> how much for just the bike? like I said earlier, we
> are mostly interested
> in a car/bongo at the moment, but we'll see.
> dale
> PS about the stabbing with a pen thing, I figure if
> you're gonna go out, you
> may as well go out in a blaze of glory ...

At this point, Dale is egging Randy Q on a bit, as he is clearly a character.

Reply from Randy Q:

> *bike 350 ... but again, you are better off with a solid*
> *vehicle considering you are married.*
> *i am a pro driver and instructor. i taught greyhound*

bus drivers for 10 years, and am also a counter
terrorist escape and evasion driver for protecting
VIP's, and yet i got hit by cars 5 times in 6 years in Korea.
Save yourself for your family :-)

as for the pen ... yes it was a blaze of glory :-)
i actually could have stabbed the guy easily and
immediately if i wanted to (i trained in philipinno
knife fighting and can use 2 knives at lightning speed)
i actually put 12 slices on him (in the air) before
pausing and letting him react, and letting him wrestle
with me
that was interpreted as me trying to kill him, when in
fact i didn't want to hurt him at all ... i just wanted
to make it clear for him to quit yelling at me, or i
COULD slice him up. such is life :-)

Such *is* life, Randy Q! As fun as he seemed, we veered in a new direction on our vehicle search.

We ended up buying a car from Michelle, a Korean lady who taught at the same Hagwon as our friends from Canada, Sandy and Sonja. On first impression, Michelle seemed like a very pleasant, but slightly clueless, lady. She walked into the teachers' office where we were waiting for Sandy and Sonja to finish teaching.

"You are here to buy my car?" she said, without a "Hello" or "How do you do?"

Sandy had only emailed us earlier that day to let us know one of his co-workers was selling their car, and we knew no other details.

"Maybe. We'll look at it," I said. "What kind of car is it?"

"Silver," she said.

By that one answer, we should have foreseen the chaos and hair-pulling the purchase of this car would bring. We should have abandoned the idea right there. But we didn't.

"What year is it?" Dale asked.

"I'm not sure. 1997, maybe," Michelle giggled nervously.

"Is it standard or automatic?"

"I'm not sure."

"How many kilometres are on it?"

"I don't know. I just drive it. My husband takes care of all that kind of stuff. I can find out for you, though. You can go look at it. It's the silver one behind the McDonald's."

She didn't know cars but we were thankful that she was proficient in English.

"How much do you want for it?"

"1.5 million."

That's 1.5 million won, which is about $1,800 Canadian – around the maximum we wanted to pay. From Michelle's wealth of information, we had gathered the car was silver (a good colour for a car, I guess) and we knew it might be a 1997 … not an antique yet. We decided to check it out.

In the McDonald's parking lot we found a silver, automatic, 1997 Hyundai Avante Wagon, a Hyundai Elantra in North America. There were a few dings on it, nothing major, and only 100,000 kilometres. We were pretty excited that it was a wagon. We envisioned ourselves on numerous camping trips, waking up in the morning in the back of our station wagon.

When we asked Michelle, she didn't think the back seats folded down. As she didn't know if the car she had been driving for a few years was an automatic or a standard, we weren't going to trust her knowledge of the seats. But what station wagon wouldn't have folding seats? That's the point, isn't it?

Michelle also couldn't give us any details on when, or if, any work was done on it, when the inspection was up, or how old the tires were. Her "husband takes care of all that stuff," and her husband wasn't available to talk. He had told her, however, that if she sold her car, he'd buy her a new one. She wanted us to take that silver car off her hands as soon as possible. *She probably has the colour picked out for her new car already*, I thought.

We told Michelle we'd think about the car and asked her to find out more details for us. By the time we left the Hagwon, without suggesting it ourselves, Michelle had dropped the price to 1.3 million.

Over the weekend we saw some sights of Busan, went to the movies, ate delicious Italian food, and spoke English to other *waygooks*. We felt somewhat normal again. At the same time, as we fought through throngs of people in the twelve-floor Lotte Department Store, we were grateful we hadn't taken a contract in Busan or any other large Korean city. Even though all the luxuries and amenities of Canada were there, so were millions of people, ninety percent of whom seemed to be everywhere we were. Dale got another huge hate-on for shopping, and malls, and being inside buildings. I looked forward to our return to the great open spaces of Hwagae.

While swapping work stories with Sandy and Sonja, we discovered we have a better work situation in Hwagae; comparatively, our Mr. Chang isn't so bad. Sonja and the other female teachers at her Hagwon have sexual harassment to contend with. Their director likes to touch the female teachers when he talks to them or walks by them. He strokes their faces and touches their behinds. Then he treats Sandy, the lone male teacher, like a king. He is forever praising him, and commenting on what a hard worker he is, and suggesting Sandy take more breaks. Sandy admits he does no more work than any of the female teachers, but also doesn't mind the special treatment he gets.

Sunday we took Michelle's silver car for a test drive. She met us on the sidewalk in front of the Hagwon and passed Dale the keys. Dale and I jumped in the car and asked who would come with us, as we had no idea where we were going. Michelle took a step away from the car, putting her hands up and giggling. "Whoa! Not me."

How helpful is she, I thought.

Sandy came with us as we did a very short test drive, and we came to the agreement that the car was what we wanted and was being sold at a very good price. We still wanted a few more details which she had yet to find out for us, so we said we'd be in contact with her that week. Scared that we wouldn't buy the car from her, she offered to drive the car to Hwagae for us.

"Do you know where Hwagae is?" I asked.

"No, but we can drive it there, no problem," she replied.

She must have really wanted to sell that silver car to us if she was willing to drive it out of the chaotic, entangled streets of Busan, and then travel hours into the sticks of Hwagae.

* * *

We tried to contact Michelle early that week. It became an arduous task. Her phone doesn't ring. Instead, it plays some annoying Korean soccer anthem song. How is one supposed to know when to hang up, when there is no ringing? I usually like to wait five to seven rings before I give up on a phone call, but all concept of phoning time is lost when you have no rings by which to judge. So we let Michelle's soccer song play and play and play that week, and not once did she answer her phone.

At last, late in the week, after Dale and I had both begun subconsciously humming the soccer anthem, Michelle phoned us back. The car sale was agreed upon, and it was decided that instead of driving the car to Hwagae, she'd drive it to the Dong Bang Hotel in Jinju that coming Sunday. We wanted to go to Jinju for the weekend anyway, and it would cut her driving distance in half.

It was early May and Korea was heating up. The temperature was quite lovely, the yellow dust was dissipating, and all plant life was in full bloom. We rode the bus to Jinju for the last time that Saturday. Over the weekend we hung out with the Jinju crowd, and I bought cleats from E-Mart so I could play soccer with the foreigner team on Sunday.

We withdrew the 1.3 million won we owed Michelle for the car, and as the largest monetary denomination available from the bank machine is equal to about twelve dollars Canadian, we stuffed pockets, purses, wallets, and cargo pants pockets with the huge wad of bills.

On Sunday I headed to the soccer field, and Dale headed to meet Michelle. I was the only female playing in the game. As the two teams lined up to shake hands at the beginning of the match, one of the Koreans we were playing against asked the guy next to me if I was playing. Me, standing there in full soccer regalia. Was I playing?

No, you sexist moron, these are my freakin' church clothes! I wanted to scream.

Instead, I smiled sweetly and said, "No, I'm just here for my looks."

The Koreans didn't catch my sarcasm, but the boys on my team chuckled, and the game began.

Anytime I made even a remotely good play the Koreans were extremely impressed.

"Good! Good!" they yelled at me. I must be some soccer prodigy.

The game went on. It was similar to other soccer games I played in before, aside from the playing surface. In the flourishing, fertile, lush country of South Korea, where people can grow things like nobody's business, they choose to play soccer on dirt. I might have seen three grass fields since I arrived here. It boggles my mind. If you fall on the dirt you suffer cuts and scrapes. The sweat on your skin accumulates layers of dust, creating a grimy film all over your body. When you run your tongue over your teeth, you discover a gritty coating of dirt in your mouth. You can just imagine the sopping, mucky mess that rainy day games become. Nonetheless, I was happy to be playing soccer instead of waiting for Michelle. After the game I went to a salon to have my hair cut and then caught a taxi back to Jenny's apartment to wait for Dale.

On the drive I noticed the taxi driver eyeing me in his rearview mirror. I assumed I must be looking quite good with my new haircut but in fact he was checking me out for different reasons. When he pulled over to let me out, he looked back and asked, "You Russia?"

"No! Canada!" I spat back at him and slammed the door.

At three p.m., the agreed upon time, Dale arrived at the Dong Bang Hotel, the same one Mr. Chang had put us up in our first night in Korea. Michelle arrived at six p.m. Her husband, who followed in his car, seemed annoyed, Dale was really annoyed, and Michelle just giggled. She gave Dale the keys and some papers, Dale gave her the big wad of cash, and they parted ways.

We drove back to Hwagae that night feeling free, confident, even powerful. I phoned an insurance agency in Seoul to arrange for insurance coverage, and we eagerly anticipated the upcoming Thursday when we would register the car in our name. Everything was going perfectly.

On Thursday I met Dale at the boys' high school, and we went together to get the car registered. I had asked Mrs. Kang to write us a note detailing what we needed done. It's amazing how much conviction a little piece of paper with some foreign words written on it instills in you. We were unstoppable, on top of the world, able to register any car you could throw at us. But we could not.

We handed the woman behind the counter all our papers and the note from Mrs. Kang. She began leafing through papers, stamping papers, printing out other papers. We really thought we were making progress. We even smiled when her co-worker came by to snap a picture of her serving the *waygooks*. Then she started talking to us in Korean.

We answered by pointing at and tapping the paper Mrs. Kang had given us, like it held all the car registering wisdom in the world, and this woman was some idiot if she couldn't read her own native dialect. But she was not satisfied. She pushed the papers back at us shaking her head. We pushed them back towards her again, pointing to Mrs. Kang's writing. She pointed to Michelle's name and mimed she wanted to phone her.

"Yeah, good luck with that," I said under my breath.

Of course Michelle didn't answer her phone. Even from across the counter we could hear the soccer anthem playing over and over.

We gave the woman our insurance agent's phone number, thinking he might be able to set her straight and make her register our car. That didn't work either.

She somehow figured out to call my middle school and tracked down Mrs. Kang, who had already left school but could be reached on her car phone. The woman talked to Mrs. Kang for a bit, and then handed me the phone. Mrs. Kang explained that the owner of the car had not provided us with the appropriate paperwork, nor had they signed the sale papers.

We collected our papers off the counter, smiled faintly at the woman, and walked out of the Hadong County Office with our tails between our legs. Our short-lived confidence had been shattered.

Later that evening, after numerous attempts at reaching Michelle, she phoned us back. Giggling between every word, she explained that the silver car she'd sold to us was, in fact, her brother's car, and she didn't know he needed to sign the sale papers, and she didn't know there was other paperwork she needed to provide us, and she didn't know her brother would be upset that she'd sold the car without him knowing, but she'd get it all straightened out soon.

Dale responded flatly, "When?"

She told us sometime the next week but said if we didn't want the car anymore, she'd give us our money back. We figured the process of returning the car to her and then shopping for another car would probably be more involved than actually following through with the silver car registration, so Dale told her we still wanted the car.

The weekend arrived, and we gazed longingly out the window at our silver car. Momentarily we were in a cartoon world, with the little devil on our right shoulder arguing with the little angel on our left. We didn't know what the legal implications of us driving the car without being registered would be. Michelle's insurance was still on the car, but would her insurance cover us in an accident?

"Maybe you'd better take the bus," the little angel said.

"What? The Loser Cruiser? Buses are for chumps! You aren't chumps. You have a car. It's yours. Go ahead. Everyone's doing it. What are you, chicken or something?" the little devil, who bore an uncanny resemblance to Biff from *Back to the Future*, piped back.

Dale did have his Korean driver's license, so legally he could drive in Korea. That had been another major hassle of a task, as there's only one building in our entire province where one can obtain their driver's license, and that building is located in some obscure place two hours from Hadong. Luckily, one of his colleagues offered to drive him there one afternoon. Dale had to do a vision test, fill out some papers, and five hours later his colleague dropped him off in Hwagae. Dale figured it would take a GPS and a miracle for him to ever locate the licensing building again, so my Korean driver's license hopes were put on the back burner.

That little devil, or rather our sense of adventure and yearning to get out of Hwagae, beat out our sensible, responsible side that Saturday.

Dale and I, in Michelle's brother's silver car, headed to the coast. Our destination was Namhae Island, the place Dale's Mr. Kim and his wife had taken us earlier in the spring. We followed road signs that, conveniently, are often written in English as well as Korean, and had no trouble finding the island.

The coastline was maybe not as dramatic but did remind us of driving the Cabot Trail in Cape Breton. There was very little flat area, and the mountains were tall and impressive. There were also many small, jagged islands peeking out of the water off the coast, and as we drove by I thought I'd like to live on one of those little islands. One acre of island, of complete solitude, maybe building an elaborate tree house village, with swings and ladders and slides grander than any *Swiss Family Robinson* could ever make. Dale doesn't seem as keen on the idea, but he does like the look of the islands. Some combination of water levels rising, and land sinking, had created these little mountainous pinnacles emerging like breaching whales from the sea.

As we drove, we discovered some of the many gems of Namhae. Probably our most exciting find was Garlic Land of Treasure Island. It's as magical a place as one could ever imagine – a whole village devoted to garlic. We couldn't believe our eyes when we read the words "Garlic Land of Treasure Island" on the road sign. And we were blown even further away as we drove into Garlic Land, with its garlic people statues, dancing garlics smiling from road signs, and the giant garlic factory that is indeed shaped like the biggest head of garlic I have ever seen.

We eventually reached Sangju Beach, a horseshoe-shaped stretch of sand that is touted as one of Korea's finest beaches. We hung out on the beach for a while, watching young Korean couples throw each other, fully clothed, into the water, and just enjoyed being at the shore.

Late in the afternoon we packed ourselves back into the car and headed for home. It was around suppertime when we crossed the bridge from Namhae to Hadong-gun. Dale and I chatted about what an excellent day of exploring Korea we'd had. We didn't get lost, and found everything and more that we'd set out to find.

We were driving up a hill at about fifty kilometres an hour, and approaching a sharp left curve in the road. A black car came flying around the curve towards us. Either the driver had taken the corner too fast, was drunk, was picking gum off his shoe, or some combination of the three. Whatever it was, the black car was centred not in his own lane, but atop the yellow line, and was rapidly crossing further into our lane towards us.

Dale saw the car but as his view of it was obstructed by the left windshield pillar, he didn't realize the car was headed straight for us. I yelled something incoherent, and pointed frantically out the windshield. Dale jerked himself forward, registered the danger, and swerved to the right.

The black car never corrected once. It kept coming towards us, and Dale kept pulling us further onto the shoulder of the road.

The black car hit us. Impact started around the front left wheel well, and it slid right down the side of our car. Our driver's side mirror exploded. Our car was bumped further off the road.

We both started yelling, "I can't believe he hit us!" as Dale brought our car to a stop.

We breathed deep, and looked back to see what happened to the black car. It was gone. It never even slowed down.

Dale jumped out and ran back down the road to see if the car had stopped out of our sight, just around the corner, but the black car had not. We surveyed our car's damage. It had fared well. Aside from the mirror being destroyed, the entire driver's side was scratched and dented. But it still worked, the alignment was fine, and we were alive. The little cartoon angel must have come along for the ride.

We didn't tell Michelle, her brother, or our insurance agent about the accident. And as angry as we were at the driver of the black car, who didn't stop to see if we were okay, we thought perhaps it was better that they hadn't stopped. Who knows how *waygooks* driving someone else's car would be treated following an accident with a Korean driver? Perhaps the driver of the black car would have turned the story around and said we had caused the accident. Would anyone have believed us?

It was our first experience with poor Korean driving, but it would not be the last. We had heard the stereotype, that driving in Korea was quite dangerous, and that turned out to be fairly accurate, at least around where we lived.

I've never once witnessed Dale beep his horn in Canada, but in Korea he uses it every few minutes. Cars pull out in front of us, cars stop on bridges in front of us to take pictures, cars drive down the middle of the road towards us, cars turn suddenly without using their signal lights, drivers here are forever doing the most absurd and dangerous things I have ever seen.

It seems that a red light is merely a stop sign. Stop, until you don't think anyone is coming, and then go while looking down to change the radio station. Stop signs don't seem to mean anything. Parking anywhere *near* a parking spot is a good parking job ... there is no regard for parking straight, for pulling all the way off the road, or for taking up only one parking space. It seems that being behind the wheel means power, selfishness, and time to catch up on cell phone conversations. I could go on and on, and so could Dale. But there's nothing we can do about it besides vent and be the best defensive drivers we can be.

I've talked about my impressions of Korean drivers to Mr. Kim the English teacher, Mrs. Kang, and Mrs. Bark. All three admitted that people drive too fast in Korea, and all three excused the dangerous driving by saying it is because people are in a rush.

"Koreans are very busy," Mr. Kim told me, proving my point of selfishness. The person behind the wheel has an agenda and schedule more important than any other person in the country. Therefore, all other people, drivers or pedestrians, had better not get in their way.

Mrs. Kang and Mrs. Bark both admitted to fleeing the scene of accidents they had caused. I had just finished telling them how angry we were at the driver who had hit us, and I realized it could just as easily have been either of the women I was sitting with, not the monster I'd imagine in the black car.

"You're kidding me? Right?" I asked.

"No," they said, both giggling and covering their mouths. They explained that they were embarrassed so they didn't stop. *To see if you'd killed anyone!* I silently fumed.

So perhaps South Korea does have some dangerous elements. I've driven in developing countries where there are no lines on the road, roads are in terrible repair and lack guardrails and other safety measures, and there seems to be no rules of the road. Yet it still seemed safer than driving in Korea. Maybe the problem is that South Korea is a little deceiving. The infrastructure is there and the roads are in impeccable condition. There are lights and signs and lines and lanes. I guess we expected the driving to be the same as in Canada and that drivers would adhere to road signs and rules and drive on their side of the road. But many people seem to drive as if lights and signs and lines and lanes don't exist.

Michelle phoned us the next week to say she'd faxed the appropriate paperwork to the Hadong County Office. Dale headed there that Friday to finally register the car. Mid-morning, I could hear Mrs. Kang across the teachers' office speaking in English. *That's strange*, I thought.

A few minutes later she was at my desk to tell me Dale had called her from the Hadong County Office. There was another problem preventing him from registering the car. Michelle's brother (or maybe Michelle) had racked up 250,000 won in traffic violation fees, and we couldn't register the car until the fines were paid.

"Ugghhh!" was my response.

We'd already planned a weekend away with the car, and we didn't want to take our chances again in a car that wasn't legally ours. Michelle, of course, could not be contacted right away. I imagined Dale was on the verge of an explosive episode in the Hadong County Office. I would have been. I told Mrs. Kang we'd pay the fine, just so we could get the car registered, and we'd get the money from Michelle later. She told me we couldn't do that.

I said, "Why not? Who cares where the money comes from?"

She was worried we'd never get the money back from Michelle. We battled back and forth for a few minutes on the issue. I wasn't going to lose, but I had to get her on my side, so she would call the county office to explain in Korean that Dale was going to pay the money. Eventually, she did call the office. The lady told Mrs. Kang that Michelle miraculously had been contacted and was depositing the money into the traffic violation fine bank account momentarily. In Korea, in 2006, you couldn't pay with a credit card or bank card in many places, and if you ordered something over the phone or needed to pay for something that wasn't in your town, you had to go to the bank and deposit the money into the business's or person's account.

Within a few hours the money had been deposited, and Dale was heading back to the county office to finally register the car. At about six p.m. that night, an SUV pulled into our yard, and Dale and a strange Korean man got out. Dale began to explain.

He'd registered the car, and then this man who worked at the county office grabbed a screwdriver and followed Dale outside, apparently looking for our car. The man didn't speak English, so he mimed to Dale that he needed to take the old license plate off our car. Dale mimed back that the car was in Hwagae. The man looked concerned, thought for a minute, indicated for Dale to wait a moment, and went back into the office. Moments later he returned with his jacket and his own car keys. He drove Dale a half-hour outside of Hadong – nowhere Dale had been before – along narrow, winding country roads deep into the mountains. Finally, they arrived at a shabby-looking house, with a baby sitting on a table in the yard and three people milling about. The man with Dale went into the house, and Dale waited outside and played with the baby.

This building, conveniently located smack dab in the middle of nowhere, was where one acquires license plates when one purchases a car. Michelle, or rather Michelle's brother's license plate, was registered in the province of Busan, and as we lived in Gyeongsangnam-do, we needed new plates. The plates were purchased, and the man drove Dale all the way to Hwagae, removed our old plates, and installed the new ones. This man was our saviour. Without him we'd never have found the license plate establishment nor been able to communicate with the folks there. Dale and I did our best charading to try to express to the man our immense gratitude, and we hoped he understood just how much we appreciated him.

NINETEEN

With the car we were able to pick up and go so easily. Pop down the road to grab something from the store. Take a spin up to the clay tennis courts that were a few kilometres away. Drive ourselves further up the valley to explore Chilbulsa Temple where Mr. Chang and Mr. Bear had taken us months earlier. Or go to the closer temple, Ssanggyesa, to hike into the beautiful Buril waterfalls. Having the car really made us feel more free, more in charge, and like we were more part of the community somehow.

The car made socializing a bit easier as well. One day, my grade three middle school student Hye Weon invited us to swim at his parents' house. The next weekend, Dale and I met Hye Weon at the middle school in our car, and we drove to his house with him guiding us along the way. His family lives up a long, narrow, winding road that meanders into the mountains. A few others had taken residence along the right side of the little road, and the mountain dropped away on the left.

That day began a wonderful friendship. We already knew Hye Weon was a great kid. He was my top student, could speak English quite well, was helpful and cheerful, humble and out-going, and always kind to others. He achieved his scholarly success without attending extra private school classes, as many of his classmates did. He just studied diligently on his own and had an amazing family who encouraged him to work hard at school, but to also be well-rounded. His mother had him listen to English radio and watch English television, and he was an integral part of running his parents' house. I don't remember if Hye Weon told us his parents' names that day, but we ended up always affectionately calling them Mr. and Mrs. Hye Weon, and referred to the family as the Hye Weons.

The Hye Weons had moved to this rural part of Korea from Seoul years ago. They didn't like city living and wanted to bring up their two sons in the fresh air of the mountains. Mr. Hye Weon is a former Korean military diver, and Mrs. Hye Weon is an artist. Now the family farms green tea, mushrooms, peppers, radishes, and persimmons at their incredible mountain retreat. Hye Weon has a brother, Jye Weon, who is a few years older. During our visit he was away, completing his military service. Hye Weon told us Jye Weon was stationed at the demilitarized zone (DMZ), the border between North Korea and South Korea.

Dale and I liked Hye Weon's parents the minute we met them. They were at ease with us and didn't try to impress us. Also, they didn't try to swing free English lessons from us, as had been the case when we were invited on outings by other people. The Hye Weons were genuinely interested in being our friends, and we very quickly felt the same. They even had a dog – a pet dog they had no intention of eating. He was a short-legged roly-poly little mutt that followed us around their property.

Hye Weon and his dad walked with us to a river near their house. The river ran down the mountain, through pools and over waterfalls, as it flowed. Mr. Hye Weon had cleared rocks out of one of the pools to create a swimming area. There were small waterfalls we could sit under and let the refreshing mountain water pour over us. There were boulders as high as trees we could jump from into the deeper pools. It was a magical place.

After swimming, Mrs. Hye Weon had a full meal prepared for us. We talked as we ate, and Hye Weon sometimes helped his parents translate. His dad didn't know much English, but Mrs. Hye Weon was quite good. We loved that they never acted embarrassed or ashamed about their English skills.

I think they liked how impressed we were with their house, and we truly were. Mr. Hye Weon showed us some of the many things he had fixed or built. There were large hand-cut logs used for stairs. Some of the windows were secured in place with mud. Beneath the rug in the living room was a cement floor which had a large fire pit underneath it. The fire was accessed from outside the house and when lit, the living room floor became cozy and warm. At harvest time they would dry vegetables by laying them on the floor and keeping the fire lit beneath.

On the walls hung some of Mrs. Hye Weon's art. One of her paintings, a thick bamboo forest with a snowy path running through it, was life-size and so realistic it seemed as though the painting was a window one could step through and take a walk along the forest trail.

The house was homey, and rustic, and remarkable, and they made us feel so welcome. The Hye Weons were proud of their home and confident in their way of life. We loved that.

* * *

I decided that enough was enough with our car's backseats. They *had* to fold down. We turned and pushed and pulled at anything that looked as though it was meant to be turned and pushed and pulled, but nothing would bring the seats down. Then we yanked and shoved and kicked, and still nothing.

I emailed our friend Harrison back in Nova Scotia, who has owned many a station wagon. He thought the seats would most definitely go down, and he suggested a few places to look for release buttons. Dale and I headed back out to the car. It was then that I noticed the leather seat covers were an addition by some person who enjoys peeling their bare legs from leather seats in the summer ... my guess was Michelle. From the trunk I reached my arm up under the leather covering, felt around along the top of the actual seat, and discovered the release button. "Take that, Michelle!" I said with great maturity, as the seats flopped forward. I really wanted to call her to tell her that she was wrong about the seats, but I knew she wouldn't answer and I didn't want to listen to her ringtone, and I'd like to think I'm a bigger person than that.

As luck would have it, the elementary school keeps all their gym mats piled under a shelter very close to where we park our car. The first nice weekend after the seat folding discovery, we "borrowed" a gym mat in the dark of night, loaded the car with blankets and pillows and beach things, and headed to Sangju Beach.

We spent a wonderful day on the beach, ate and drank at a nearby restaurant, then slept in the car for the first time.

While sleeping in the car is convenient and free, it's not as amazing as we thought it would be, not like sleeping on an air mattress in our old Toyota Previa van, with a space heater and Keno to keep us warm. Sleeping in the back of the Avante was significantly less romantic. The seats don't fold down to the point of being completely flat, so we're always sliding towards the trunk door on the slippery gym mat. And the gym mats aren't as cushiony as we'd imagined, so we spent the night turning every few minutes to relieve aching body parts. Mosquitoes attack us if we have the windows down even a crack, and the small interior of the Avante gets mighty smelly when we sleep in it following a big pork dinner. Think extreme "Dutch Oven."

Within a month of registering the car, we'd accomplished three traffic violations. The first we knew of was a parking ticket we received outside the E-Mart in Jinju. Dale and I were both fit to be tied, as we'd parked on the side of the road, as everyone else does, to avoid the long lineup of traffic heading into the E-Mart underground parking. That ticket cost us about forty-five dollars Canadian.

As we pulled out of the parking spot, Dale made a u-turn, and immediately we were pulled over by a cop; infraction number two. Luckily, he knew no English. He yelled at Dale in Korean and made wild hand gestures, and Dale just responded, "What?" The cop eventually got frustrated and waved us off without giving a second ticket.

The next Tuesday, while I was working at the elementary school, the vice principal informed me of the third violation.

I was sitting with my back to him on the other side of the room, preparing for my classes, when I heard him say something loudly. Eun Hye, the administration lady, who was sitting near me, looked up and then looked at me. He repeated what he said, and this time I heard, "Bess-uh, drive-uh fast-uh." I had absolutely no idea what he was talking about. It sounded like he was saying that I drive fast, but I rarely drove as I didn't have my license, and I couldn't imagine how he would know how fast or slow I drove. Again, he repeated, "Bess-uh, drive-uh fast-uh."

I looked at Eun Hye, who unpredictably had the best English of all school staff, for help. She spoke to the vice principal in Korean, and then he came over to me and handed me an envelope. It was addressed to Dale, and it was already open.

Inside was a speeding ticket that had occurred while I was driving. I knew this because the ticket had a picture of me driving the car at the time of the incident: not my head but an overhead pic looking down through the windshield. They were definitely my legs, and not Dale's, in the driver's seat. The date on the ticket said it was from a couple of weekends earlier, and I remembered that it was another day we had gone to Sangju Beach in Namhae. Dale had consumed a few beers, so I had driven home. I had noticed traffic cameras in different areas on the roads when we were out and about, but must not have noticed this one. I was clocked going seventy-eight kilometres an hour in a sixty-kilometre zone. That fine cost us about thirty-five dollars Canadian.

It seems as though barely anything with regards to traffic is policed here, but somehow we end up with two fines in a week. Motorcycles and scooters drive down the sidewalks and through crowds of pedestrians at crosswalks. People on motorcycles and scooters are required, by law, to wear helmets, but many do not. It is illegal to have more than two people on a motorcycle or scooter, but we see three or more, none of whom are wearing helmets. We see babies in women's arms instead of car seats, truck beds laden with people, and vehicles going through red light after red light.

I guess I should consider myself lucky that I was caught by a camera, and not actually pulled over, as I didn't have a license. Still, I was a little angry about the speeding ticket. And *really* angry that the vice principal had opened our mail and read it.

But our little silver car has given us so much freedom to explore and do it on our own schedule that our car-owning spirits could not be dampened. Even repairs didn't get us down. That might be because our car repairs have been more convenient, and less expensive, than any work we've ever had done in Canada. The first thing we needed to do was replace the driver's side mirror which had exploded in the collision. Parts and labour cost less than a hundred dollars Canadian.

Since then, we've had a flat tire just about every other week. Each time it was from driving over a nail. We're not sure where all the nails are coming from. If we had that many flat tires in Canada, we'd be broke. But each flat tire we've had in Korea has taken a brusque, yet kind, mechanic less than fifteen minutes to repair, and cost us only five dollars. The tire is quickly taken off, nail found and removed, a piece of something shoved in the hole with some goo, and we're on the road again in no time.

June Man's dad has been our tire repair guy a number of times. Dale's limped the car to downtown Hwagae, by the bus stop, where June Man's dad has a garage. As with all other mechanics we've encountered in Korea, he works quickly, cheaply, skillfully, and gruffly.

Next to the garage is June Man's mom's store. The family lives in the apartment behind the store so often we encounter June Man or one of his sisters while we're shopping there. His mom, like his dad, seems very serious and most times she doesn't even use her calculator to total our purchases or tally the change. We try to win her over by acting gracious and using our limited Korean vocabulary when we speak to her. Despite her sober façade, the corners of her mouth curve up ever so slightly when we smile and bow and tell her "*Kamsahamnida!*"

* * *

On a weekend adventure to Busan, our radio stopped working during the drive. Then the lights on the dash went out. The next time the highway took us through a tunnel in the mountains, we realized we had no headlights or taillights. I don't like driving through tunnels in the best of circumstances and often find myself holding my breath until we've emerged on the other side. In this tunnel I was on the verge of hyperventilating. Oncoming traffic couldn't see us until the last second and cars flashed their lights at us in warning – as if we didn't know our lights weren't on. Dale could barely see the road and I worried we'd get rear-ended. There was nothing we could do but drive and hope we found a garage before dark.

At the next city, which was Masan, Dale took the first exit and miraculously we immediately came upon a little garage. Through gestures and pointing at things, we told the mechanic what we suspected to be wrong – the alternator was done. He nodded in understanding and got on the phone. After a quick call, he looked at the clock on the wall and held up two fingers. We guessed he was telling us it would take two hours. Then he led us into the waiting area, which was also the living room of his family's home. A woman we assumed to be his wife brought us a tray of watermelon slices, and we sat with her and her two children to wait. They shyly spoke a few words of English to us, and we drew pictures and coloured with the kids on their coffee table. Eventually, a van careened into the driveway, and a driver delivered the new alternator. Shortly after that the mechanic was finished. He charged us less than a hundred dollars, and the whole family was there to wave us off – giving us bottles of juice as we departed. It was possibly the most pleasant experience I've had at a garage.

After getting our new alternator, we continued on to Busan. It was surprising that we were even on this trip, because after we'd visited big cities like Busan and Dajeon by bus, we'd vowed we'd never go there by car; they were too busy and confusing. Little road trips from Hwagae got our confidence up, though, and we started getting used to the road signs and driving customs. Nevertheless, Busan was not an easy city to navigate. Dale was the driver, and I was the map and sign reader, and between us we managed to arrive at our destination, Haeundae Beach – a one-and-a-half-kilometre-long stretch of sand at the southeastern end of the city.

Busan, and specifically Haeundae Beach, is famous for waves and Dale wanted to go surfing. We found the only surf shop, Surfer's Dream, rented inflatable boards, and walked a couple of blocks to the beach before deciding where the waves looked best. We'd never used inflatable surfboards before, but they seemed solid and Dale was able to catch lots of waves and I caught some too. There were a few other people surfing and some young people burying each other in the sand.

I was taking a break on the beach when I heard a whistle blowing. A lifeguard was frantically waving at someone in the water. I looked out and saw it was Dale. He looked at the guard, waved, and then turned back to the ocean to watch the swell. The lifeguard blew on his whistle once more, and continued to wave at Dale, indicating he should get out of the water. Dale looked at him again, shrugged, and again turned away. The lifeguard continued to hail him. Dale caught a wave towards the beach, and the lifeguard stopped whistling and waving, and walked towards him. As soon as Dale's wave ended, he hopped back on his board and started paddling back out.

The lifeguard started blowing his whistle again.

I walked over to him and asked what was wrong.

"He must come out of the water," he replied.

"Why?"

"Because surfers must wear shirts."

"Why?"

"For safety."

"You mean a life jacket?"

"No, a shirt, for safety."

"A shirt isn't going to save him."

"The surfers must wear shirts so we can see them."

"But you can see him. Does everyone who goes in the water need to have a shirt on?"

"No, not swimmers. Only surfers."

I thought about that for a second. Nobody was swimming, and there were only a handful of *very* visible surfers in the water. Also, I knew Dale didn't have a rashguard or any shirt appropriate for swimming to put on.

"You must get him to come out of the water," he told me, blowing his whistle and waving again.

"Me? How am I supposed to get him?"

"He must come out of the water. You must get him," he insisted again.

I didn't feel like going into the water so I turned and went back to my towel to watch. The lifeguard finally gave up whistling and waving, and quietly watched as well.

When Dale did come out of the water, the lifeguard went to him and gave him a stern lecture. Dale promised to wear a shirt next time.

Another spot we enjoyed in Busan was Seongjong Beach, a short drive from Haeundae. Seongjong was smaller and a bit quieter, but also had good waves. Randomly, and perhaps part of the reason we liked this beach so much, was that there was a restaurant you could see from the beach that advertised Nova Scotia lobster. It had a large Nova Scotian flag on the side of the building and each time I looked at that flag I felt a bit like I was home.

* * *

Because I didn't have a driver's license, I didn't drive the car very often. Sometimes I'd switch with Dale if we were on a long trip and the stress of the drive had tired him too much. Really both roles were stressful and tiring. The navigator had to do some very quick street and city name translation, and had to manage our giant map. The driver had to constantly be defensively driving, always expecting cars to do the unexpected. To make navigating even more difficult, sometimes the street names or driving instructions were painted on the street, in the lane in front of you, so you had to get it read before you drove over it.

One day as we were driving, with my window down halfway, the map I was reading was suddenly sucked out the window and gone. My hands didn't even move. The shock of it left me sitting in the map-reading position, without a map to read.

Sometimes I took the car on my own for an errand in Hwagae. On one such occasion, as I drove along, I be- came aware of a movement near my left hand (which was on the steering wheel). I glanced in that direction, and emerging from one of the vents, was a big, ugly, leggy, menacing praying mantis. It didn't matter at all that I knew the insect was not dangerous. It was big and scary, and it was staring at me.

I would rather have a bee or a wasp in the car any day. I can manage getting stung and safely pulling over. I could not manage a stare-down with a praying mantis. It crawled on the dash until it was just in front of both of my hands and sat there watching me, perched like it was about to attack. The few glances I stole at its little alien face led me to believe that it was waiting for the right moment to leap onto me, wrap its six legs around my face, and suck my blood.

I removed my left hand slowly from the steering wheel, cranked my window down, and gripped the steering wheel again. I then removed my right hand and, staring just above the praying mantis's head at the road, picked up a book from the passenger seat beside me. In a swift movement, still keeping my eyes on the road, I whacked the praying mantis out of the window. A quick glance at the dash and another at the back of the book assured me that it was indeed gone.

I started breathing again.

TWENTY

One sunny day, we discovered the Jirisan Spa, a huge public bath facility. I'd read about Asian public baths in our Korea book: about relaxing in various types of saunas, soaking in mineral baths and green tea baths, and scrubbing away all the yellow dust and dirt of life.

There was a bath house in Hwagae, but I wasn't ready for that one. I needed practice before I bathed publicly in our little town, where everyone knew me. It wasn't that I was shy. I had been to Europe and exposed my bits and pieces to the beach breeze. But public nudity in Asia was a first for me. I worried that perhaps I was different – perhaps my muff was crooked or my breasts were oddly shaped. And what if I ran into a co-worker, or a student? With my luck, one day I'd walk into my classroom and find a nude caricature of my atypical Canadian anatomy exaggerated all over the chalkboard. So we decided on the Jirisan Spa. It was a bath house in a neighbouring province, miles from Hwagae and my students, and a place where we could discreetly break ourselves into bath house culture.

Dale and I drove into Jeollanam-do, the next province to the west, and towards the signs for the Jirisan Spa. While the skies were clear from clouds, we noticed patches of yellow haze suspended above the mountaintops. It was the first time we could actually see the yellow dust in the air, coming to get us. We'd been breathing it for two months, but I'd read in *The Korean Times* that sweating and scrubbing the skin was the best way to rid the body of the yellow dust's toxins. This visit to the spa would benefit us in more ways than one.

From the outside, the building looked like a big sports complex. We paid the 7,000-won fee (about eight dollars Canadian) and parted ways; Dale headed off to the male spa and I to the female. I went through turnstiles, up stairs, and into a large locker room. There was a counter just inside the door, and a woman behind the counter gave me two hand towels and a locker key. I found my way to the locker, stripped down, and stuffed my clothes inside.

At the entrance to the baths, I looked around. It was a large room ... the size of a room containing an Olympic-sized pool, but instead it was comprised of a variety of smaller wading pools. I stood there, stark-naked, surrounded by equally naked Korean women. As the lone naked Caucasian, in a sea of naked people, I began to reevaluate how discreet I was being.

To my left, three sauna doors lined the wall. To my right stood a row of toilets – no stalls, no doors, just toilets. I looked away as a lady chose a bowl and lowered her bottom. Across the room were rows of shower heads mounted at chest height. I watched as a woman turned on one of these mini-showers and crouched beneath it on a red plastic stool. *Sitting down to have a shower?!* I scoffed at her laziness.

At the far end of the room was a wall of windows looking out onto a small patio area. The patio boasted beautiful flowers and shrubs, and it backed onto a large natural rock formation. There were another two wading pools outside, one with a waterfall that was spewing water straight from mountain springs. Women soaked in the baths or lounged around on benches, under the sun.

I was one of about a hundred women visiting the Jirisan Spa, and I appeared to be the youngest by a number of years.

Feeling a bit watched, I tried to act as normal as I could, as though I'd been to the bath house hundreds of times before.

I sauntered around and stuck my hand in various pools. Some were hot, some were frigidly cold, and some were just tepid. I was Goldilocks, and each pool was my porridge. I chose a lukewarm bath tucked into a corner of the room, slipped into the refreshing water, and began looking around to see what everyone else was doing. My attention was immediately drawn to the groups of women who were viciously scrubbing the living life out of each other. Women bent over plastic stools, while others straddled them and savagely scrubbed their backs. Veins protruded from arms and back muscles bulged.

I had questions. *Did they know each other? Was everyone okay with what was being done to them? Did they have a safe word? Am I going to be involved?*

My hand protectively went to my lower back, thinking of my sun tattoo – the one my dad had said resembled "bird shit." Fearing they might throw me face down and try to scrub it off, I backed up against the wall of the pool, so nobody could see my posterior. Then, as sneakily as I could manage, I pulled myself out of the pool and sidestepped my way to a sauna.

I couldn't remember if I'd ever been in a sauna. I knew sweating would be involved, but I just wasn't familiar with the degree of sweating, or the feeling of dying.

I had brought a magazine along to pass the time, and planned on spending a good forty-five minutes to an hour sweating out all those nasty toxins from my body. Within five seconds in the tiny room, I was sweating profusely. Sweating was happening from the usual places, as well as some new ones … fingertips, end of my nose, toenails. Before long, the perspiration was dripping onto my magazine, the pages became soaked, and I no longer had the dexterity to turn them. I put the magazine down. It was intense to say the least. When I breathed, I could feel my lungs perspiring, *or were they expiring?* I couldn't be sure, but I knew it wasn't good. My nostrils burned when I inhaled, and my skin burned when I fanned it with my magazine. I started to see stars. I started to feel panicky.

What if I lose consciousness? I felt an uncomfortable sweltering sick feeling deep in my gut. After mere minutes I was stumbling towards the door. I threw it open and gasped for air. I scanned the crowd to see if anyone noticed my laboured exit. *Had they been timing me, and did they know that I was a sauna failure?* Defeated and dizzy, I staggered to a mini-shower, collapsed on a plastic stool, and doused myself with cold water until I was no longer faint. *So this is why there are stools and sit-down showers.* The realization came as I started to feel myself again.

I'd forgotten to bring my own washcloth, so I used one of the spa's hand towels and started to scrub the sweat and filth from my skin. I was in my own little scrubbing world when a woman, two stools down, began making a deep guttural noise. I jumped a little. *Did she need medical assistance?* Nobody seemed to be too concerned for her and she continued. It seemed she had some major phlegm she needed to get rid of, and she was going to do it four feet from me.

I watched women coming and going from the three saunas, and none of them appeared to be in any kind of medical distress. Determined not to be defeated, I headed towards a different sauna, the middle one.

It was a dry sauna, lined with some type of wood. There was a woman sitting cross-legged on the floor sipping from a canister. She offered it to me. I know it's rude not to accept things when offered, but I was fearful it was a canister full of that horrible ginseng juice Mr. Chang had fed me months ago, and with the heat of the sauna I feared I might vomit. Smiling, I bowed and waved no. She appeared mildly disappointed but began a calisthenics routine as I sat down. The heat was different in this sauna, not as harsh. I set my watch and for ten minutes I persisted, watching the lady on the floor sip her drink and stretch herself into various naked positions.

Feeling confident that I had mastered the sauna, I headed out for another scrub and soak, and then through the doors to the outside area. What a wonderful feeling it was to be naked in the great outdoors, feeling the warm sun and breeze all over my body. I was surprised by how many others were also bathing in the sun. Women in Korea often carry parasols on sunny days, and wear dark visors and gloves to protect their hands and faces in the summer. But at the bath house, the women were relaxing under the sun and splashing around in the outdoor pools unreservedly.

I sat near the waterfall for a few minutes, but my competitiveness got the better of me and I went inside to see if I could conquer the third sauna.

On my way I discovered a reflexology path – a strip of floor with rocks protruding from the cement. A poster on the wall diagramed how walking on the rocks activated pressure points in the soles of the feet which triggered health benefits elsewhere in the body. Of course I needed some of that! I made it three steps along the path. Sharp pain shot through my feet and up my legs, my waist and knees buckled, and my arms fanned out like a large awkward emu trying to take flight. I figured with all the time spent barefoot along the rocky coastline of Nova Scotia, this little rock path would be a piece of cake. It was not. I stepped off the path and righted myself. Just then an elderly woman passed me, walked gracefully to the other end of the path, turned around and came back. I went to find a tub to soak away my shame.

I never mastered the rock path, but I considered our visit to the Jirisan Spa a success. I liked the pattern of soaking, sweating, scrubbing, and repeating. And I found that the Asian female body was no different than mine. Every bit and piece was located in the same place, and their muffs were not unlike my own. I was ready for the Hwagae Bath House.

I headed there two weeks later, on a Sunday evening when I was feeling particularly grimy. Hwagae's bath house was a smaller version of the Jirisan Spa – a cozy locker room, a bathing room with mini-showers and three pools (hot water, hot green tea water, and frigid cold water), and two saunas. I nabbed a plastic stool and began the cleansing process.

The place seemed fairly busy for its size, but when I entered the sauna to begin my first bout of sweating, I was pleased to find it empty. I sat on the bench and relaxed. After a few minutes I became aware of someone looking at me through the window of the sauna door. I turned my head to find one of my grade five students with her nose and hands pressed up against the glass, smiling and waving at me. I smiled and waved back. *Please don't come talk to me. Please don't come talk to me,* I repeated over and over in my head. The little girl now had her head turned and was speaking to someone else, beckoning for them to come. Moments later the sauna door opened, and in walked my student and her mother.

There's really nothing more horrific than a naked parent-teacher meeting. I was mortified. The encounter became especially interesting because my student was too shy to use any of the English she had learned, and her mother, who seemed very eager to talk to me, didn't know any English. *What should I say? Where should I look?* The conversation became one of charades and gestures, the naked mother running naked on the spot to indicate she's seen me jogging in Hwagae, with naked me tapping my head and giving a naked thumbs-up to indicate I think her naked daughter is a good student.

After this first Hwagae Bath House experience, I surprised myself by becoming a regular visitor. I did, however, think that perhaps Friday morning visits might be less risky for encounters with people I knew. I could go after the students had started school and still be on time for my ten a.m. class.

My plan worked. The mornings were much less busy at the Hwagae Bath House and I was always one of only five or six women, none of whom I knew. However, I soon came to recognize the other Friday morning regulars. As I never did get comfortable with naked conversations, I didn't get their names, but I fondly thought of them descriptively: Buddhist

Monk Lady, Coughing and Spitting Lady, Naked Calisthenics in the Sauna Lady ... This last woman was very surly-looking, so I always tried my best to stay out of her way in the tiny little sauna while she did naked push-ups and 1980s-style naked aerobics. When finished she sat down next to me and proceeded to stretch and burp.

There was also Swimming Lady, who became my bath house hero. Every Friday morning, she swam lengths in the little pool of frigid water. I wanted to be like her.

At first, I could only get my feet in the cold pool. The water was numbing like the Northumberland Strait in May. I knew, though, that cold water baths offer tremendous health benefits. So, as with the sauna, I was determined not to give up.

After a few weeks of dipping my body further and further, I was able to get my whole self entirely in the pool. I immediately kicked and flailed like mad, so I wouldn't lose feeling in my extremities. Total body ice cream headache ensued. When I exhaled, I could see my breath, my skin became tauter than ever before, and my heartbeat was deafening in my ears. *Is this what health feels like?* I wanted to get out, but worried I hadn't received all the health benefits yet, so I eyed the red button on the wall.

Swimming Lady had pressed the red button numerous times, and then frolicked beneath the water that gushed from the ceiling. However, when I pressed the button a torrent more powerful and painful than I could ever have imagined was unleashed upon me. It pounded and pelted me. It might have bruised me. I cowered below it, and by the time it was finished with me, I felt battered and nearly drowned. On the plus side I was no longer bothered by the freezing water. I was now numb from the thrashing. Gasping, I draped myself over the side of the pool to recover.

After the red button incident, I was no longer willing to try anything new at the Hwagae Bath House. I steered clear of the lineup for The Body Buffer – the machine that had women rubbing their bodies against a spinning disc attached to the wall, like a cat rubbing against someone's leg.

I also avoided The Earthquaker. Like The Body Buffer, I didn't know the actual name of the machine but named it myself. The Earthquaker stood in the locker room and had a little platform for women to stand on. Users wrapped the machine's wide belt around their waist, leaned back to make the belt taut, and pressed go. Much naked jiggling ensued. The belt vibrated the naked person, particularly in their naked abdominal area, and this would lead to health benefits, I assume.

My Friday morning retreats at the Hwagae Bath House have become one of my favourite experiences in Korea. For one hour a week, amongst the pools and the saunas, the scrubbing and the sweating, I become one of them, just another one of the bath house ladies. *Which one?* you might ask. I'd like to think Canada Lady or Teacher Lady. But I would be happy with Bird Shit on Her Back Lady.

TWENTY-ONE

We made it through yellow dust season relatively unscathed, although I did end up with a nasty cough that wouldn't go away. Eventually, I asked one of my colleagues where I should go to see a doctor, and later that day Mr. Kim the English teacher drove me further up the valley into the mountains, to a little building where a woman gave me a shot of something in my bum, and a handful of pills. She wanted to put me on an IV, but I declined. I didn't really notice any difference after the injection, and I didn't take all of the pills, mainly because I wasn't sure just what they were. I did a lot of coughing, and slowly as the yellow dust went away, so did the cough.

I had to miss some of my morning jogs, because I couldn't jog and cough at the same time. As well, I was starting to believe that my exposure to the yellow dust on my morning jogs might have been the main contributor to the cough. Not being able to run was very disappointing for me, but I'd like to think that the person who was even more disappointed was Dale's bus driver.

He was a man who I wouldn't be able to recognize if I saw him standing on the street, but someone I recognized by the giant bus he drove past me every morning during my run. He was also a man who, at some point, without ever meeting me, made a connection with me; we were kindred spirits of the early morning hours. I knew we had connected when one morning, as he passed me, he flashed his lights. I kind of noticed the first day. The second day when it happened, I looked around to be sure there was no car he might be flashing his lights at – to let them know their lights weren't on or to warn of a cop down the road. There was only me. The third time he flashed his lights at me, I got a warm and fuzzy feeling inside, and I waved and smiled back.

I told Dale about my new morning relationship, and the next time when he came home from school, he told me he'd sat near the bus driver so he could watch. He confirmed that the bus driver, as he passed me, both flashed his lights and smiled shyly.

I was a little bit in love with the bus driver.

*　*　*

The end of yellow dust season meant that summer was approaching. Public school teachers in Korea, as in most countries, enjoy a paid vacation over the summer and winter. In contrast, most Hagwon teachers only got seven days off over their entire year contract. Dale and I were so thankful to have public school contracts as it meant we were to have four weeks off during the summer *and* winter. I don't think Mr. Chang had completely thought this through when hiring us, and was quite surprised to learn we were planning a trip outside of Korea for our vacation time. I think he assumed we'd want to kick around the school with him during this time.

Well, perhaps he knew better than to assume we'd want to hang out with him. That ship had sailed. I did my best to avoid him at school, and he interacted with me very little. Each time he was awkward or rude, or some combination of the two. So no, we decided not to knock around Hwagae for our summer vacation but instead planned a trip to Bali, Indonesia.

We'd explore the island, Dale would surf, and I would relax on a beach.

Hwagae Middle School did manage to rope us into working for a few days before we left. Mr. Kim the English teacher had organized an English Summer Camp for the students, and Dale and I would be camp leaders. It was still "school" but it was more casual school. The kids got to wear their regular clothes, no school uniforms, so the event had a fun and less formal vibe to it. Activities included English classes each day, a "beach day" where we walked to the river behind the school and swam in a pool where it was deep enough, a Hwagae Idol singing competition, and a games day.

Thankfully, "games day" was relatively tame compared to what we'd experienced previously. At the middle school I'd been involved in a competition amongst teachers where we all had to jump on one foot, while holding the other foot in our hands. The object was to ram each other hard enough to make someone else let go of their foot – or fall over. I anticipated I would be quite good at this game, being athletic and having pretty good balance. But I had no idea just how vicious and powerful my female co-workers could be. I also didn't really expect anyone to take it seriously. I was wrong!

It was a frenzied, hopping throng of grown women dressed in business casual, ricocheting off each other. Young Miss Kim, always so timid and quiet, lined me up and took me out, with one solid ramming. I saw her coming, but was completely unprepared for how hard she was going to hit me. The jolt sent me flying, scaring the bejesus out of me. I assumed she must do this in an amateur league somewhere. The rumble continued until there was only one left standing – on one leg. It was truly one of the most ridiculous yet aggressive things I'd witnessed in Korea – possibly anywhere – and I was shocked that we all emerged unscathed. And despite my competitive nature, I was not at all upset that I was the first one out. I was terrified.

Games days at Dale's schools were not much different. At the girls' high school, Dale had asked if they would play soccer.

"No, Mr. Knowles, they are girls," was the response.

So instead of a friendly game of soccer, the girls engaged in barbaric activities such as "chicken" competitions, where two girls wrestle while sitting atop two other girls' shoulders. This was okay for girls, but soccer was not? There was also a sumo-like competition, where girls wrestled until the winner slammed the loser hard into the dirt. And there was a game where girls threw water balloons to their partner, thirty feet away, who was to catch it in a basket atop her head. I don't believe one balloon was caught successfully.

Our English Summer Camp games day yielded zero injuries, and it capped off a pretty good time with our students.

The only game even remotely violent was called "Shoot the Tish." This was Mr. Kim the English teacher's idea. He talked about it excitedly the previous day, so Dale and I were eager to find out what shooting a "tish" involved, and what exactly a "tish" was. *Was something going to die?* We'd been told there were wild pigs in the mountains that everyone considered a menace. *Were those tishs, tishes, tishi?*

When Shoot the Tish time came we were left quite underwhelmed. A tissue, your basic everyday Kleenex, was tacked to a target and the kids had to shoot the tish with a water gun. The winner of the game was the person who soaked their tish first, causing the tish to deteriorate and fall limply to the ground. It was not an idea we would be bringing back to Canada.

Hwagae Idol was decidedly our favourite English Summer Camp activity. The kids were very into it, and they had so much fun. One of my students, who has a very serious personality, did a rendition of "The Lion Sleeps Tonight." When he got to the part where he needed to "*aweem away*," he did it with the least gusto and intonation he possibly could, like a record was stuck on those two words. His voice neither rose, nor did it fall.

Hye Weon did an amazing performance of the Turtles' "Happy Together." Not only was his pronunciation excellent, he had a beautiful singing voice, and performed with confidence and a commanding stage presence. Dale and I and Mr. Kim all voted Hye Weon to be the winner of Hwagae Idol.

* * *

I had often mentioned my excitement of the coming summer to my students. I love summer. I've always been a summer person. I talked about hot sunny days, going to the beach or riding bikes, or just playing outside. My students always seemed confused. I wasn't using difficult vocabulary, so I was confused about their confusion. Then I learned what they all knew and I had yet to find out – that summer is rainy season in Korea.

It is humid, it is wet, it is a truly terrible time of year. I couldn't believe that I could ever be that annoyed, and disgusted, by weather. But I was. I was a horrible person to be around.

We had to run our air conditioner constantly in order to be comfortable and to be able to dry our clothes inside. We'd shower in the morning but be wet by either rain or sweat (or both) within minutes of leaving the house. We'd shower the minute we came in the door from school, and we went through more umbrellas than I have ever owned in my life. Some just wore out from overuse, but many were left on the bus by Dale. He'd made a habit of leaving his things on the bus: umbrellas, gloves, hats. He did manage to get one toque back, but never any umbrellas.

I was just a miserable person leading up to our summer vacation, and I couldn't wait to get out of Hwagae. We bused to Seoul and spent a couple of days at Rod and Crystal's apartment in Incheon, an adjacent city. Dale had worked with Rod in Nova Scotia, and he and his girlfriend Crystal had invited us to crash at their place.

While Incheon was still rainy and humid, it was a nice

change from Hwagae. The first day we were there, Rod and Crystal went to a Black Eyed Peas concert, so Dale and I amused ourselves. Our main goal of the day was to buy supplies to make nachos, something we hadn't eaten since leaving Canada. Cheese, salsa, and chips – we didn't think it would be a huge task in a big city with lots of amenities.

It was Saturday, however, so the stores were incredibly busy. Everywhere we went we had to fight through throngs of people and Dale's patience was wavering as he hates both stores and throngs. We went to Lotte Mart first. There we found nachos and salsa but no cheese. So we set out in search of another store and discovered an E-Mart. This store did sell cheese, but we didn't have enough cash to buy it, and the bank machine in the store wouldn't work for us. Back to Lotte Mart we went to find a bank machine that would give us money. Returning to E-Mart with our nachos, salsa, and cash, we bought the cheese and eagerly made our way to Rod and Crystal's to indulge in our victory.

Oh, how our mouths watered for those nachos. Oh, how we couldn't wait for the cheese to melt and drip around the sweet salsa and crispy salty chips. Oh, how hard we'd worked for them – yet another grocery expedition that challenged the bond of our marriage.

The toaster oven chimed that the nachos were ready and as Dale carried the tray of piping hot, mouth-watering nachos to the table, the most scrumptious-looking nachos I had ever seen, he dropped them. All over the floor! I was in tears. Dale was in a rage.

Thankfully we hadn't used all of our nacho supplies in the first tray, because there was *no* way we were going shopping for more. Our marriage couldn't survive it. Begrudgingly we assembled another tray, sat silent and awkward as they baked, and held our breaths while Dale gingerly and carefully transported them to the table. They were the most delicious nachos I have ever tasted. It might have been one of the most delicious meals I have ever tasted.

In the evening, Rod and Crystal returned home, covered in mud from the rainy outdoor concert. We relayed our nacho saga to them, every detail and every emotion. Perhaps they were too tired and muddy, or perhaps they took for granted their city conveniences. Rod and Crystal did not seem to find the story anywhere near as climactic or impressive as it seemed to us.

The great nacho disaster of Incheon closely rivalled the great ramyeon disaster of Hwagae from a month earlier. On a day when I was feeling completely done, done with Hwagae, done with Mr. Chang, and done with my students, all I wanted was to tuck into a piping hot bowl of ramyeon concoction that Dale had made. Once that food was in my belly all would be right with the world again.

All I needed to do was to take my bowl of soup from the kitchen to our bedroom and find a comfy seated position on my side of the bed so I could see the movie we were about to watch on our computer. As appalling as it was, we'd made it a habit to eat dinner in bed while watching a movie. It was the most comfortable way to do it, as our living room chairs were sticky and weird and the little kitchen table and chair set was not comfortable nor conducive to watching a movie and so we ate in bed. And we were not ashamed of it one bit. Well, perhaps a little bit.

One day, months into this nasty habit, I had recalled aloud that *Sesame Street* sketch where Ernie eats cookies in bed and Bert explains that it is a terrible idea because he'll get crumbs in the sheets which will result in crumbs in his pyjamas which will cause itching and then Ernie won't be able to sleep.

Despite Bert's warnings we continued to eat food in bed and this night in particular I moved a bit too rapidly, perhaps a bit too eagerly. As I neared the bed I faltered and I dropped the bowl of ramyeon all over my side of the bed. Noodles, vegetables, pieces of egg, and all that spicy broth in my bed, in my sheets, soaking into the pillow and the mattress.

And so I cried. I stood and stared at the mess and I cried over my spilled ramyeon that I just wanted to eat. And that's when Dale came and he took the bowl and the spoon and he put them in the kitchen and he got paper towels and rags and cloths and he gathered up the chunks of food, and he removed the sheets and put them in the washing machine, and he scrubbed the mattress and the box spring, and the base of the bed, and the floor, and everywhere that ramyeon ended up and he told me to sit on his side of the bed and he got me another piping hot bowl of ramyeon and served it to me and if that isn't true love, I don't know what is.

*   *   *

The day before our flight to Bali I phoned a transportation line to ask what time we should catch the airport bus. The lady asked where we were located, and I said Incheon. She told us a time, and the next morning we set out, excited for our trip.

What I hadn't accounted for was that she might have not known exactly where we were in Incheon. The city is the third biggest in Korea, smaller only than Busan and Seoul. Wherever we were when we caught the bus, it was a *very* long way from the airport. Or perhaps the bus we caught did not take the most direct route. Our drive to the airport took a painful hour and a half when we were anticipating about twenty minutes. We meandered through industrial park after industrial park and arrived at the terminal with no time to spare.

Grabbing our bags, we ran to the check-in counter and waited in line there only to find out we had to go somewhere else first. We needed to fill out paperwork stating that we would, in fact, be coming back to the country after our trip. It was a step we hadn't anticipated, so our anxiety was at a max as we raced around the departure terminal.

Once the extra paperwork was completed we ran back to the first lineup, through check-in, sprinted to Security, and on through the airport towards our gate. I've never had to run like that for a plane. It was a horrible feeling. A feeling of utter helplessness. If we weren't about to miss our flight, I might actually have enjoyed it. Dodging in and out of people, just trying to keep Dale's backpack in sight. It was like we were in a video game, and we played it so well that we did manage to make our flight.

On our way to Bali we had a stop in Singapore. I wasn't looking forward to this, as the layover was twelve hours long, but it turned out to be quite enjoyable. The Singapore airport has been voted the best airport in the world many times. We took a bus tour of the city and watched a free movie in the airport movie theatre. If we'd had more time, we could have toured the city on foot or worked out at the free gym.

Bali was both a wonderful and horrible trip. We did all the things we wanted. Dale bought a surfboard and surfed some of the breaks he'd dreamed about. At the end of the trip, he got the tattoo he'd been wanting for years. I had a massage and a facial, relaxed in the sun, and shopped. And we both loved the sights and adventures.

We took a boat over some of the deepest waters in the world to the island of Nusa Lembongan. We visited temples, enjoyed the amazing coastline, and watched world-class surfers on world-class surf breaks, like Dreamland and Uluwatu. It really was a dream vacation. Except for the fact that I went a bit crazy.

I didn't sleep at night. I lay awake listening to the ocean … and thinking we would be devoured by a tsunami at any moment. I was paranoid, and often cranky. It was strange and uncomfortable and confusing and very frustrating, for both of us. Toward the end of our stay, I started suspecting that the malaria medication we'd been taking might have had something to do with it. And then I made the discovery.

The medical clinic we went to in Hadong, prior to our trip, prescribed us Lariam for the prevention of malaria. A little research online told me that in the U.S. and abroad, numerous cases of psychosis, aggressive behaviour, homicide, and suicide had been linked to Lariam. I didn't usually experience side effects when I took medication, but Lariam definitely affected me, and I couldn't wait for it to be out of my system.

* * *

When we returned to Hwagae we found our house had been taken over by an intruder. Mold covered the sticky fake leather chairs in the living room. Mold was growing in large patches on the walls. Mold covered most of the clothes we had left behind. It was appalling. Rainy season hadn't let up and we hadn't thought to run the air conditioner while away to keep the house dry.

On the air conditioner went, the washing machine was fired up, and I began scrubbing.

It took days of listening to the washing machine singing, and wading through dirty water each time we had to use the washroom, before I had all the clothes clean. Garments were strung up here, there, and everywhere throughout our house, as it was too rainy and humid to dry anything outside.

I considered returning the small herd of Thirsty Hippo dampness eaters to the grocery store in Hwagae and asking for a refund. I had bought the pink boxes that depicted smiling hippos and contained kitty litter or some other moisture absorbing material, thinking they would fend off the moisture in our house while we were away. I was wrong. The herd I had bought was no match for Korea's humidity in the summer. It left me wondering just how many herds of hippos it would have taken to save our house from the mold infestation.

It was around this time that I started going down to the river to cool off. The difference in temperature due to elevation was dramatic. As I walked down the hill and onto the valley floor I immediately felt more comfortable. There was a cement pathway with rice paddies on one side and the riverbed on the other and it was like there was an invisible fogbank of cool air luring me towards the riverside of the path. I'd climb down onto the rocks and find a place to sit and soak my feet in the refreshing water. Even just dipping my feet seemed to lower my body temperature and cause an immediate improvement in my mood.

One day, as I soaked my sweaty feet, I discovered a man skinny-dipping a little upstream from where I was sitting. The river wasn't very deep where we were so he was doing less skinny-dipping and more skinny-wading. I was sure he hadn't been there when I walked past earlier, but he and and all of his naked parts were definitely there now.

In silent commitment, neither of us decided to acknowledge the other's presence. Without gawking too much I watched as he, my naked accomplice, waded around in knee-deep water, splashing and cleansing himself. For my part I continued to sit on my rock perch and soak my feet, letting the air and water return me to a person that could be tolerable to live with.

After I was feeling my normal self again, and a bit after that because I was waiting for him to depart first, I gave in and stood to leave. Pretending that naked men in rivers is an everyday occurrence for me, I climbed back up onto the cement path and walked towards home. I didn't look towards him as I passed, honouring our secret pact that he didn't see me and I didn't see him. Instead, I stepped over his clothes that he'd laid out on the lane and kept looking straight ahead.

That marked the last day that I went down to the river to soak my feet and cool off. And I never saw my naked friend again, although I don't know that I'd recognize him with his clothes on.

TWENTY-TWO

Returning to work after summer vacation was sobering. I could sense there was something wrong as soon as I walked into the elementary school. All the teachers and staff were very quiet, and the vice principal was crying. Eun Hye came over to me and told me one of the teachers had died the week before. He had been on a camping trip with a group of children and got into a car accident after he'd returned the kids to their homes. She described to me which teacher it was – the man who worked with children who had special needs.

He was a kind and gentle-looking man, likely in his late forties. He always spoke to me on Tuesdays when I was at the elementary school, extending to me a warm greeting and a smile. He seemed very patient, a calm and quiet soul, as he helped his students. It was a tragedy.

* * *

As with all tragedies, the hardest part passed. Weekly routines were re-established and school life went on.

Our fall progressed much more ordinarily than our spring. Perhaps it was because we had become accustomed to life in

Hwagae, or perhaps it was because Hwagae had become accustomed to us. Probably it was a little of both.

Mr. Chang eventually decided that teaching math in English was no longer a good approach, and he tasked me with developing a conversational English curriculum. This gave me lots of work to do at my desk in the teachers' office. I wrote everyday scenarios, such as going to the bank and taking public transportation, developed PowerPoint slides and worksheets, and gave the students tests. The kids really seemed to prefer the new format and material.

I got to know Eun Hye better, and we talked every Tuesday when I was at the elementary school. She and I were about the same age, and she was so fluent in English that we could have conversations like two old friends. And we *were* friends ... as much as two people who share an office space once a week can be.

Dale and I got back into our after-work routines. We often played basketball with my students following school on Fridays. Only the boys came, but there was always a crowd, despite the stipulation that they had to speak English during the game. The kids learned sports terms like, *Pass. Shoot. Dribble. Good shot!* and it was really fun to bond with them in that setting.

If we didn't go away on the weekend, we usually ate at our favourite pork barbecue restaurant in Hwagae. It was owned by a lovely young couple, who had a son in the first or second grade at the elementary school. They were always very welcoming when we dined there, and the experience of the meal was wonderful. As with many Korean restaurants, the meat was brought to us raw and we cooked it on the grill that was set into our table. By this time, we'd learned the ins and outs of this style of dining, and we loved it. Perilla leaves were served with our meal, and we wrapped the cooked meat, kimchi, and other side dishes in the broad leaves, before eating the delicious bundle.

Sometimes we headed southwest from Hwagae, to a little city called Suncheon. We'd go in the afternoon, shop for anything we needed in one of the big department stores, indulge in a meal at Outback Steakhouse, go to a movie, and then drive home.

Dale connected more with Kimon and started jamming with him. The two of them, along with some other foreigner friends, played a few gigs at a bar in Jinju.

The middle school added new bathrooms at one end of the school, and each stall contained an actual sitting toilet. And the elementary school tore out the old, squeaking, metal playground equipment and replaced it with a colourful, safer, and quieter playground for the kids.

We fit back into our life in Hwagae quite well, and we noticed that our days had come to feel perfectly normal.

* * *

One week, Candace emailed to ask if she and some friends from Daejeon could visit for the weekend. That same week, the Hye Weons invited us to their house again. I explained to Hye Weon that we had guests coming for the weekend. When I saw him next, he said he'd spoken to his parents and they would love to have all of us to their house.

Saturday morning Dale drove to Gurye, about a twenty-minute drive west of Hwagae, to collect the crew from Daejeon from the train station. There were six of them, plus Candace's two dogs — she had gotten a second little one named Charlie. We knew Candace and Sarah from home but now there was also Chris from Compton, Sopheap from Ontario, Joel from Wisconsin (who looked just like Leonardo DiCaprio), and Kevin. Kevin was a surprise.

I had gone to school with Kevin and his brother since I'd moved to Dartmouth in grade four. He lived in my neighbourhood, and we even went to the same church, back when we both went to church. I found it remarkable that three of us – Kevin, myself, and Sarah – who went to the same junior high and high school, all randomly ended up in Hwagae for a weekend together.

We were a party of eight, ten with the canines, when we parked at the bottom of the Hye Weons' road and walked up the mountain to their house. I worried there might be too many of us, and I didn't want the Hye Weons to have to feed us all, so we'd brought rolls of kimbap (similar to sushi but made with Korean flavourings) with us to share.

Mrs. Hye Weon had not only planned to feed all eight of us, but also five more of my students, friends of Hye Weon who shyly grouped themselves off to the side through most of the visit.

We all swam and jumped in the mountain springs as Hye Weon had done with Dale and me during our earlier visit. When we finished swimming, Mr. Hye Weon lit a fire on the bank above the swimming holes, and over the open fire Mrs. Hye Weon cooked a feast of meat and vegetables for us all.

It was an amazing afternoon filled with cultural learning and appreciation for everyone. Our friends from Daejeon were grateful for the rural Korean experience after spending all their time in the city.

*   *   *

A few weeks later we invited the Hye Weons to dinner at our little house, to return the generosity they had shown us, and to spend time with them again. We served the rice mixture we'd been perfecting over the past months. In that time, we'd added hot pepper paste (called *gochujang*) to the recipe, as well as a mystery liquid Mr. Bear had given us. Other than knowing it was edible, we weren't sure what the liquid was or how to use it. It was thick like molasses, very sweet, and it may or may not have contained alcohol. We decided to add it to our rice stir-fry, and the result was delicious. The Hye Weons seemed to enjoy it as well.

Dessert was apple crisp that I'd nuked in the microwave, as we didn't have an oven. I learned this method of cooking apple crisp from my mom, who always cooks hers in the microwave. Dale finds this method appalling, but he doesn't seem to have any trouble eating it.

The bigger problem with dessert was that I couldn't find butter in Hwagae, so I'd made the crisp with olive oil, giving it an unfortunate olive oily flavour. Some vanilla ice cream might have masked that flavour, but I'd been tricked by desserts in Korea one too many times. On numerous occasions I'd purchased ice cream and other sweets that contained what I thought to be chocolate. I was then horrified to discover the chocolate was actually beans – "sneaky beans" as we learned to call them. Apparently the beans I'd coveted so much when we first arrived in Korea had been there all along, hiding in the desserts: throughout ice cream and ice cream bars, inside pastries and other baked goods. I started feeling uncomfortable anytime I bought sweets and the only time I felt truly secure that I was buying sneaky bean-free ice cream was when we went to Baskin Robbins.

Missing decadent chocolate desserts from home, I even commissioned my mom to mail us her famous Rice Krispie Rollup. It took over a week to arrive and we were thankful that it didn't accidentally get shipped to North Korea first, like another package she'd sent. Despite being less fresh and crisp than we were used to, that entire Rice Krispie Rollup, infused with chocolate frosting and containing zero sneaky beans, was devoured in one evening.

I didn't want to risk serving apple crisp with vanilla ice cream only to discover the ice cream had been implanted with sneaky beans. So we all ate the crisp, sans ice cream, and kept any complaints we might have had about the olive oil taste to ourselves.

The five of us chatted through dinner, sometimes with the help of Hye Weon's excellent translation skills. At one point the three of them started talking very seriously in Korean. They spoke rapidly for a minute or two, as Dale and I watched, and then they seemed to come to a decision. Hye Weon explained to us that there was a little stray puppy living around the middle school. I knew of the dog, as I had seen this puppy a couple of times in front of the Old Lady's Store. Hye Weon had just told his parents about the dog and asked them if he could take it home as a pet, and his parents had agreed. We liked them even more.

*   *   *

The first week in October was Chuseok. This is one of the most important celebrations in Korea, and it occurs on the fifteenth day of the eighth lunar month, in either September or October. Traditionally, families gather to celebrate the harvest, share food and stories, and honour loved ones who have passed away.

For Dale and me, Chuseok meant more time off from work, so we decided to take a road trip. We packed a gym mat and headed to the east coast. Dale brought the new surfboard he'd bought in Bali, and he hoped to catch waves from a storm that would pass through during the Chuseok holiday.

We spent a little time in Busan before heading up the coast, passing Korea's industrial capital, Ulsan. Some nights we slept in the car, and some nights we found a room. Finding a hotel room was always an interesting task. We had discovered that some hotels are known as "love hotels." It's not their actual name – just what they are referred to. These were often the cheapest accommodations available but weren't always the nicest. We weren't picky and had stayed in many "love hotels" in Jinju and Busan. We just considered them crappy hotels. But, one day, when inquiring about the availability of a room, the person at the front desk asked us how many hours we'd like the room for. That's when we learned about "love hotels."

During Chuseok, we visited small towns, so we took what accommodations we could find. While none of them were "love hotels," none of them were very cheap either. But the night the tropical storm blew through we were happy to pay anything to not sleep in the car.

Unfortunately, the surf didn't pan out much for Dale, but we enjoyed driving along the beautiful coast, ate lots of delicious Korean food, and discovered some amazing hikes.

*   *   *

Later in the fall, some of our Daejeon friends came to visit again. Dale, Kevin, and I had signed up for The First White Sand Green Pines Hadong Seomjin River Marathon Festival and Challenge. Dale was running the ten-kilometre race, while Kevin and I would run the half marathon. Miss Kim, from my middle school, had told me about the race and then helped us register for it. She and her brother were running the ten-kilometre event. Also running with us was Craig.

Craig was an Australian, in his thirties or forties, I had met when I attended an event with teachers from my middle school. He was an English teacher in Sacheon. Both being foreigners, we had gravitated to each other and sat at the same table. In our brief conversation, the Hadong race had come up, and we exchanged contact information as he was interested in signing up for it as well.

Over the next few weeks, Craig started calling our house. Each time we spoke there were things that seemed a bit off about him. He expressed to me the frustrations he had with his co-workers, as well as his students. He told me he'd thrown a desk.

When I told Dale about Craig, he thought he was likely just lonely. I wasn't so sure but maybe getting to vent to another

English teacher might help him. As the race approached, Craig talked about the logistics of getting to Hadong early enough for the race. I let it slip that friends were coming to stay at our house the night before and we'd be travelling to the race together in our car. Craig seemed interested in that plan, so I felt I had to invite him to join us.

The night before the race Kevin, Candace, Sarah, and Sopheap, along with Candace's two dogs, arrived. There was one queen-sized bed in our spare bedroom, and we took some gym mats from the elementary school, so everyone had a place to sleep. I made a big pasta dinner to help us carb load for the race, and Dale lit a bonfire in the yard.

Craig arrived in the midst of it all. He had gotten a drive to our place with one of his colleagues. He seemed a little awkward at times, but then again, he didn't really know anyone in our group. I continued to give him the benefit of the doubt.

The next morning, we all piled into the Avante (some in the trunk!) for the drive to Hadong. My race did not go as well as I would have liked. I'd overdone it on the carb loading the night before and had consumed a bit too much junk food, which made me feel sluggish during the run. It was too bad that I didn't feel better, as the race was a great route. All flat, out and back, leaving from Hadong and snaking towards Hwagae along the Seomjin River. Aside from being one of the few *waygooks* in the race, it all felt much like any race I'd done back in Canada, with people lining the route to cheer us on and water stations which kept us hydrated. My race time was two hours, four minutes, and forty-nine seconds. It was great to have completed the race, but I had been hoping to better my personal best of one hour and fifty-one minutes.

Everyone else was happy with their race performances. Dale had never run ten kilometres in his life before that day, and Kevin ran his personal best. Sweaty and a little sore, we all made our way back to Hwagae.

When we got to our house, Craig discovered that Candace's dogs had gotten into his bag. There didn't appear to be any mess, other than a few things strewn about the floor, one item being his toothbrush. Craig flipped out. He threw the toothbrush across the room, and his voice went up an octave as he ranted about the dogs getting into his stuff. Things became uncomfortable. My doubts had been correct.

A short time later, after Dale and I had a quick, private meeting about Craig, Dale informed him that it was time to leave, and he would drive him to the bus stop in Hwagae. Craig didn't want to leave. He hadn't had a shower yet, he told Dale. Dale told him again it was time to go … and opened the door for Craig to follow him. Late in the afternoon the group of us walked to town to have supper. All of us were nervous that Craig might still be lurking around Hwagae but we didn't see him anywhere. We never saw or talked to Craig again.

On the Monday after the race, when I arrived in the teachers' office, Miss Kim came right over and congratulated me.

"Thank you. Great job to you too," I said to her. We had seen each other immediately following the race and had expressed our congratulations then, so I thought it was odd that she was congratulating me again.

"No, you came third!" she said excitedly.

"No I didn't, my time was terrible," I told her.

"No, look. You are third!"

She showed me a newspaper with the race results, and in my category (under thirty female), I had indeed placed third. I eventually received a race booklet and on the cover I could see myself in the crowd of runners. Mostly I could see Kevin, because he is a lot taller than me, but once I spotted him I could kind of see me beside him. Listed in the booklet were all participants' names, written in Korean, speckled with a few English names, including mine. Eventually a prize and a special certificate arrived for me. It said *3 위* (third place). That third place felt a little more special.

TWENTY-THREE

On the 22nd of December we went to Daejeon to have a little Christmas celebration with Candace and our friends there. A bar owned by two Canadians hosted a full turkey dinner, and after our night of festivities we walked out of the bar to find a couple of inches of snow had fallen. If our Christmas had just been the snowball fight we had that night, and the turkey dinner with friends, I would have been happy. But we were fortunate enough to have a Korean Christmas as well.

The next day we travelled back to Hwagae and on Christmas Eve, Hye Weon and his dad picked us up. Their SUV had no backseats, so we bumped around on the floor for the ride up the mountain. When we got to their house, I was thrilled to find the dog they had rescued a few months earlier. It had grown a little taller and fatter, and was enjoying its mountain life immensely. Their friends from Jinju were also there to celebrate Christmas Eve. They were a kind young couple, with a ten-year-old son.

We spent much of the afternoon making homemade *mandu* – Korean dumplings. Mrs. Hye Weon had made the dough for the outer shell of the dumplings, and her husband was using a glass bottle to roll the dough flat. The bottle was so old and had been used for this task so many times that you could see the wear on it. A mixture of meat, vegetables, and kimchi had been prepared as a filling for the dumplings. Mrs. Hye Weon taught us to take a spoonful of filling, place it on the flat dough shell, wrap the edges of the shell around the filling, and then mould and pinch the shell closed to create a perfect little dumpling. With expert hands she showed us that the shape the dumpling formed should resemble the head of a person wearing a bonnet.

In Korea it is said that if you can make a beautiful dumpling, you will have beautiful children. We tried our best, but our dumplings did not resemble a person wearing a bonnet. I silently apologized to any future progeny we might produce.

Once made, the dumplings went right into a big pot of soup to cook, and soon after we ate them. They were delicious and incredibly filling. Perhaps Dale and I were still full after breakfast and lunch, or perhaps everyone else had been fasting all day in anticipation of the dumplings, but we were able to eat far fewer than everyone else. Little Mrs. Hye Weon must have eaten at least fifteen. I wanted to eat more but could only manage about five.

The family from Jinju left in the evening and we all went to bed. Dale and I were given the room above the living room and kitchen area. We ascended the log steps Mr. Hye Weon had built to a room with massive windows framing an amazing view of the mountains.

Christmas morning, Dale and I, along with Hye Weon and his mom, went for a hike further into the mountains. The scenery was even more magical than usual, as there was snow in places and the air was crisp and clear.

Before we'd gone too far, we came upon a yard where a TV crew stood amongst a large collection of clay kimchi pots. A man with a video camera and another with a microphone were interviewing a lady in her fifties or sixties. The man with the microphone saw us and waved us over. After talking in Korean with the TV crew, Hye Weon explained that they were interviewing the woman about her kimchi and they asked if we could taste it, *on camera,* and give our impressions. Dale volunteered me.

I stepped forward towards the camera and its bright light. The woman reached into a kimchi pot, pulled out a long piece of kimchi, dripping with spicy red sauce, and held it toward my mouth. *Was she serious? Did she want to feed it to me – with her bare hands?* With the camera right in my face, I tried my best not to look too shocked or disgusted by the hand feeding. I managed a half smile and opened my mouth as she shoved the kimchi in. I chewed and smiled and nodded and eventually swallowed. Glancing around I saw the kimchi lady, and Dale, and Hye Weon, and Mrs. Hye Weon, and the camera and microphone guys, all looking at me with anticipation. I stared directly into the camera lens and gave my heartiest *"Mashisoyo!"* along with two enthusiastic thumbs-up.

* * *

Just prior to winter vacation we sold our car, the guitar, Dale's skateboard, and the surfboard he bought in Bali. Dale took the surfboard to Surfer's Dream in Busan to sell on consignment, and a guy named Eben bought the skateboard and guitar. We felt there was a bit of fate happening, as he had the same name as one of Dale's closest friends back home.

The only person who responded to our car ad was a guy named Fernando Montenegro. *What an amazing name!* we thought. He too lived in Busan. Conveniently, the same weekend we got rid of the skateboard, surfboard, and guitar, we met with Fernando so he could test-drive the car. He didn't commit to it that day, so we were forced to drive it back to Hwagae. We heard from Fernando later the next week and he told us he'd purchase our car. Dale made another trip to Busan where he and Fernando spent hours in the vehicle registration office trying to get the sale and transfer sorted out. It was then Dale discovered that because the process was so complicated and arduous, there were actually people you could hire to help navigate the paperwork and lineups. He and Fernando managed to figure it out on their own and in the end, the car was Fernando's and Dale took the bus back to Hwagae with 1.6 million won in his pockets – about four hundred dollars more than we paid for the car.

* * *

After our Korean Christmas with the Hye Weons, we made our final preparations for winter vacation. School was shut down for the month of January, and we had booked flights to Southeast Asia. On New Year's Eve we flew to Bangkok, ringing in the New Year in a taxi on our way to our accommodations. For the next four weeks we travelled by taxi, boat, train, bus, bicycle, scooter, motorcycle, and tuk-tuk. We went from Bangkok, overland to Siem Riep, in Cambodia. Then by river to Battambang, and overland down to Kampot. We crossed into Vietnam and made our way from Ho Chi Minh City, all the way up to Hanoi.

By this point in our relationship and our travels it had become obvious that we each had our own strengths and weaknesses. Dale was the money guy. He could figure out currency exchanges, and totals, and what our change should be, just as fast as a shopkeeper using a calculator.

I was the navigator and the language gal. I had become quite adept at reading maps and I also had a great sense of direction. If we'd been somewhere I remembered exactly how we got there. And I did well using the little bits of foreign language we needed to get by. I could listen to a native speaker and do a pretty good job of matching the accent to help us be better understood. This division in labour and roles served us well. But if Dale had to do the talking or find our way back to our lodgings, or if I had to figure out how much that purse in Bangkok was going to cost me in Canadian money, we'd be sunk.

Our strong bond and teamwork abilities also served us well during a harrowing experience in Cambodia. We were in Kampot, a small town where we'd spent a day volunteering at a school. Late afternoon we walked from our accommodations to a restaurant about a kilometre away. There we ran into another Canadian named Warren, whom we'd travelled with when crossing the border from Thailand into Cambodia, and for that long dusty drive to Siem Riep.

The three of us ate and chatted throughout the evening, catching up on each other's travels. After darkness fell we decided to return to our accommodations and Warren offered to drive us both on the back of the motorcycle he was renting. We declined. I wasn't comfortable squeezing three of us onto a bike, even though it was common practice in Asia. Dale and I set out on foot and the further we got from the lights of the restaurant the darker the night became. There were no streetlights and no houses had any lights turned on. Had everyone gone to bed? We could barely make out the faint glow of our accommodations in the distance so we walked hurriedly in that direction.

Soon the growling began. At first we could hear just one dog but one dog quickly became many. We'd seen lots of dogs along this street earlier in the day. They were all mutts, many of them likely strays. In the heat of the day they barely moved, spending their time cooling off in the shade. By daylight they weren't the least bit intimidating. However, in the dark their presence felt much different. We couldn't see the dogs, only hear them, and they seemed to be getting closer. Walking beside me, Dale said we needn't worry – the dogs were definitely behind fences. I didn't remember seeing any fences during the day and was not reassured.

The dogs got closer and closer and the growling became more vicious and I knew there were no fences and I was fairly confident that the dogs weren't tied or restrained in any way. Soon there was at least a dozen dogs circling us. I could feel a hot wet nose touch the back of my leg. This was not good.

As we continued walking Dale and I simultaneously shifted our posture so our backs were slightly angled towards each other. We each had a half-filled bottle of water and we hit it as hard as we could with our free hand, trying to be loud and intimidating. And we started yelling. My voice came from an intense mixture of fear, anger, and adrenaline. I had never been this scared in my life. We kept walking and banging and yelling and the dogs kept circling us. They growled, and barked, and gnashed their teeth at our heels. Fur brushed my legs. Their breath was on my skin.

Finally, as we neared the lights of our accommodations, the dogs started to drop off. The growling lessened. And by the time we arrived the dogs had quieted and become part of the night again.

The relief that swept over us was incredible. I don't know how long the episode lasted, perhaps only a few minutes, but it felt like forever and once the adrenaline wore off we were left exhausted.

Dale told me he thought it was funny that I had been yelling in Korean.

"What do you mean?" I asked.

"You were yelling in Korean. At the dogs. '*Hajima!*' and '*Sikkeureowo!*'"

"Really?" I replied.

"Yeah, you actually sounded really angry and scary. I hope you don't talk to your students like that," he said jokingly.

I hadn't even realized I was yelling in Korean. At this point I still only knew a handful of Korean words and phrases. But, when I thought about it, the Korean translation of "Don't do that!" and "Too noisy!" did seem much harsher and more intimidating than yelling the same thing in English.

It was likely the lights from our accommodations and the fact that the dogs were getting further from their territory that made them eventually leave us alone. But I like to think it was my Korean fight or flight response that saved us.

*   *   *

There was a lot of excitement in the air when we returned to school following winter vacation. Some of our students had gone on trips of their own and were keen to share their experiences. The music teacher at my middle school was eager to relay that she'd seen us during our vacation. I assumed she meant at the train station in Gurye or perhaps in Seoul catching the plane. But she had actually seen us from her tour bus at Angkor Wat in Cambodia.

Hye Weon had also gone travelling and sadly wouldn't be returning until after we were back in Canada.

Even Eun Hye had some vacation news for me. When I went to the elementary school on the first Tuesday after the holiday, she told me she'd gone on vacation and gotten married.

"What? Congratulations!" I replied with shock.

She showed me an album full of wedding photos. I couldn't even recognize her. Eun Hye, like me, doesn't wear any makeup, and often her hair is pulled back in a ponytail. Mostly she wears jeans with t-shirts or baggy sweaters. She is a beautiful woman but again, like me, is very plain and not fancy. The woman in the wedding photos was *very* fancy. She was dressed in a beautiful traditional Korean wedding gown, but she wore so much makeup, and the pictures were so retouched, that it could just as easily have been *me* in the photographs.

I told her how beautiful the pictures were, and then I made the comment that I couldn't keep to myself. "I didn't even know you had a boyfriend!"

"Oh yes, I had a boyfriend," Eun Hye replied.

"How long have you been seeing each other?" I asked.

"Oh, not long," she said.

Then she got very quiet beside me and glanced around to see that nobody was looking or listening.

"I have baby," she said, barely above a whisper, and pointed to her stomach.

"Oh. OH!" I tried my best to hide my shock and keep my voice quiet like her. "That is wonderful news, Eun Hye. Congratulations again!"

* * *

The Hye Weons invited us to celebrate Chinese New Year with them in February. Hye Weon was still away but his brother Jye Weon was there, having time off from his military service. Their friends from Jinju came as well, and again we made delicious dumplings.

According to the Chinese Zodiac cycle, 2007 is the year of the pig, so we rang in the new year with a bottle of champagne and a pig-shaped cake. We didn't think about it at the time but this visit would mark our last time at their home, as well as the last time we'd see Jye Weon and the lovely family from Jinju.

Over the next days we did more and more "lasts": taught our last classes, bowed and left the teachers' office for the last time saying, "*Annyeonghi gyeseyo!*", waved one last time to the bus driver ...

For our final weekend in Korea, Candace and our friends from Daejeon came to visit again. This time eight of them made the trip and we did one last tour of Hwagae with them. We visited the market, watched a man forging knives, and wandered down onto the parts of the Seomjin riverbed where the winter waters were low in anticipation of the spring thaw.

We dined once more on *pajeon* and *dongdongju* and even *soju*, and at the end of the weekend we walked with them to the bus stop in Hwagae and watched them leave.

With a mix of sadness and excitement, I began filling up our suitcases. Dale thought we should leave everything except our clothes behind, but I found room for my new soccer gear as well as the towels and bedding we had bought. After all, we weren't lugging his skateboard back to Canada and I'd managed to use up a few bottles of the moisturizer I'd brought.

The night before our departure from Hwagae, Mr. and Mrs. Hye Weon stopped by our house to say goodbye. She had told me she wanted to give us one of her paintings and I had told her I would like to buy one. We decided to do both so she brought the two paintings with her and I safely packed them away. We hugged and bowed and promised to keep in touch, and then said our final goodbyes. We would miss the Hye Weons most of all.

In the days leading up to our final exit from Korea, we had wondered aloud what our actual departure would look like. *Would Mr. Chang come?* We didn't think so, and we were right. Instead, and much more to our delight, Mr. Bear came to see us off. If we had any regrets in Korea it would have been that we didn't spend more time with Mr. Bear. There were still many things we wanted to know about him and his family.

One day, when exploring downtown Hwagae, we happened upon a little store filled with toys and stationery and candy. A handsome young man we guessed to be slightly younger than us asked, in perfect English with a North American accent, if we needed any help. We were floored. Where had this guy come from and why wasn't he already our best friend? We complimented him on his second language skills and introduced ourselves as the ESL teachers in town. He said, "Yeah, I know. My father works at the middle school. This is his store."

"Who is your father?" we inquired.

"Mr. Bear."

I'm sure we startled him with our overly excited reaction and gushes about how much we loved his father, but he didn't seem startled – indifferent and bored, but not startled. In fact he didn't seem to find us even the least bit interesting. The interaction left us with a bit of wanting: wanting him to like us and to want to hang out with us, like everyone else seemed to. But he did not. We decided he might just be the coolest guy in Korea, second to his father of course.

We never saw Mr. Bear's son again so we never got another chance to win him over. But Mr. Bear being present for our Hwagae departure more than made up for it. We still couldn't communicate with him very well, but we tried to express to him through gestures and simple language that we really appreciated him and had great respect for him. He smiled and nodded and as our taxi pulled away he waved. Mr. Bear capped off our year in the most perfect way.

In the airport after check-in, we found a restaurant and ate our last meal in Korea. It was *kimchi chigae*, a delicious traditional stew served in the traditional way – piping hot in a stone pot with a bowl of rice on the side. It was a dish we'd grown to love.

And so it was with our noses running and Korean spices still on our tongues that we boarded a plane and left Korea for good.

EPILOGUE

It would be fourteen years before we'd eat *kimchi chigae* again. Back in Canada, Dale and I started new jobs and changed to other new jobs. We had Keno back, along with a second dog, Lixie.

I returned to Asia one time, not to South Korea, but to China. I was part of a group of ESL teachers who won a trip through the company we worked for. I was surprised to again be asked to pose for pictures with complete strangers. There were seven of us but for a reason none of us could figure out, I was singled out of the group to have my picture taken.

In fact, as we were exploring the Forbidden City with throngs of other tourists, a man walked right up to me and thrust his very chubby sleeping baby into my arms. My first thought was that he was going to run and this boy was now mine. My second thought, as I gazed down at this adorably squishy bairn, was that I was totally fine taking him back to Canada with me. But the man didn't run. Instead, he wanted to take pictures of me holding his child. After a few photos, a lady I assumed to be the baby's mother arrived on the scene and seemed much less enthusiastic about the fact a strange woman was holding her baby. I'm not sure if her anger was directed more at me or her husband, but she quickly took the child from me and I was forced to return to Canada with some new chopsticks instead.

Dale continues to avoid grocery shopping, shopping of any kind to be more accurate, and I am still plagued with random and embarrassing injuries. Just this week, while jogging lightly across a parking lot, my ankles momentarily forgot to function and I found myself flat on my face on the asphalt – jeans, knees, palms, and pride all torn.

Candace stayed in Korea for several years before moving back to Nova Scotia with her dogs. We see her occasionally and when we do we reminisce about our adventures in Korea and how much we grew to love Korean food.

Every so often I hear from Eun Hye. She no longer works at Hwagae Elementary School, but has become a stay-at-home mom to a little boy. And Mrs. Kang emailed once to say she and her two sons had visited Canada in the summer.

In the fall of 2008, I discovered I was pregnant and around the same time, we got a call from Hye Weon. We'd kept in touch regularly through email and the odd phone call since we'd returned to Canada. Hye Weon was finishing up his second year of high school and wanted to visit Canada during his winter vacation. He and his mom were calling to ask if he could stay with us for the holiday.

Dale and I talked it over and agreed we would be happy for the visit.

We exchanged many emails with Hye Weon, help-ing him work out the logistics of his trip, but at some point there was an oversight by one of us. When flying to Korea, it doesn't matter if you land at the Seoul airport or the Busan air-port. There are trains and buses that transport you all around the country rather quickly. When flying to Canada the airport where you land makes a *huge* difference.

Shortly after Christmas, I received a phone call from Hye Weon. He was at the Toronto airport.

"Wonderful!" I said. "Welcome to Canada! What time is your flight to Halifax?"

"I don't have a ticket to Halifax," Hye Weon replied, "just to Toronto."

This wasn't good. I explained to him that Toronto was almost 1,800 kilometres from our house. We couldn't pick him up from the Toronto airport. His options were to buy a plane ticket from Toronto to Halifax or take the train from Toronto to Halifax. He said he'd try to figure it out. Less than an hour later he called back and told me a very kind woman in the airport was going to help him get to the train station. He would take the train from Toronto to Halifax – another full day of travelling.

On the evening of December 29, amongst the hordes of travellers departing the train at the station in downtown Halifax, I found Hye Weon. He was weary and in need of a good night's sleep, but was excited to be with us in Canada.

Back at our house, Hye Weon began to unpack his things. He'd brought with him a backpack as well as a traditional Korean drum, a large instrument in a large carrying case, and both the backpack and the drum bag were stuffed with clothes and gifts. On the middle of our kitchen floor, with Dale and I looking on, Hye Weon pulled out bags of dried mushrooms, loose tea, and dehydrated fish. Our eyes widened and our jaws dropped.

"Hye Weon, how did you get all of that through Customs?" I asked.

"The man on the plane next to me just said to say I didn't have anything to declare," Hye Weon replied casually.

We couldn't believe how lucky he was that his bags hadn't been searched. Firstly, his gifts very much resembled marijuana and magic mushrooms. Secondly, he was required by law to declare all food items he brought into Canada. And thirdly, we weren't sure if he was even allowed to bring any of it into Canada.

The next night we hosted a New Year's Eve party at our house, and we were able to introduce Hye Weon to many of our friends. When our friend Sam arrived, Hye Weon looked at him with surprise and asked, "Aren't you from the train?"

Sam looked at Hye Weon and said, "Yeah, I remember you!"

Sam works on the train and does the route between Halifax and Montreal. As luck would have it, he and Hye Weon had seen each other on Hye Weon's journey from Toronto. I think Hye Weon started to assume everyone in Canada knew everyone else in Canada.

A huge snowstorm hit that night, and the party moved outside with people riding one of Dale's surfboards down our steep driveway. Hye Weon loved it.

Soon after New Year's, Hye Weon revealed to us that he planned to bike across Canada. He had made this goal back in Korea and his parents were aware of it. We were not. Dale was blunt with him. "Hye Weon, you'll die! It's winter! You'll get hit by a snowplow, or you'll have a flat tire and die from hypothermia while you try to fix it. You can't do it!"

Hye Weon was disappointed by Dale's response. He really wanted to do a bike trip and was determined that would happen, so he and Dale came up with a different plan. Dale suggested that Hye Weon could fly to British Columbia and bike down the west coast of the United States, where temperatures in the winter are much milder. Hye Weon agreed it was a good plan, and we called his parents to make sure that they too were definitely okay with his bike trip.

We also convinced him not to bike for too long: that he should get back to Korea in time to start his final year of high school in the spring. He had expressed his unhappiness with school and the Korean education system in general. He really didn't want to go back, but we assured him that finishing high school was important and he would most definitely regret it if he didn't graduate.

Next, he needed a bike. I took him to a shop in Halifax that builds bicycles from used parts, and Hye Weon made an order. A short while later he had a bike and began training.

Every day, after Dale and I went to work, Hye Weon went biking. He'd return at night and tell us the places he'd discovered on his ride. Each time he managed longer and longer distances. A few times he got lost but he always made it back to our house eventually. Sometimes Hye Weon biked to the house of a man who gave him free English lessons. Sometimes, when he wasn't biking, he cooked for us.

We'd discovered a Korean grocery store where Hye Weon helped me find the ingredients to make the rice mixture we'd created in Korea. One day, he used some of these ingredients to make a giant pot of soup. It smelled so good – the pungent Korean spices filled our kitchen. I imagined it would be much like the dumpling stew we ate at his parents'. However, when I scooped out my first spoonful, instead of dumplings I found the little dried fish Hye Weon had brought with him on the plane. My stomach lurched. It might have been a bit of pregnancy nausea or the fact that I still hadn't developed a taste for fish eyes. I couldn't eat it. I felt terrible but tried my best to eat around the fish.

We persuaded Hye Weon that taking the drum with him on his bike journey, as he planned, was not a good idea. In the end, he decided to leave it with us, and finally the day came that Hye Weon would depart. I drove him to the airport, gave him some energy gels and bars, hugged him, and said goodbye.

I wasn't yet a mother, but some maternal instincts were starting to kick in, and I desperately hoped he'd be okay. He was only sixteen years old and came from a country vastly different than Canada and the U.S. But Hye Weon was a remarkable kid. He was wise beyond his years and he had common sense. He was open-minded and adventurous, willing and excited to try new things – very much like his parents. Nothing ever seemed to be able to dampen his spirits.

The only real logistical preparation he had done prior to leaving was join a website called couchsurfing.com. His plan was to either camp or find free accommodations by "couch surfing" along the west coast, and he did just that.

On January 30th, he emailed that he was in Bellingham, Washington.

On February 2nd, he emailed from Tacoma. *My bike is now awful, I think I have to fix it here.*

February 18th his message said, *I fixed and bought some stuff in tacoma and I'm now seaside. Oregon. I'm very easy going now.*

February 22nd, from Coos Bay, Oregon, *I met crazy heavy rain from reedsport to coosbay, and now it's fine. Yeah I camped few days, it was nice to see the gorgeous blinking stars, but it was miserable to face to wake up with wet sleeping bags.*

February 26th, from California, he wrote, *yeah I'm still alive don't worry about it. And I slept at bunch of crazy place (like abandoned ban, day use area, church etc).*

We weren't sure if he'd slept in an abandoned barn or an abandoned van.

On March 3rd, his email said he'd be in San Francisco in a couple of days. He also wrote, *I got injured since I fall down on the road and my bike is broken little but there is a lot of beautiful people in here.*

The next we heard from him was March 19th: *I'm in here in public library in the city named Lompoc in California. It's only 300 miles left to get to San Diego. I got first flat tire yesterday afternoon. And tried to fix it but it didn't work (even spare tube popped). Eventually, I hitchhiked and one of the truck driver offered me a ride, couple of tubes, shower, dinner, and place to stay (actually he was the president of the shipping company). Yeah there are a lot more fun and funny stories so far, let me tell you later.*

With each email he sent, more people were included in the recipients list – some of the people he met and stayed with along the route.

On March 30th, his email was sent to eleven addresses. *How are you doing? I'm Hye Weon, I'm doing very good now. I wanna tell you that my journey is almost done! I'm very glad to meet you and I was very happy with you. Finally I crossed the Mexican border and my journey's end. Right now I'm in LA Korean*

Buddhist temple. I booked the flying ticket for April 2nd from LA to Vancouver. And I'm gonna fly back to Korea in 3rd. Well thank you so much for your help and regard. I'll always remember you. Thank you!

Sixteen-year-old Hye Weon, from the mountains near Hwagae, South Korea, biked for two months on his own, from Vancouver, British Columbia, to Tijuana, Mexico, and then back to Los Angeles. We were so thrilled and proud that he'd achieved his goal, and relieved that he was still alive.

* * *

Since his bike trip Hye Weon has finished high school, attended the Korea National University of Arts, majoring in TV and multimedia, and completed his military service. He's done more travelling, worked as a carpenter, and made documentary films.

Jye Weon got married. He and his wife live in Seoul and have a beautiful little girl.

Mr. and Mrs. Hye Weon are still living in their mountain home near Hwagae. They've added more rooms and rent them out to travellers. Each winter they go travelling – Southeast Asia, India, France … Often Hye Weon stays at their house while they're gone. He tends to the fire under the living room floor and keeps the dogs company.

We exchange letters each year with the Hye Weons, and we keep in touch through email and social media. We miss them.

I realize now that we've become them, in a way.

Our dumpling making must have been decent because, like the Hye Weons, Dale and I are parents to two very handsome boys. I'm not exactly the mother I thought I'd be or that I'd said I'd be; we own an X-Box. I don't love the thing, but when the boys play Minecraft in the living room and I'm in the kitchen cooking and I hear the Minecraft cows lowing, I am immediately brought back to our little house in Hwagae.

After walking many times hand in hand through Hwagae's "cherry tree tunnel," Dale and I are still happily married. We've left the city behind and live, not up a mountain, but a pretty steep hill. Dale is always working on our century-old house, fixing and building, while I try, unsuccessfully, to grow food. I no longer own toe socks or teddy-bear slippers, but this past year we did purchase our second Korean vehicle, a Hyundai Tucson.

Aside from Hye Weon, we haven't kept in touch with any of our students. I still picture them the way they were years ago, the same ages and the same shy smiles.

The two paintings by Mrs. Hye Weon still hang in our house, and to this day we love and cook Korean food. Years ago, I even started making my own kimchi, and from a very young age our kids loved it. And recently, I tried a recipe for *kimchi chigae* that has become *the* favourite meal in our house.

We're regular shoppers at the Korean grocery store, the one we found back when Hye Weon visited us thirteen years ago. We love shopping there because it reminds us of the little supermarket in Hwagae, packed with wonderfully random things. I make sure to greet the owners with *"Annyeong haseyo!"*, hand them my money with two hands, and bow and say, *"Kamsahamnida!"* in thanks.

And we often think about it all: about Mr. Bear, the old lady and her store, the nice couple from the pork restaurant, and my friend the bus driver. About Mr. Kim the English teacher, and the temples, and the bath house ladies, and even about Mr. Chang.

We think about the little things. Like the drinks we were offered everywhere we went, and how every gas station was full service and each fill-up included a gift of tissues or work gloves.

We think about the rich traditions and ceremonious practices we learned during our time in Korea. How it all seemed so strange to us when we arrived but how wonderfully special the gestures and customs were. How it all became normal to us.

We'd love to go back there one day. We'd love to take our boys around the Hwagae Market and walk beneath the spring cherry tree blossoms. We'd love to stroll with them along the river, and watch the farmers tend to their rice paddies and tea fields. We'd love to show them the schools where we taught, and see if any of our students still live in the area.

But mostly we'd love to take our boys up the mountain, to the Hye Weons' magical retreat. Maybe we'd sip green tea and make beautiful dumplings together, or maybe we'd swim in their mountain stream. We'd love to have just one more day with our Korean family in Hwagae, sitting on the floor, talking and laughing, warmed by their fire beneath.

ACKNOWLEDGEMENTS

Thank you to all family and friends who have cheered me on over the years and supported my writing.

Thank you to our Korean family: Hye Weon, Jye Weon, Bae Yoon Cheon (Mr. Hye Weon) and Yang Jin Wook (Mrs. Hye Weon), for being so welcoming and open.

Thank you to the people who read my early emails from Korea and suggested they might be book-worthy or asked for more: Marc Cyr, Harrison Wright, Matt MacInnis, Leanne Rankin, Daina Deblette.

Thank you to Jeremy Parent and Mairi Fraser for watching our house. And to Cathy Simpson and my parents for watching Keno.

Thank you to Mary-Anne Donovan, C-J Ward-Askey, Jen Zwicker, and Dale Knowles for edits and feedback, and of course to Dale for being my partner in Korea, in travel, and in life.

Thank you to Mowat and Malloy for your interest and pride in everything I create, no matter if it's a story or a funny-looking birthday cake. And thank you to Gordie for helping me walk out some sticky words and ideas.

Thank you to Stef Walker, Heather MacNeil Mills, Mary-Margaret Keating and your families for years of support and drives and meals, and also to Allyson Marshall and her family, especially for Christmas letter requests.

Thank you to Jay Miller and Tobi Dwyer for being two of my loudest cheerleaders.

Thank you to Karine Gautreau for giving me great writing advice.

Thank you to Julie Chisholm for being my earliest reader as my penpal, and for always being a great friend and supporter.

And thank you to Lesley Choyce and everyone at Pottersfield Press for seeing potential in my little book.

ABOUT THE AUTHOR

Beth Ann Knowles is an online ESL teacher, teacher mentor, and mom. When she's not working she can often be found on a trail in the woods or writing in her car while she waits for her boys' practices to finish. Her work has garnered much attention and won esteemed literary awards. Beth Ann's debut publication, *Row Bot*, was a children's book that she wrote and illustrated. *The Kimchi Experiment* is her first full-length, non-fiction title. Beth Ann lives on the South Shore of Nova Scotia with her husband, two sons, and their dog Gordie.